Let's Talk A...

A Critical Examination of the New Psychotherapies

Anthony W. Clare
with Sally Thompson

BRITISH
BROADCASTING
CORPORATION

Published by the
British Broadcasting Corporation
35 Marylebone High Street
London W1M 4AA

ISBN 0 563 17887 6

First published 1981

Printed and bound in England
by Whitstable Litho Ltd
Millstrood Road, Whitstable, Kent

This book is typeset in VIP Palatino,
10pt leaded 2pts

The numbers in the text
refer to bibliographical information
given at the end of each
chapter

Contents

Introduction

Patient's name:	Psychiatry
Age:	In middle years
History:	European born; after sickly youth in the US travelled to Vienna and returned as Dr Freud's Wunderkind. Amazing social success for one so young. Strong influence on such older associates as Education, Government, Child Bearing and the Arts, and a few raffish friends like Advertising and Criminology.
Complaint:	Speaks of overwork, loss of confidence and inability to get provable results. Hears conflicting inner voices and insists that former friends are laughing behind his back. Patient agrees with Norman Mailer: it's hard to get to the top in America but it's even harder to stay there.
Diagnosis:	Standard conflictual anxiety and maturational variations crisis accompanied by compensatory delusions of grandeur and a declining ability to cope. Patient averse to the therapeutic alliance and shows incipient over-reliance on drugs.
Recommended treatment:	Requires further study
Prognosis:	Problematic

Time Magazine, 1979[1]

Thus did that faithful recorder of America's pulse sum up the state of psychiatry in that part of the world. Allowing for the characteristic flamboyance of the American diagnosis, the state of British psychiatry is not all that different. Psychiatry at the beginning of the nineteen-eighties is in a period of profound self-questioning and self-doubt. The grandiose claims made on its behalf in earlier years have become the object of satire and ridicule while psychiatrists themselves are alternatively portrayed as sinister agents of the State and glib, complacent gurus.

During a period in which psychiatry has become self-obsessed and its public image somewhat blurred and murky, there has been a bewildering proliferation of therapies, alternately described as 'new' and 'fringe'. Such therapies have tended to originate in California and gradually spread east across the United States and thence to Europe. Many of these 'new' therapies stress their orthodox psychiatric roots, others take pride in the extent to which they have thrown off the constraints of established psychiatry and have ploughed genuinely virgin ground. All offer rich prizes – self-discovery, self-perfection, maturity, holism, earthly salvation, a community, a place in the sun.

America, as Gore Vidal once remarked, is a society which has always chosen 'to groove along emotional lines'. New therapies arise there with the same ingenuity and rapidity as new automobiles. When the Controller of Radio 4 accepted the proposal put forward by Sally Thompson for a six-part series, to be presented by me, on the origins, claims and achievements of the so-called new psychotherapies, it provided both of us with a unique opportunity to meet and question many of the people who have originated or developed those psychotherapies in the United States of America. The time available was necessarily limited and we had to restrict our survey. Accordingly, the radio series ('Let's Talk About Me') and this book paint an unavoidably partial picture. It is also a highly personal one.

One of the more attractive aspects of these therapeutic movements is their openness. With one or two exceptions, we encountered enormous goodwill and co-operation throughout our journey and we welcome this opportunity to express publicly our gratitude to the many therapists, clients, commentators and critics who so readily gave of their time and their opinions. We are especially grateful to Carl Rogers and Rollo May who provided us with a detailed historical perspective regarding psychotherapeutic developments within the United States since World War II, to the late Gregory Bateson who both entertained and educated us during our stay in Esalen, and to Cyra McFadden and her husband who did much to correct our impression of Marin County, California as a community made up entirely of clients and therapists. We are also indebted to James Bugental, Arthur and Etta Deikman, Werner Erhard, Vivian Janov, Stanley Keleman, Ted Long, Don Miller, Zerka Moreno, the late Ida

Rolf, Michael Salveson and Claude Steiner. We appreciated the forebearance of the staff at the Esalen Growth Center, Big Sur who tolerated our presence and, in particular, Janet Lederman and Richard Price. Other individuals who provided valuable insights concerning the role and value of the new therapies were Paul Brown, Professor Hans Eysenck, Louise Fletcher, John Maher, William Murray, Tudor Parfitt, Valerie Singleton, Dr Robin Skynner and Professor R. Bruce Sloane. To all of these and to the many clients we met during the course of our enquiries we say a heartfelt thank you.

The bulk of this book is devoted to the less orthodox forms of psychotherapy. One chapter (Chapter 9), however, is concerned with a number of recent developments in psychotherapy which while novel are hardly unorthodox for they have been readily taken up and absorbed into the mainstreams of psychiatric theory and practice in Britain, the United States and elsewhere. While our account of these trends is brief we have included it because many of these new approaches in family, marital, sex and behaviour therapy incorporate a number of techniques and ideas pioneered within what might be termed the 'fringe'. Readers interested in a more detailed exposition of such therapies are advised to consult some of the references to Chapter 9.

This book, like the radio series which preceded it, subjects the developments in psychotherapy since the War to a broad and critical examination. The questioning tone, however, should not be taken as evidence that we believe what we have earlier described as 'orthodox' psychiatry to be without blemish. Sadly, there is much that is lamentable concerning psychiatry. There is an excessive emphasis on drugs and physical treatments, there is a remarkable lack of humility on the part of many of the spokesmen of contemporary psychiatry concerning its therapeutic shortcomings and limitations and there is more than a tendency for orthodox psychiatrists and classically-trained psychoanalysts and psychotherapists to see the mote in the eye of the unconventional therapies while remaining blind to the beam in their own. I have already written a critical account of psychiatry as practised in the United States and within Britain's National Health Service which makes it plain that criticism of the unconventional does not imply an unshakeable faith in the efficacy of drugs, ECT and psychosurgery.[2] Nor are we insensitive to the needs of many miserable and unhappy people, over and above the seriously mentally ill, who seek support and assistance from the so-called 'caring' services. However, as emphasised in a 1971 report on Scientology, 'those who feel they need psychotherapy tend to be the very people who are most easily exploited; the weak, the insecure, the nervous, the lonely, the inadequate and the depressed, whose desperation so often is such that they are willing to do and pay anything for some improvement of their condition'.[3] In the final analysis, it is to these people that this book is dedicated that they might be able to make better sense of the wares that are offered as panaceas for their problems.

Anthony Clare
Institute of Psychiatry
London 1981

References

1 Psychiatry on the Couch. *Time* Magazine 2 April 1979, pp.40-47

2 Clare, A. W. 1976 *Psychiatry in Dissent: Controversial Issues in Thought and Practice*, Tavistock, London

3 Foster, J. G. 1971 *Enquiry into the Practice and Effects of Scientology*, HMSO London

1 Psychotherapy – the New and the Old

In addition to the need for psychotherapeutic services in the treatment of mental illness, a burgeoning interest among US citizens in self-actualisation and emotional fulfilment has created a powerful demand for diverse forms of psychotherapy. As affluence and leisure time expand, the demand will almost certainly grow. The human potential movement, represented in its most concrete form by the encounter group and a variety of new psychotherapies, has become the primary vehicle through which to participate in this development.

Daniel B. Hogan 1979[1]

Few words in the lexicon of psychiatry are as ambiguous as the term 'psychotherapy'. It was first used by J. C. Reil in 1803 in an article somewhat colourfully entitled 'Rhapsodies in the Application of Psychic Methods in the Treatment of Mental Disturbances'.[2] Since that time major problems have surrounded attempts to define quite precisely what is meant by the term. Many experts argue that it should only be applied to verbal therapies, thereby eliminating such therapeutic methods as dance, music or art therapy. Others doubt the wisdom of extending the notion of ameliorating mental suffering to include self-growth and 'self-actualisation'. In spite of these and other difficulties, attempts are continually being made to arrive at some consensus concerning the meaning of the term and a popular definition is that provided by the respected American psychoanalyst, Jerome D. Frank which says that psychotherapy 'encompasses all those chosen activities by which one person seeks to relieve the distress and beneficially affect the behaviour of another through psychological means'.[3]

Given such a wide mandate, it is hardly surprising that psychotherapy appears to subsume an apparently endless list of human activities. Everything sooner or later becomes defined or redefined as psychotherapy. Chatting with friends becomes psychotherapy, jogging with colleagues is psychotherapy; according to a story in the British newspaper, the *Daily Mail*, the psychotherapeutic blessing has even been given to prayer! An American psychotherapist, Dr Herbert Benson, is of the firm opinion that prayer is good for high blood pressure, anxiety and stress. Instead of the celebrated apple a day, Dr Benson's patients are advised to close the eyes, breathe deeply and pray for twenty minutes daily. Daily prayer, declared redundant in a confidently agnostic society, has made its inevitable come-back, no longer, however, to erase the sins of the soul but to ease the pain of the psyche.

A British psychotherapist, Dr Anthony Storr, attempts a similar definition. Psychotherapy, for him, is 'the art of alleviating personal difficulties through the agency of words and a personal, professional relationship'.[4] Here Storr introduces two rather specific features – 'words' and 'professional' – which Frank, familiar with the more unorthodox variegation of therapies sheltering under the term in the United States, avoids. Some therapies, as we shall see, do not lay particular emphasis on the healing power of words *per se*, while the extent to which others are 'professional' or involve the participation of 'professional' psychotherapists introduces the extremely sensitive issue of what is a 'professional' psychotherapist.

However, as Lewis Wolberg, the author of one of the definitive textbooks on the subject, points out,[5] common to most respectable definitions of psychotherapy is the view that it is a treatment by psychological means of emotional problems in which a trained person deliberately established a relationship with a patient with the object of removing or modifying existing symptoms, altering disturbed ways of behaving, and helping to promote positive development of the individual's personality and social life. At the heart of 'psychological means' is talking, although other means, some remarkable for their unorthodoxy, are employed. The notion that talking can help ease psychological pain and personal distress is one of the more distinctive features of the second half of this century. People are everywhere in search of someone who will spare the time to listen to their troubles. The most quoted statistic about the British General Practice system is the one which says that the average GP can only spare five minutes for each patient that he sees. The fact that the statistic is erroneous is beside the point, which is that it is used not to demonstrate the likely inadequacy of the GP's physical examination and medical diagnosis but to criticise a system which allows the doctor such a short space of time to listen to his or her patients talking about their problems.

We must, after all, have the time to talk. To talk about what? What is it that so many are going on about, examining their own and each other's psychological navels, in groups, on couches, under massage, in primal scream sessions, with counsellors, social workers, encounter facilitators, gurus, pastors, est trainers, Indian mystics and the hundred and one varieties of 'experts' who have mushroomed to meet this apparently inexhaustible, insatiable and perhaps even instinctual need? Tom Wolfe, who coined the phrase 'The Me Decade' to describe the 1970s, provided a trendy, albeit cynical, guide-list to problems in an article in *New York Magazine*:

> What did they want to eliminate from their lives? Why, they took their fingers right off the old repress button and told the whole room: my husband, my wife, my homosexuality, my inability to communicate, my self-hatred, self-destructiveness, craven fears, puking weaknesses, primordial horrors, premature ejaculation, impotence, frigidity, subservience, laziness, alcoholism, major vices, minor vices, grim habits, twisted psyche, my tortured soul.[6]

Not everyone believes that talking, however the activity is carried out, can necessarily alter or affect some of the items on Wolfe's list. The extent to which one has confidence in the efficacy of psychotherapy is not unrelated to the particular side of the Atlantic on which you live. Indeed, one of the new therapists whose work we will be considering, Arthur Janov, who 'invented' primal scream therapy (Chapter 5), believes that the British are psychologically infantile when it comes to baring the soul and getting down to the nitty-gritty of being born again, achieving a transformation and attaining self-perfection. It does appear as if the well-known reserve of the British will ensure that this part of the world remains relatively barren soil for the new, and even for some of the old, talking therapies. However, as we shall see, it will not be for want of trying on the part of the enthusiastic transatlantic salesmen of these new post-Freudian wares.

The corollary of Janov's observation is that Americans are psychologically adult and adept at getting to grips with the monsters that lurk just below consciousness. As a land renowned for its belief in progress, the better life and the pursuit of happiness, America does seem the obvious culture in which therapies dedicated to notions of self-perfectibility and growth might flourish. But it has to be said that the therapy from which they originate, the father as it were of the noisy, colourful, extrovert, irreverent and combative children that swarm around the therapy nursery, was anything but positive and optimistic. The new therapies may indeed promise heaven on earth – most of them do – but Freudian psychoanalysis offered no such heady hope and Freud himself took a decidedly jaundiced view of his fellow men. Nor, indeed, did he take a particularly benign view of the nation which adopted him so wholeheartedly. According to Ernest Jones, Freud's biographer, who shared Freud's opinion on this point, Freud had

> a feeling that commercial success dominated the scale of values in the United States and that scholarship, research and profound reflection . . . were lightly esteemed . . . he came later to take the rather cynical view that it was a country whose only function was to provide money to support European culture.[7]

It certainly supported Freud. By 1952, 64% of the members of the International Psychoanalytic Association were in America. Yet Freud's main fears concerning the future of psychoanalysis focused on that country. He was shocked by the tendency to commercialise and sensationalise his ideas and was convinced that Americans lacked intellectual creativity, observing in his introduction to the *Special Psychopathology* number of *The Medical Review of Reviews* that, 'the contributions to our science from that vast country are exiguous and provide little that is new.'[8]

He even worried that the American reception of his theories would only result in their being crucially and perhaps fatally amended, the great American sin being 'to shorten study and preparation and to proceed as fast as possible with practical application'. In retrospect, he seems to have been remarkably perspicacious. All his worst fears that psychoanalysis, far from being understood as a science of the complex nature of man, would be emasculated and diluted into a wonder treatment were to be fulfilled. In some cases the change took place without any overt admission that Freud's views had been altered. In other cases the change was accompanied by an explicitly defiant rejection yet the new therapies shamelessly borrowed terminology, concepts and mechanisms from orthodox psychoanalysis without so much as an acknowledgement. Freud, for all his psychologising, remained firmly wedded to a biological perspective on the human race. For him, man was first and foremost a biological organism and in following man's vicissitudes he was primarily interested in what happened to his biological needs in the course of his growth and development. All of man's subsequent needs were conceived by Freud as outgrowths, reflections, or 'sublimations' of those basic biological drives. In many respects, as Judd Marmor one of America's most respected analysts, has pointed out, Freud's thinking was Hobbesian in its portrayal of man's innate tendencies as essentially selfish, animalistic and antisocial. The chief function of society was to 'inhibit, forbid and suppress' those impulses which could otherwise destroy it. Freud's pessimism concerning human nature is legendary – he once wearily observed that mankind, taken as a whole, are a wretched lot, and in one of several passages of similar pessimism in *Civilisation and its Discontents* he lays this gloomy vision on the line:

> . . . men are not gentle creatures who want to be loved and who at the most can defend themselves if they are attacked. They are, on the contrary, creatures among whose instinctual endowments is to be reckoned a fair share of aggressiveness. As a result, their neighbour is for them not only a potential helper or sexual object, but also someone who tempts them to satisfy their aggressiveness on him, to exploit his capacity to work without compensation, to use him sexually without his consent, to seize his possessions, to humiliate him, to cause him pain, to torture and kill him. *Homo, Homini lupus* (Man is wolf to man). Who in the face of all his experience of life and history will have the courage to dispute this assertion?[9]

As it subsequently turned out, quite a few of those who followed him were prepared to dispute it, not the least of whom was Carl Rogers, one of the founding fathers of the so-called encounter movement. To Rogers, such a gloomy view seemed more appropriate to puritanical Christian fundamentalism than to any self-liberating psychotherapy worthy of the name. Rogers was not alone in noting the curious similarity between Freudian psychoanalysis and the puritan Christian ethic it seemed to believe it was supplanting. In the place of original sin Freud installed the turbulent id. Where once man was to be redeemed from his sinful state by religious redemption, now it was to be through psychoanalysis. But each approach involved a philosophical position based on a view of man as flawed, forked and failed.

The extent to which Freud pondered the possibility that the vast intellectual and moral edifice he was building might resemble not so much a science of living as a religious blue-print is touched on in Chapter 8. The only optimistic note that Freud permitted himself concerning the future of mankind involved the unseating of religion by science, a revolution he outlined in *The Future of an Illusion*. 'In the long run', he declared, 'nothing can withstand reason and experience'.[10] Religion, to Freud, offered a contradiction to both. However, he did see one escape outlet for it. If religious ideas were to be confined to 'a belief in a higher spiritual being whose qualities are indefinable and whose purpose cannot be discerned, they will be proof against the challenge of science but they will also lose their hold on human interest'. He also believed that religion would only be expelled from European civilisation by means of another system of doctrine and one which from the outset would take over all the psychological characteristics of religion itself – 'the same sanctity, rigidity and intolerance, the same prohibition of thought' – for its own defence. He never appeared to notice that his own creation, psychoanalysis, and a number of its branches contained the seeds of a metamorphosis into just such a doctrinaire religious system. And yet he had been warned. In the first decade of this century, Freud and his close followers became convinced of the need to form an association of psychoanalysts, a sort of closed-shop union whose leaders would decide what was and what was not psychoanalysis, would hand down the approved line on controversial issues and would function like a latter-day Inquisition when it came to declaring any dissenter a heretic. One who demurred and who resigned from the newly-formed International Psycho-Analytic Association within months of joining was Eugen Bleuler, the distinguished Swiss psychiatrist, the man who gave the world the term 'schizophrenia' and at whose hospital, the Burgholzli in Zurich, Jung studied. Explaining his resignation, Bleuler drew attention to his view that while 'the principle "all or nothing" is necessary for religious sects and political parties . . . for science I consider it harmful'.[11] Sixty years later, in the attractive Californian coastal resort of La Jolla, Carl Rogers was to express views which even if only partially accurate testify to Bleuler's prescience. (Chapter 2).

But it was not just the atmosphere of the secret society, the papal-style leadership of Freud, the classification of disciples as true or false, the regular conferences which, like conclaves of cardinals dogmatically ruling on the acceptability or otherwise of the latest example of theoretical scholarship, emphasised the similarity between psychoanalysis and religion. Nor was it merely the fact that the analytical training resembled nothing so much as the initiation and training entered into by novices in some of the more demanding religious orders. It was the fact that, unlike medicine, psychoanalysis operated with a model of universal disease. To the doctor, man is presumed healthy until a disease is diagnosed. Psychiatrists who adhere to the so-called 'medical model' are characterised less by their emphasis on a biological view of man (which they may or may not manifest) than by their assumption that there is a state of relative psychological health from which their patients deviate. The psychoanalyst, however, like the priest, is confronted by the evidence of flaw in us all. The conflicts of infantile life, the lot of Everyman, are never definitely resolved. Some manage to develop appropriate defences, attain the requisite degree of ego strength and succeed in engaging in relatively mature interpersonal relationships. Others come to grief in one or other of these areas. But one and all bear stigmata and scars of pathology. None of us is without oedipal sin. There are healthy organs and there are diseased ones. But in psychoanalytical psychopathology, there is only illness and the best we can hope for is to keep it within bounds.

One man who has written extensively of the relationship between psychoanalysis and religion is the analyst and philosopher, Rollo May. When researching this book, the producer Sally Thompson and I, met him at his summer cottage in New Hampshire and we put to him the often-repeated view that psychotherapy, and particularly psychoanalysis, is the secular religion of a civilisation which has rejected God. He agreed promptly. Indeed, he reminded us that the whole psychotherapy movement began at a time when the medical profession was moving into areas hitherto considered the preserve of the priest. The developments in present-day California are not just the outgrowths of psychotherapy but of what May calls 'psycho-religious therapy'. There was, as he pointed out, always a push behind psychoanalysis to get it to move into religion. Many of the early practitioners had religious training. May himself was a student at the Union Theological College in New York. So too was Carl Rogers. Jung was only the most noted of the early analysts who attempted a synthesis of religion and psychoanalysis while Adler, in May's words, was writing a book 'a clergyman might write' when he died. May believes that psychotherapy is something that occurs when civilisation disintegrates. 'Everybody then is thrown on his own. He has no community that is made to order, and so he has to look inside'. May is convinced that the beginning of the disintegration of the modern period, the First World War, also marks the beginning of the tremendous impact of psychology. 'That is why,' he says, 'our psychology departments in this country have grown tremendously. This great growth was not because of any inherent value on their part but because psychology was the nearest science to a defunct and bankrupt religion, and they had to grab something. It was to tell them how to live.'

Some of the trappings of orthodox medicine do linger in psychoanalysis particularly in the notion of expertise. The therapist is seen as a potent, knowledgeable and trained professional holding all the powerful cards in contrast to the passive, ignorant and dependent patient, helpless and waiting to be 'cured'. Many of the newer psychotherapies, on the other hand, emphasise a vigorous populist egalitarianism, and reject orthodox psychoanalysis along with orthodox psychiatry. Instead they hold out a model in which there is no 'expert' and in which the client has as much to teach the therapist as the therapist has to teach the client. (Often, of course, this is no more than the dismal truth. In many of the new therapies the level of ignorance is indeed shared, though like so much else in this general field, it is unclear whether the mere sharing of such a situation is as beneficial as its protangonists insist.) Coupled with such an egalitarian emphasis is an often openly stated hostility to learning. Rogerian psychotherapy embodies such a hostility. Rogers makes no secret of the fact that he rejected orthodox psychoanalysis not merely because it had, to his way of thinking, become a petrified religious orthodoxy but because it was élitist, had incorporated a body of inchoate and opaque ideas impenetrable to the average man and because it was superfluous. For Rogers, love, otherwise known as caring, genuineness and empathy, is all you need (Chapter 2).

It is over twenty years since Rogers first began to produce what has since become a string of books, all of which emphasise the essential simplicity of psychotherapy, its accessibility to ordinary people, the redundancy of complicated training and the equality between the counsellor and the client. Yet again one is confronted by the fact that these are quintessentially American values. They permeate every one of the bewildering array of psychotherapies flourishing on the West Coast of America. They form its creed. It is paradoxical to discover that in America, psychoanalysis finds itself increasingly under fire for being what it is criticised in Britain for not being, namely a system of highly structured, scientific theories capable of testing and refutation. Even worse for the analysts is the fact that psychoanalysis is increasingly lumped together with behavioural psychology and biological psychiatry as a technology. At the moment, the fashion is to regard technology with contempt bordering on dread. Technology in the land of technological wizardry is a dirty word. Reason follows, hard on its heels.

The word *experiential*, on the other hand, is in. What Rogers fuelled, even if he did not actually start the engine, was the movement away from rational values and critical enquiry and towards intuitive experience, trusting 'gut feelings' and suspending, if not totally eliminating, one's critical faculty.

Experience is the watchword of many of the new therapies. It is proclaimed with the certainty of religious belief that experience can save, that it promotes growth, another sacramental word, and that hitherto it has languished in the shadow of that betrayer of hopes and of humanity, reason. Thus do the new talking therapies energetically set about secularising many aspects of religious practice and belief and not merely the disagreeable ones. Where once birth, marriage, death, the confessing of sins were sacramental moments, presided over by the men of God, so now they are opportunities for experience and self-growth solemnised by the man of therapy. As one belongs or does not belong to this or that religious creed, so one consecrates oneself or forgoes the latest therapy. As Cyra McFadden, the author of *The Serial*, that wickedly satirical novel on the psychological explorations of the citizens of Marin County, California, put it when talking to us about this aspect of the new therapies: 'There is an enormous air of sanctimony, a strong secular religiosity about it – you are either saved or you are not and if you are not saved there are a great many people there who are willing to help you but not to discuss with you the value of being saved or remaining resolutely unsaved.' In her words, there is 'the collective reek of a great many joggers' about the new movement and nowhere more than in Esalen, that self-styled university of experientally-based psychotherapy, nestling high over the Pacific Ocean, half-way along the Big Sur coast between San Francisco and Los Angeles. Indeed, Esalen could well be understood as a particularly twentieth-century version of the religious retreat house, a place for the recharging of spiritual batteries, out of the hurly-burly of the mainstream of life. At first glance, any resemblance between this oasis of sensual enjoyment and, say, an Irish retreat house might seem somewhat fanciful. I once spent two days at a place called Lough Derg, which for my less religious readers I should explain is a centre of pilgrimage, poised between Northern Ireland and the Irish Republic, to which people go to perform penitential exercises, fasting and good works. The actual name of the place is St Patrick's Purgatory which is a singular euphemism since it actually bears more than a passing resemblance to Dante's Inferno. The weather is appalling. You have to clamber about in your bare feet while reciting innumerable decades of the rosary (a Roman Catholic version of the Indian mantra) while going without sleep for forty-eight hours and consuming in the meanwhile only black tea, burnt toast and 'soup' (pepper and salt in hot water). Now Esalen is not quite like that. For one thing the weather is magnificent. Instead of penitential rocks, there are hot mineral baths in which naked nubile American bodies loll while being gently massaged with scented oils to the sound of the rolling surf (impossible to replicate in Ireland not merely for fear of a belt from a bishop's crozier but the danger of contracting pneumonia). Nutritious foods abound and the entire atmosphere from the sun-soaked log cabins to the waving palm trees, exudes a sensual quality which doubtless accounts in part for Esalen's popularity.

So wherein lies the similarity? In both places the self is the object of attention – in the orthodox religious retreat centre it is to be denied, frustrated and disciplined; in Esalen it is to be discovered, liberated, fulfilled. The language of Esalen, in common with the language of many of the therapies which pass through it, is the language of inverted religion. Where once it was through prayer that man was to be liberated from himself, now it is through experiential therapy that he will be liberated from others. Gestalt therapists, rolfers, assertiveness trainers, transactional analysts, all stress the particular, the idiosyncratic nature of what they have to offer but all preach the healing power not of prayer or sacrifice or denial but of – experience. The central religious message having been turned on its head, all else remains the same, the same air of moral hygiene, the same earnest goodness, the same insistence on the intrinsic lovableness of every man, the same benevolent regard for the dissenter as a straying sinner to be pitied.

There is, too, a puritanism about a place like Esalen which, for all its nudity and apparent hedonism, marks it out as a somewhat dreary, self-conscious place. It is as if the only way the renegade puritans from those stolid mid-Western towns with names like Billings and Kalispell, who seem to make up so many of Esalen's clientele, can actually taste the forbidden fruits of sensuality is to transmogrify them into therapy, which at Esalen is actually hard work. So eating, swimming, breathing, making love, are all therapeutic and are all earnestly discussed, analysed, formulated and dissected with the same degree of moral seriousness as a bevy of monks might discuss the liturgical modifications of the Second Vatican Council. And, as in the case of religious belief, the notion of establishing the truth of falsity of the new therapies by means of scientific enquiry is a futile endeavour. It does seem that there is no way that what happens at Esalen and the hundreds of other growth centres throughout the United States, can be tested (although as will be seen later, there have been one or two ingenious attempts) any more than it is possible scientifically to evaluate a monastery or run a double-blind controlled trial of Lourdes.

Freud never seemed to have foreseen the crowning achievement embodied in the new therapies which is the final obliteration of the notion of original sin. Gone are those dark primaeval passions whose existence so troubled Freud. In their place is a vision of man as a virtuous, competent, triumphant ego, an ego whose flaws are always the product of a crippling, headtripping (Esalen jargon for 'thinking'), authoritarian society. Where poor, misguided Freud saw the constraints of society holding man back from indulging his polymorphous, perverse and psychopathic tendencies, the new dewy-eyed fraternities of

California see them as inhibiting man from holistic growth, sensual fulfilment and mutual love.

However, John Maher, a blunt-speaking Irish-American who runs a remarkable centre in San Francisco for delinquents, the Delancey Street Foundation, sees the notion that perfection can be achieved within one's lifetime, as a typically American example of self-delusion. He also believes that the obsession mental health is itself a form of mental illness.

> They even have this psychotic notion, [he told us,] that every man and his wife have to work out their problem, which is totally crazy. My grandmother raised ten children. A couple of them were undercover homosexuals and joined the church for a free lunch. A couple of them were tough guys, because they had a hard life, and became gangsters. The dumber ones got city jobs and the smarter ones went on to make a few bucks in the American culture. All in all, they had a good batting average. The old lady was totally bananas. She wanted to see her dead children in the world beyond, and no matter where you went in the house there was a saint, preferably covered with blood, staring at you from the wall. Her husband, Patrick, understood that she was totally out of her mind, but she was a wonderful woman and he loved her; and she, on the other hand, realised that he was a man who had come from a different country, one who had a hard time adjusting in American culture, and was not quite sure which one he was. And to blow off steam, Patrick would have to go out on a Saturday night and punch a cop. They loved each other until they died, and didn't separate because they viewed each other as human beings in whom they did not expect perfection. Here in the United States we have this obsession with perfection. One dare not have a wrong attitude around anyone else or you have to go through this incredibly complicated nonsense of 'working it out'.

Another observer of the American scene, Martin L. Gross, also identifies the desire for perfectibility as the mainspring behind the rise of psychoanalysis in the US. Such a search is common to both the new psychological and the old Protestant ethic. As Gross points out in *The Psychological Society* such self-perfection 'was once sought through the intervention of God but is now accomplished by supposed scientific adjustment of the psyche'.[12] Gross recalls how Alexis de Tocqueville, the nineteenth-century social historian, interpreted this hunger for perfection in the American character. 'Aristocratic nations are liable to narrow the scope of human perfectibility', observed de Tocqueville, 'democratic nations to expand it beyond reason'.

Britain, it would seem safe to say, remains in this respect at any rate, an aristocratic nation. Yet, paradoxically, it is to the creation of its Welfare State with its National Health Service that social historians point to explain why psychoanalysis never managed to take root to any significant extent in this part of the world. Not merely, as we have seen, is Britain not a psychoanalytical society. It is not a psychological one. Psychiatry has stayed close to its medical base and, at least until recently, has appeared content to concern itself with the more extreme end of the psychopathological spectrum, that is to say with the severe mental disorders such as schizophrenia and manic-depression together with the more crippling neurotic and personality disorders. The provision of a National Health Service for all meant that treatments which could be widely and cheaply applied across the nation acquired popularity. Psychoanalysis, being time-consuming and therefore expensive, was relegated to the more exclusive suburbs of the major metropolitan areas. It is, of course, true that even in the United States, it is restricted to the more affluent areas with the majority of psychoanalysts practising in a handful of States, of which New York, Massachusetts, and California are the major beneficiaries. In Britain, drug therapy, behavioural methods of treatment and techniques, and strategies of social rehabilitation took pride of place in the immediate post-war years. In so far as psychotherapy flourished, it did so in the form of group therapy which offered the possibility of treating more patients more economically than one-to-one therapies. (See Chapter 9).

Another cultural explanation for the popularity of psychotherapy in the US relates to the observation that although the therapist appears committed to the patient first and foremost, in fact his major role is as a purveyor of crucial social values. Psychotherapy is particularly suited to the American milieu because it endorses one of the central tenets of American life, namely the notion of the autonomous individual as the ultimate bearer of responsibility for his or her psyche, or should we say soul. Therapy unashamedly aims at reinforcing the American ethos that all men are basically equal and should function independently. Indeed, two psychiatrists, Wen-Shing Tseng and McDermott, writing in the *American Journal of*

Psychiatry back in 1975 and looking at Western-style psychotherapy mainly through Eastern eyes, observed that within a society in which self-sufficiency and responsibility are highly idealised, it is often difficult to find opportunities for the satisfaction of dependency needs except in the setting of a relationship with one's therapist.[13] (Where else but in California, could a marriage which has lasted longer than a year be referred to, only half-jokingly, as a state of mutual interdependent fixation?) It is a most curious state of affairs whereby countless clients for psychotherapy earnestly rummage about in their minds for memories of their first utterly dependent relationship, trying to unravel what went wrong so that they might thereby be able to engage as adults in adult, non-dependent relationships, and end up, in the process, highly dependent on a therapy which continues to hold out the notion that individuals can and should attain a state of independence *before* engaging in a relationship with others.

A related notion is that until you know yourself you cannot know others. In the name of such a dubious proposition, people have left wives or husbands, have fled responsibilities, thrown up careers, walked out in the middle of contracts, each time stilling the nagging voice of guilt with the glib reassurance that before all else one must be true to oneself. As we shall see, this philosophy propels many in a search whose repetitiveness and remorselessness is justified by an idealisation of the very process of searching. Therapy no longer becomes a means to a particular end. It is the end itself. Asked in a television interview, how his psychoanalytic therapy was going after twenty-two years, Woody Allen replied 'slowly'. Quite right. There is plenty of time once therapy becomes life and life becomes therapy.

The newer therapies, however, those talking treatments derived from encounter principles and the ideas of Carl Rogers, have little truck with lifetime searches for the very understandable reason that the object of their particular search-and-locate mission is the self itself, the 'real me'. There is the general assumption at the heart of most of these new approaches that if I can obtain the courage and the skill and the desire to strip away all the superficial social face creams, the personal lipsticks, the ideological mascaras and the phoney veneers that have accumulated since birth and the indoctrination that passes for childhood and adolescence, then and only then will I find the 'real me'. Once I have found me, then I join the ranks of the chosen, the élite, the righteous ones who quietly bear the satisfaction of knowing that they know who they are, and the even more delicious certainty of knowing that others do not know who they are not. Understandably, such a state of superiority is difficult to hide. It can usually be seen in the knowing smiles of the chosen and can be witnessed in the ready earnestness with which they helpfully guide those who have not yet found their real selves to the correct therapeutic path to self-enlightenment.

Such a search can become overpowering. Indeed, life becomes a somewhat wearying process of utter self-absorption. In Cyra McFadden's opinion, the search for the elusive self makes it difficult to engage in the most mundane of activities without simultaneously checking the emotional responses to make sure they are 'authentic'.

> There is something dreadfully wrong [she told us] with the notion of health as we define it here. You never get out of bed in the morning and say 'Today I feel reasonably OK. I think I might be able to bumble through. If I have a stiff drink at lunch, and go about my business, I might conceivably make it through till five in the afternoon'. One is too busy taking one's emotional pulse, all, all, all the time. It is a cumbersome preoccupation. It takes away a lot of time that one could spend more profitably, seeing friends and doing things that involve more gratification and far less earnest, cumbersome endeavour.

Other critics are even more condemnatory. Christopher Lasch, Professor of History at the University of Rochester in New York State, insists that when they speak of 'meaning' and 'love' the new therapists define such terms simply as the fulfilment of the patient's emotional requirements. Given the nature of the therapeutic enterprise, there is no notion of any need for the subject to subordinate his needs and interests to those of others. Love as self-sacrifice strikes the therapeutic sensibility as intolerably oppressive and injurious to personal health and well-being. 'To "liberate" humanity from such outmoded ideas of love and duty has become the mission of the post-Freudian therapies' argues Lasch, 'and particularly of their converts and popularisers, for whom mental health means the overthrow of "inhibition" and the non-stop celebration of the self'.[14] Ah, yes, the elusive self. Next to the word 'pain' it was the word 'self' that we were to hear most frequently during our trip through California exploring the new therapies and their adherents. That 'non-stop celebration of the self' takes remarkable forms. The menu list is vast and varied – est, bioenergetics, rolfing, psychodrama, primal scream, Reichan massage, jogging, acupuncture, tai chi, chanting, modern dance – the resultant psychological indigestion inevitable. Everybody is in search of their true self, everybody is in the process of becoming somebody else. Like Lewis Lapham's San Francisco, the new therapies have often impressive façades, yet it is difficult to avoid the feeling that every door opens into an empty room.

Yet as we shall see in subsequent pages, there are those, other than the therapists themselves, who implicitly and in some cases explicitly endorse California's claim to be the New Athens and who, like Theodore Roszak, discern in what Lasch dismisses as 'narcissism' a 'transformation of human personality in progress which is of evolutionary proportions', a shift in our consciousness as 'epoch-making' as the appearance of speech or the invention of tools.[15] An example of this transformation is Michael Murphy, one of the co-founders of Esalen and the Esalen Institute Sports Center, whose claim to our attention is that he 'nicely adapts the mystic intention of these oriental exercise meditations to the game of golf'. Indeed Roszak's latest book *Unfinished Animal* is a veritable guide-book to the gurus, heroes and seers of the new search for transcendence and self-hood. Yeats rubs shoulders with Madame Blavatsky, Blake, Rudolf Steiner. Even dotty George Gurdjieff with his verbal gymnastics and his incoherent ramblings on cosmic forces and 'feeding the moon' merits inclusion as guru and therapist. Uri Geller is there, so is Timothy Leary. To what illustrious end can such powers be directed? In what common cause can Carl Jung and Jack Sarfatti, Doris Lessing and Aleister Crowley, Thomas Merton and Carlos Casteneda be counted as comrades-in-arms? It is the role they play drawing *meaning* out of *strangeness*:

> All are valued for the access they give to uncanny realities, regions of experience that transcend conventional science, standard intellect; each is surrounded by that special luminosity which only belongs to an ultimate human concern. The choices may be banal, the efforts flawed but the intention is clear.[15]

Roszak's view of what this intention is merits analysis. It is that we accept the transcendent potentiality that is the essence of our human nature. In this new vision man is not a fallen angel but the possessor of a whole and healthy spirit. He glows in an original splendour, aspires to transcendence and succeeds often enough 'to sustain a Godlike image of human being'. The psychotherapy of the future, declares Roszak, 'will not find the secret of the soul's distress in the futile and tormenting clash of instinctual drives but in the tension between potentiality and actuality'. Man's task, no less, is to become what he is. 'What is most significantly and pathologically unconscious in us is the knowledge of our potential godlikeness'. At the present time only a talented, artistic élite are allowed to experience this exalted state. But when Everyman seeks his lawful inheritance by turning inwards in the only search that has any intrinsic meaning, namely the search for his true, authentic self, he finds his puny efforts at self-expression, his glaring paintings, his misshapen sculptures, his banal poetry mocked as pretentious and meretricious by the liberal, cynical élitist Laschs of this world.

It would be unwise to dismiss Roszak, as so many dismiss the new therapists, as a crank. Equally, it would be unwise to see the new psychotherapies as some kind of encapsulated phenomenon, unrelated to the wider trends and fashions of contemporary society. At the time of the Jonestown massacre in Guyana it was fashionable to look for psychological explanations, to see the bizarre happening as symptomatic of a wider sickness, a symbol of impending moral and social collapse. The Manson murders, the Patty Hearst 'conversion', the morass of the Moonies have all provoked similar speculation and interpretation. Such theorising can prove tricky yet it would be foolish to ignore the common theme of *conversion*. 'Conversion', wrote William James, 'is in essence a normal adolescent phenomenon, incidental to the passage from the child's small universe to the wider intellectual and spiritual life of society'. A number of critics, observing the growth of cults of bewildering variety, have suggested that the unique social pressures of the 1970s made the passage from adolescence to maturity particularly difficult. These pressures they identify as the mechanical quality of much education, a tightly competitive job market, a sense of obsolescence felt by many young adults and the menaces of an overly materialist and eroticised society'. Through membership of a cult, the adolescent's anguish about being marginal to society is suddenly replaced by a sense of cosmic purpose and corporate power.

And what of the claims of the cult to be 'therapeutic', to be delivering 'treatment' in the medical sense of the word? Some of the new psychotherapies, it should be said at once, insist that they are not in the business of *treatment*. Treatment conjures up notions of illness and patients and doctors. The psychotherapies antagonistic to such notions insist that they are not providing treatment for the mentally ill, but are in the business of helping individuals to discover themselves as mature beings. Words like 'growth', 'transformation', 'self-actualising' and 'mature' abound and at times the therapies that employ them sound much more like courses of philosophy than methods of treatment. Yet it is a rare approach that forgoes absolutely the description of being a therapy. Perhaps it is difficult to throw off a mantle which carries with it an aura of respectability, selflessness, professionalism and reliability. For example, even psychodrama, which does seem at the outset to lay little claim to therapeutic pretensions, earns its first endorsement from Zerka Moreno, widow of its founder, by virtue of its alleged superiority over more orthodox psychiatric approaches in curing the mental illness of her sister (Chapter 5), while an overtly anti-therapeutic approach like *est* cannot resist having its effects evaluated against other 'therapies' in research journals and cannot forgo making claims on behalf of its proven superiority in all manner of situations from alcoholism to running a supermarket (Chapter 7).

These then are some of the hopes raised by the new therapies – the possibility of healing, of rebirth, of religious meaning, of growth, of perfection – hopes which hold out the simultaneous and beguiling promise of fulfilment here on earth, and not in some ethereal and possibly mythical heaven. It may seem a long way from Freud and, of course, it is. Yet the transformation of psychotherapy from a treatment of limited applicability and efficacy into a philosophy of life applicable to all has directly contributed to the present situation wherein the activity of talking about oneself and one's feelings has become highly prized.

But there is one more promise held out by the talking

therapies, the promise of 'holism' (Chapters 3 and 4). Holism emphasises the intricate relationship between man's biological and psychological systems and stresses the contribution of good physical health, nutrition, exercise, environmental influences and spiritual replenishment to good mental health. The approach, enshrined in gestalt therapy but also reflected in somewhat more esoteric approaches, is a reaction against what is seen as a disastrous split in the way Western man views himself, a split between his rational, cerebral, intellectual powers on the one hand and his emotional, visceral, physical essence on the other.

Technological medicine is a particular target for criticism and is unfavourably contrasted with approaches stressing holistic health as revealed in the following advertisement for an Esalen one-month course entitled *Inner Road to Health*:

> This is a workshop about health – learning how to get well and stay well, and helping others to do the same, all by natural means. Sessions held during the day will focus on a variety of holistic health practices. We will cover acupuncture and acupressure, herbal systems, homeopathic systems, rolfing, nutrition and diet, different forms of massage such as shiatsu, polarity, Esalen massage and deep-tissue massage, and topics in anatomy, physiology, organic gardening etc. The sessions will be both experiential and didactic. As different systems are introduced, we'll explore ways of experiencing and embodying this knowledge, using our hands as well as our minds. For example, we'll gather our own herbs to prepare powders, salves, infusions, tinctures, and herbal baths while at the same time learning the medicinal uses of various American, Chinese and Indian herbs. Evening sessions will focus on individual and interpersonal process work, based on gestalt and psychosynthesis approaches. A principal emphasis throughout the month will be on discovering and awakening inner resources. In this connection regular meditation, chanting, yoga, tai chi, massage and other quieting practices will help still the mind and relax the body, permitting new sensitivities to emerge.

From Freud to organic gardening – it has been a long and tortuous road, so long and so tortuous that many at this end of the journey are unaware of where it all began. All the 'new' therapies stress their novelty. Yet all embody ideas, values, techniques even, which have been seen before. What they all hold out, however, as we shall see remains tantalisingly elusive.

References

1 Hogan, Daniel B. 1979 *The Regulation of Psychotherapists*, Vol I. p.2 Ballinger. Cambridge. Mass.

2 Reil, J. C. 1803 'Rhapsodies in the Application of Psychic Methods in the Treatment of Mental Disturbances'

3 Frank, J. D. 1978 'General Psychotherapy: The Restoration of Morale' *The American Handbook of Psychiatry* 2nd edition. Editor, S. Arieti, Chapter 7, Part 2, p.117 Basic Books. New York

4 Storr, A. 1979 *The Art of Psychotherapy* p.vii Secker and Warburg/Heinemann. London

5 Wolberg, L. 1977 *The Technique of Psychotherapy* 3rd edition. Part 1, p.3 Grune & Stratton. New York

6 Wolfe, T. 'The "Me" Decade' *New York Magazine* 23 August 1976 pp.26-40

7 Jones, E. 1959 *Free Associations: Memoirs of a Psychoanalyst* Basic Books. New York

8 Freud, S. 'Introduction' to the Special Psychopathology Number of *The Medical Review of Reviews* p.255

9 Freud, S. 1964 'Civilization and its Discontents' In: *The Standard Edition of the Complete Works of Sigmund Freud* Editor, J. Strachey. Hogarth. London

10 Freud, S. 1964 'The Future of an Illusion' In: *The Standard Edition of the Complete Works of Sigmund Freud* Editor, J. Strachey. Hogarth. London

11 Bleuler, E. 1980 Quoted in *Freud: The Man and The Cause* (R.

Clark) p.294 Jonathan Cape and Weidenfeld and Nicolson
12 Gross, M. L. 1978 *The Psychological Society* Simon & Shuster. New York
13 Tseng, W. and McDermott, J. F. 1975 'Psychotherapy: historical roots, universal elements and cultural variations' *American Journal of Psychiatry* 132: pp.378-384
14 Lasch, C. 1976 'The Narcissist Society' *New York Review of Books* 23 (15): pp.5-13
15 Roszak, T. 1976 *Unfinished Animal* Faber Paperbacks

2 Encounter Therapy – Love is What You Need

. . . the whole movement towards intensive group experience in all its forms has profound significance for both today and tomorrow. Those who may have thought of the encounter group as a fad or phenomenon affecting only a few people temporarily would do well to reconsider. In the troubled future that lies ahead of us, the trend towards the intensive group experience is related to deep and significant issues having to do with change.

Carl R. Rogers[1]

When the definitive history of psychoanalysis comes to be written, the most intriguing chapter will probably be that which attempts to explain how the United States, that land of legendary optimists, 'the only idealistic nation in the world' as Woodrow Wilson once characteristically proclaimed it, successfully ingested what is at heart a pessimistic theory based on man's fallibility and imperfection and regurgitated it in the form of a manual of self-growth and positive thinking.

More than any other country, America took psychoanalysis not merely to its medical bosom but to its very cultural heart. There one finds the highest *per capita* ratio of psychoanalysts. It is there that medical psychiatry has been infiltrated to the most significant extent by what W. H. Auden called 'a whole climate of opinion'. It is into everyday American life that the high-flown jargon of psychoanalysis has seeped out of the clinics and the consulting rooms.

No one, in our view, has been more crucially influential in this regard than Carl Rogers. Indeed, when the self-same psychoanalytical history appears we venture to suggest that next to Freud himself the name of Rogers will stand as one whose effect on the way Americans perceive and make sense of their lives and life in general has been most influential. For it was Rogers who partially demythologised psychoanalysis. He stripped it of its secrecy, its élitism and its theoretical complexity, all features which jarred unpleasantly with the American faith in instant understanding and the ready accessibility of even the most complex of ideas to even the most simple of minds. He substituted instead a sort of Sears Roebuck catalogue of instructions for living. At the heart of Rogers' theory is his belief that the primary human drive is towards self-actualisation, a need for enriched human experience. Psycho- or talking therapy is successful in so far as it embodies three qualities – so-called Communicated Authenticity or genuineness, Regard or warmth, and Empathy or understanding. All you need, in other words, is not love but the acronym CARE.

So when we set out for California to take a look at the newer forms of therapy it was to the man we regarded as the father of the modern talking therapy that we first journeyed. We found him living with his wife in a small, simply furnished, sun-splashed bungalow, perched high on the hill which hangs over the sandy beaches of La Jolla, near San Diego in Southern California. Balding, bespectacled and shirt-sleeved, Carl Rogers welcomed us both into a shaded lounge, full of the trappings of a busy life as a world-renowned psychologist and guru. Despite the fact that at the time of our visit his wife was unwell, he gave freely, too freely indeed, of his time, an act which seemed typical of a man who exuded such decency and genuine goodness as to make it difficult to voice any reservations about his basically optimistic and idealistic philosophy of man.

Before we spoke of Encounter therapy and the movement associated with his name, he talked a little of his background, of where, as they say in California, 'he was coming from'. He had spoken of this before in a lecture to Brandeis University, and a more detailed exposition of the relationship between his background and his ideas can be obtained in his book *On Becoming a Person*.

Rogers, like a number of the influential American psychologists and psychiatrists of the 1950s (Burrhus Skinner is another), comes from the strict and somewhat uncompromising religious and puritan atmosphere of the mid-West. The fourth of six children, Carl quickly learned the virtues of thrift, abstemiousness and hard work. Dancing was sinful, even carbonated beverages were slightly wicked. Life was tough, purposeful and ordered and there was no lack of experts, secular and religious, to tell you how to live it. He went to college in Wisconsin to study agriculture where he learned, among other things, that the storing of encyclopaedic knowledge for its own sake was a pointless exercise. 'Don't be a damned ammunition wagon,' exhorted his agronomy professor, 'be a rifle'.

He then changed from agriculture to history, but an even more significant change occurred when a trip to China for an International World Student Christian Federation Conference presented itself. According to Rogers, it was a turning point. He saw Germans and French hating each other (it was 1922) and he realised to his astonishment that 'sincere and honest people' could actually hold different and often incompatible views. Following the China visit came several years at the Union Theological Seminary in New York. He intended to train for religious work but, in common with the majority of his contemporaries, he found that in thinking his way through the philosophical questions raised there, he thought himself 'right out of religious work'. 'I felt', he told us 'that while I would always be absorbed by questions concerning the meaning of life, its values and its purposes, I would not be able to give to any specific religious doctrine my assent'. It was his reluctance to profess a system of belief that also led him out of Freudian psychoanalysis, after he had been exposed to its influences during his period of psychology training at Teachers' College in Columbia University. Initially he 'soaked up' the dynamic Freudian views and was a convinced if not card-carrying devotee when he became a psychologist at the Child Study Department of the Society for the Prevention of Cruelty to Children in Rochester, New York. He spent twelve years there and, initially at any rate, he functioned in a fairly orthodox way if his contributions to the literature are any guide. *Social workers and legislation, Three surveys of treatment measures used with children, The clinical psychologist's approach to personality problems* and *A diagnostic study of Rochester youth* do not suggest any clues to the fundamental disenchantment with clinical psychology that was to come, but one paper which appeared in 1939 entitled *Authority and case work – are they compatible?* raised one of the issues that was to preoccupy Rogerian psychotherapy for several decades.

For him the crucial issue, was the question of expertise. He recalled, in his Brandeis lecture, the case of a youthful fire-raiser whose unaccountable impulse to indulge his alarming habit was, in classic Freudian style, traced back to a sexual impulse concerning masturbation. 'Eureka! The case was solved. However, when placed on probation, he got into the same difficulty.'

Freudian theory, Rogers discovered, didn't always work. Worse, it actually got in the way. To us he related the case of the harassed mother whose adolescent son was giving her hell. Applying Freudian theory again got Rogers nowhere and, in a sudden burst of Rogerian genuineness, he told her so. She agreed, got herself together to leave, then turned and asked 'Do you ever take adults for counselling here?' Back she came, sat down and poured out her misery about herself, her fragmenting marriage, her sense of failure – all very different from the sterile 'case history' she had given before. 'Real therapy began there', observed Rogers, 'and ultimately it was very successful'.

Several such incidents began to insinuate the seditious notion into Rogers' brain that it might be the *client* and not the *analyst* who is the expert, who might know best about what is wrong, what needs to be done and how to do it. In Ohio State University, where Rogers went in 1940, he began to develop his distinctive view subsequently to be published in 1942 as *Counselling and Psychotherapy*. Over the next twenty-two years (five at Ohio, twelve at the University of Chicago, and four at Wisconsin), in a score of books and dozens of papers, Rogers put together the bones of Rogerian psychotherapy and laid the foundations for the Encounter movement that was to proliferate through North America, finally flowering, if that is the precise word, in the 'Me Decade' of the 1970s as a major leisure activity, cultural force and language of social intercourse, displacing in the process the formidable Freudian monolith.

So what were the revolutionary tenets that Rogers, like some latter-day Luther, nailed to the clinic door in his act of rebellious reformation? If the religious analogy offends, and in these relentlessly secular days it tends to, then in defence let it be said that it was precisely this analogy which Rogers used when talking to us of his rejection. To Rogers, Freudian psychoanalysis has all the trappings of a fossilised religious ideology while psychoanalytic institutes, in his own bitter words, 'have become the most orthodox religious institutions I know and the way they have frozen analytic thought into a dead form is horrible.'

From the outset Rogers, the mid-Western, religiously trained, Calvinistically steeped, Freudian, one-time believer in hell-fire, primitive impulses, infantile neuroses and oedipal conflicts, threw over the gloomy vision, shared by the sage of Vienna and the Pope of Rome, of man as a flawed, forked animal. Instead of a fallen angel or the battleground of savage passions warring for supremacy, the Rogerian vision of man is reassuringly positive.

'Man, at the core,' he told us, 'is essentially trustworthy and constructive. Evil behaviour, which we see and of which the world can give plenty of examples, is really the outcome of social conditioning'.

Client, patient, analysand, and sinner – they are all potentially, essentially, intrinsically good. And what of the analyst, expert, therapist, counsellor? In orthodox Freudian psychoanalysis the therapist appears possessed by and in possession of enormous power. Freud himself, in addition to explaining the horse phobia of Little Hans and unravelling the psychological disturbances of Gustav Mahler, interpreted Leonardo da Vinci's artistic genius in terms of a conversion of primitive sexual energy, and Woodrow Wilson's compromises prior to the Treaty of Versailles as a consequence of an infantile fear of his father. Freud was in no way inhibited by the disagreeable fact that in both the latter cases the subjects of the inquiry were dead and had never actually met Freud let alone unlocked the secrets of their respective psyches. The enigma of Antigone, the blindness of Oedipus, the childhood of Hitler, the novels of William Golding – the audacity of analytic interpretations is rivalled only by their fertility. Is it surprising that even today, with Freudian analysis in intellectual crisis, the figure of the analyst is surrounded by fantasies of omnipotence, fantasies fed by the knowledge that to become a high priest involves years of indoctrination, learning a complicated language and rite, and adopting an air and posture of aloof, confident and critical detachment concerning the activities and pastimes of one's fellow-men?

It is all of this that Rogers rejects. He insists that it is not the psychotherapist's own expertise that matters in therapy, nor even the techniques that he uses. What is important in talking therapy is quite simply the relationship between the patient and the therapist and more particularly three personal qualities in the therapist himself. The first of these is *empathy*, or very sensitive listening:

> This is something that is very rare in our lives. We usually listen in order to respond, to make a judgement, to express our own opinion in contrast to the one that is being expressed. Really to sensitively listen to this other person, to try to get inside the world of that other person, to sense and feel it as if you were inside that world, is a very rare thing, but a very powerful thing.

Rogers believes that a relationship is more likely to be growth-promoting if, in addition to empathy, there is real *caring* on the part of the helping person. 'I like to use the word "prizing" – the way a parent prizes a child. It does not mean that the parent approves of everything the child does, or anything of that sort, but the worth of the person is very real and prized.'

The third quality necessary in a therapist is *genuineness*, or what he sometimes calls realness. 'That means that there is no façade, no professional white coat. If the person I am at this moment comes in contact with the person the client is at this moment then things are certain to happen.'

What sort of things? By means of applying his 'person-centred' approach the therapist or counsellor enables or facilitates the development in the client of a new self-confidence. This is achieved by treating the client not as a defective object to be manipulated and repaired (Rogers' view of medical interventions), nor as a bundle of complexes to be interpreted and explained (his view of psychoanalytic interventions), but as a person to be valued. In the encounter group the crucial activity is not treatment, interpretation, revelation, or advice, but listening, listening 'acceptantly to myself', listening to 'the richness in each other'. In this way can be developed 'a deep trust in the capacity of the individual to be himself, to accept himself, to express himself'. The paradox, which runs through so many of the newer therapies, that we cannot change, we cannot move away from what we are, until we thoroughly accept what we are, is a central notion in the Rogerian view of the person. Rogerian psychotherapy has its techniques, of which more later, but its essence is as a system of values, a philosophy for living. It can be summed up in a series of statements which bear a resemblance to a religious credo, a resemblance which does not seem to be accidental or coincidental.

In my relationships with persons I have found that it does not help, in the long run, to act as though I were something I am not.

I find I am more effective when I can listen acceptantly to myself and can be myself.

I have found it of enormous value when I can permit myself to understand another person.

I have found it enriching to open channels whereby others can communicate their feelings, their private perceptual world to me.

I have found it highly rewarding when I can accept another person.

The more I am open to the realities in me and in the other person, the less do I find myself wishing to rush in and 'fix things'.

Life, at its best, is a flowing, changing process in which nothing is fixed.[2]

We have come a long way from the mid-West. But there is more. We have claimed that Rogers is the father of most of the cults and creeds and therapies that jostle, compete and thrive in the great psychological supermarket that is California. It is doubtless a contested claim and there will be those who will argue the case for Wilhelm Reich or Fritz Perls or even Abraham Maslow, individuals whose roles are mentioned in subsequent chapters. But Rogers was the first to marry the following two assertions, a coupling of which was to prove exceptionally bountiful during the succeeding thirty years:

> Persons have a basically positive direction.
> Experience is for me the highest authority.

Such consummately positive endorsement of the goodness of the human spirit might strike some observers of a more cynical persuasion as a little naïve. It seems a trifle disingenuous not to say superficial to relegate the horrors of the human condition, Auschwitz and Buchenwald, Hiroshima and Nagasaki, My Lai and Kampuchea, Manson and Jonestown, to the outcome of social conditioning! At the very time that Carl Rogers exhorted us to shrug off our European scepticism, born of an over-exposure to the grim historical memory of two appalling conflagrations in this century alone, the psychotherapy-obsessed citizenry of California were resolutely voting in Proposition 13, which, whatever its long-term benefits to the capitalist economy of the USA, owed much of its appeal to the fact that it cut welfare programmes, health care and urban development plans in favour of handing back taxes to the relatively affluent. Offered such an opportunity to exhibit their inherent 'positive direction' most of the newly enriched population, it was being predicted, would not embark on personally-inspired programmes aimed at helping the less fortunately endowed in California (of whom there are still surprisingly plenty) but would use the opportunity to become still richer (while doubtless spending a little more on finding their true selves through therapy).

While Rogerian utopianism flourishes best in America, it is quite clearly detectable across the Atlantic too. Anthony Storr's latest book *The Art of Psychotherapy* illustrates the extent to which such ideas have penetrated even the very citadel of psychoanalytically derived psychotherapy in the NHS. While acknowledging the fact that he himself was originally trained as a Jungian and underwent a period of analysis with a Freudian analyst, Storr, declares:

> It is my belief that we shall soon see the disappearance of the analytical schools as discrete entities. Although personal analysis will continue to be an important part of training for those who wish to specialise in psychotherapy, the labels of 'Jungian', 'Kleinian', 'Freudian', will become less and less important as research discloses the common factors which lead to a successful outcome in psychotherapy, which to my mind is largely independent of the school to which the psychotherapist belongs.[3]

It is quite clear from what Storr subsequently writes that these 'common factors' have more than a passing resemblance to Rogerian notions of empathy, caring and genuineness. In *Psychiatry Observed* Baruch and Treacher in the course of a sustained attack on the medical foundation of British psychiatry, extol the virtues of 'psychotherapy' which, mysteriously, they refrain from defining until close to the end of the book. When it eventually emerges it turns out to be about relating to patients as human beings, and ensuring that the therapist operates:

> within a self-reflexive framework which enables him to understand the contribution that he makes to the personal interactions in which he is involved. He must also treat his client as an equal – as somebody who also strives to make sense of his own world and his own behaviour. The medical model inevitably carries with it a set of assumptions about patients that is hostile to psychotherapeutic approaches.[4]

Storr teaches psychotherapy to trainee psychiatrists in Oxford; Treacher is a lecturer in the Department of Mental Health at

Bristol University, Baruch being a one-time sociology student in the same Department. In the fields of social work, marriage guidance, pastoral counselling, vocational training up and down the country you will hear the self-same solemn endorsements of the essential goodness and equality of man and the curative effects of understanding and love.

How is such a system of values actually implemented in practice? After all, the psychoanalyst, by virtue of the theoretical structure underpinning his work, has a ready-made system of interventions. He explores his patient's dreams, early childhood memories and parent-child experiences. He examines in intimate detail the client's handling of the relationship involving the therapist himself, looking for clues concerning the unresolved conflicts and crippling patterns of unconsciously motivated behaviour.

The medically-trained doctor, with his biological and social framework, explores his patient's physical status, evaluates the possible role of environmental and social stresses, modifies symptoms by means of straightforward advice and reassurance and intervenes with drugs and related physical treatments to ease discomfort and pain. But what do Rogerians do? If it is based on listening, to what do they listen? If counselling is truly non-directive then is the counsellor merely a human tape-recorder into which the client pours his woes to be played back if and when the client chooses? How do Rogerians demonstrate their love, empathy and genuineness?

On such points Rogers tends to be somewhat vague. The practical aspects of therapy are however straightforward enough. Most Rogerian work these days is done within the so-called encounter group. The group, whose optimum size ranges between six and ten (there have, however, been groups of upwards of a hundred people), has a counsellor or facilitator whose task is to encourage the participants to express their true feelings about themselves and each other. Drugs are not used, interpretations are avoided.

> No one is ever pushed to express anything. There is an opportunity for expression. If they [the clients] express something there is an attempt to understand it. There is no attempt to force a person to disclose anything, no goal that complete openness is a must. I think every person needs their own private thoughts and feelings, the ones they are comfortable with. It is the thoughts and

feelings they are not comfortable with that by expres
benefit.

The foundation of Rogerian therapy revolves aroun
tionship with the facilitator and other members of
This relationship is based on what Rogers calls m
actualising tendency' by which he means that tende..., inner-
ent in all of us to want to develop our potentialities, to expand
and to grow. Despite the fact that the Rogerian approach is
generally practised in groups, therapy is still person to person as
he described in *On Becoming a Person* in 1961:

> The therapist feels the client to be a person of unconditional
> self-worth, of value no matter what his condition, his behaviour,
> his feelings . . . . the therapist is genuine, hiding behind no
> defensive facade but meeting the client with the feelings which
> organically he is experiencing . . . the therapist is able to let him-
> self go in understanding this client . . . (senses) what it feels like
> to be the client at each moment of the relationship.[2]

Such a therapist enters into a relationship with each client comfortable in the fact that he knows not where it will lead and
satisfied with the knowledge that he is providing a climate
which will permit the client 'the utmost freedom to become
himself'. The authors of a comparative study of psychotherapies
described what optimal Rogerian therapy means to the client
thus:

> an exploration of increasingly strange and unknown and danger-
> ous feelings in himself, the exploration proving possible only
> because he is gradually realising that he is accepted uncondition-
> ally. Thus he becomes acquainted with elements of his experience
> which in the past have been denied to awareness as too threaten-
> ing, too damaging to the structures of the self. He finds himself
> experiencing these feelings fully, completely, in the relationship,
> so that for the moment he is his fear, or his anger, or his tender-
> ness or his strength. And as he lives these widely varied feelings
> in all their degrees of intensity, he discovers that he has experi-
> enced himself, that he is all these feelings. He finds his behaviour
> changing in constructive fashion in accordance with his newly
> experienced self. He approaches the realisation that he no longer
> needs to fear what experience may hold, but can welcome it
> freely as a part of his changing and developing self.[5]

.t may help to explain the nature of Rogerian interactions by providing an example which Rogers himself has described again in *On Becoming a Person*. It is the case of a Mrs Oaks who, embittered by marital and family troubles, admits that she feels hostile to humanity. She distinguishes between feeling love towards people and caring for them:

> *Client:* It might be expressed better in saying I care terribly what happens. But the caring is a – takes the form – its structure is in understanding and not wanting to be taken in, or to contribute to those things which I feel are false and – it seems to me that in – in loving, there's a kind of final factor. If you do that, you've sort of done enough. It's a —
>
> *Therapist:* That's it, sort of.
>
> *Client:* Yeah. It seems to me this other thing, this caring, which isn't a good term – I mean, probably we need something else to describe this kind of thing. To say it's an impersonal thing doesn't mean anything because it isn't impersonal, I mean I feel it's very much part of a whole. But it's something that somehow doesn't stop . . . it seems to me you could have this feeling of loving humanity, loving people, and at the same time – go on contributing to the factors that make people neurotic, make them ill – where, what I feel is a resistance to those things.
>
> *Therapist:* You care enough to want to understand and to want to avoid contributing to anything that would make for more neuroticism, or more of that aspect in human life.
>
> *Client:* Yes. And it's — (pause). Yes, it's something along those lines.[2]

Rogers, in providing this excerpt, points out that in struggling to describe her own feelings, the client is probably describing the therapist's attitude towards her as well. What the therapist is supposed to be feeling is 'a caring enough about the person' such that he has no wish to interfere with her development nor to use her in any self-aggrandising goals of his own. The satisfaction comes in having set her free to grow in her own fashion. The therapist does not restrict himself to expressing understanding (conventionally conveyed by uttering 'mm-hmmm with just the right intonation!') but restates what the client struggles to say in such a way as to enable her to reassess its meaning and acknowledge to him and to herself that this is indeed her actual view.

In Rogerian group therapy, the participants are encouraged to create a climate of trust in which each can express his or her most intimate feelings so that helping and healing relationships may be constructed. In one encounter group, the facilitator or leader suggested an 'exercise' in which one of the members was cradled by the others. 'Do you have any feelings that we might drop you?' asks the leader. 'What I was trying to convey with this was that the group was willing and able to cradle one of its members . . . and that person can give herself to the group'.[6] In another group, an exercise is employed in order to give concrete expression to the actual relationships within the group:

> I'd like to have you try visualising who you feel close to and distant from. Try to place each of us in the group according to how you feel to us. In other words, those that you feel closest to put close to you; those that you feel furthest from put far away from you. Just put us where we go; anywhere you choose. Move us around and change us as you see fit, like an interior decorator. Now let the rest of us look around as she places us and think in terms of how close we feel to her. Where would we put ourselves, one at a time?[7]

However, not all encounter groups are necessarily caring and supportive. Rogerian approaches, as modified by Synanon, the drug addict rehabilitation movement that flourished in North America until quite recently, emphasises the value of ripping away façades. Participants were verbally attacked and abused for fencing, parrying, keeping others at bay and retreating into verbalisations and intellectualisations. In recent years Synanon has changed its goals from offering an unorthodox yet apparently effective treatment for drug dependence to offering an alternative way of life. Small groups are the preferred way of working and the Synanon counsellors refer to the 'Synanon game' which takes place in these groups as a verbal dog fight. A Synanon group was included in the Stanford study of encounter group efficacy (see Chapter 10) and the following verbatim extract gives some impression of the dog fight in action:

> Like you've got this bird nest on your head, you know, and you're kind of spastic and you jerk and then you've got these cowboy boots you've been wearing for a long time and that dirty shirt. Do you have any socks on when you get up at night? Don't you sort of stand your clothes up? Then I ask you about public

figures and you name a couple of white authors . . . I ask you about yourself as a man and you want to take me on a god-damned trip. And this trip, you are so fucked up, you are trying to be white . . . I don't want to know about your background, I can tell you about your life . . .[7]

A participant in that same group commented that the group 'was really heavy. They attacked very viciously. In fact, all the girls were attacked on sexual issues. If they were virgins, they were attacked about that; if they weren't virgins, they were attacked for that.' The aura around Synanon has affected the whole encounter movement. Wherever we went in California we were struck by the extent to which most therapists were anxious to assure us that their groups did not practise such crude tactics. It may be relevant (it may not) that Synanon is now enveloped in allegations of chicanery, widespread intimidation involving whole communities, and fascist bully-boy tactics employed on a grand scale.

But such 'shock' tactics are by no means exclusive to Synanon. In the same Stanford study, there was a group led by a disciple of Jacob Moreno, the founder of psychodrama (Chapter 5). In one meeting, this self-styled 'tourist guide' and 'antenna' for the group, challenged a relatively silent member thus:

How come you don't say anything? Why do I always have to come to you? What's going on in your gut? . . . Why don't you be direct? Why do you use sarcasm like that? . . . We've got to find out who you are and what you feel? . . . I get so fuckin' tired of having to push you and find out what you're like. Do you want us all to be like you? How long do you want us to go? Twenty-four hours without saying anything?[7]

The leader then threw his cup of coffee across the room, slapped the unfortunate participant's face and, in the words of the authors of the study 'pushed him around a bit'.

However, there are other methods employed in encounter groups of somewhat more subtlety. Participants are often encouraged to close their eyes and touch each other's faces, imagine they are particular animals, split into groups to invent ways of introducing themselves to each other, wander around the group, find the person they know least and have a 'back-to-back' conversation and so on. All of these and other 'exercises' are designed to get behind the social and intellectual façades to find the 'real' feeling 'me' within each and every encounter participant.

We shall see later the evidence for and against the usefulness of these approaches (Chapter 10). Rogers, in his discussion with us, made much of the fact that his particular work has, over the years, been subjected to evaluation, and noted that as much could not be said of many of the other therapies in this general area. In one sense he is right. There have indeed been numerous studies of the therapeutic impact of caring and empathy, of the alterations in people's self-evaluation following exposure to encounter groups and of the characteristics of therapists which seem related to bringing about such changes. But much of what has been conducted can be faulted by virtue of the lack of properly selected samples, the failure to include a matched control (i.e. a group of people similar to those receiving therapy but who are not treated but are evaluated before and after an equivalent period to that of the therapy) and the possibility of bias (e.g. therapists participating in the treatment also acting as 'impartial' judges of the treatment's efficacy). Bearing such reservations in mind, one approaches with some caution the fairly extensive literature supporting the Rogerian view of the importance of empathy, genuineness and caring in the therapist. It is still far from clear whether such attributes are sufficient in their own right or are merely supplementary to additional attributes such as professional skill, theoretical knowledge, and specific techniques. The more demanding and complicated the problem, be it schizophrenia or a highly disorganised family relationship, the less likely that such attributes on their own are effective.

At this stage it is worth noting that some of the more enthusiastic proponents of the approach decry the usefulness of asking whether they bring about any degree of measurable change. Some go further and reject the whole notion of change or improvement or recovery in favour of the notion of *process*.

The good life is a process; it is a direction not a destination, and the direction which constitutes the good life is that which is selected by the client when there is psychological freedom to move in any direction. One of the key elements in that freedom is what Rogers terms an 'openness to experience'. Married to the vigorous anti-intellectualism of the movement, such an 'openness' might seem synonymous with a lack of critical judgement. In practice it is difficult to avoid concluding that such is the case. Jonestown happened after we had visited Rogers. Had it happened before we would undoubtedly have put to him the proposition that his own unqualified endorsement of 'gut feelings' and 'experiential openness' indirectly contributed to the exposure of drifting and psychologically vulnerable people to the blandishments of a manipulative charlatan and to following him to the ends of earth and beyond. Perhaps it was understandable, even forgivable, to write in 1961 that 'doing what "feels right" ' proves to be a competent and trustworthy guide to behaviour which is truly satisfying, though it betokens a somewhat shallow understanding of human nature. Two decades later can such boundless confidence in the essential untrammelled goodness of man be sustained without a judgement of monocular vision being visited on the seer in question?

Even introducing evidence of man's inhumanity to man into the discussion of Rogerian theory that sunny summer day in La Jolla seemed incongruous somehow. As suggested earlier, Rogers' basic decency makes it seem in some way dishonourable to mention the extent to which some of our fellow-men have fallen short of the noble expectations placed on them by this placid, honest and unpretentious man. His writings seem likewise to shun the blood, the passion, the rough beast in human relationships, so that when he does bring himself to discuss actual case histories the individuals concerned never seem to be warm, vibrant, flesh-and-blood people but sanitised and colourless. A typical example is provided in Rogers' latest book *Carl Rogers on Personal Power*[8] in which a case-history is provided on that old green-eyed monster itself: sexual jealousy. The actual account reads like the script of Bob and Carol, Ted and Alice, a movie which took Rogerian theories to their inevitable and hilarious conclusion. Fred loves Trish, Trish loves Chip, Janet loves Fred. They all have tremendous opportunities for mutual growth, support and personal maturation and Fred takes an overdose. Poor Fred feels threatened by Chip, threatened by Janet, threatened by his colleagues. The permutations and associated microscopic analysis of feelings is intermittently reviewed by Rogers, but the most illuminating comment comes from an observant friend who notes that what is missing from the entire account are 'the emotions of anger, fear, rivalry, lust and neediness'.

Rogers' contemporary, the philosopher and analyst Rollo May, shares these reservations. In his view Rogers fails to understand the tragic elements in the human condition. He told us how he once challenged Rogers, in the light of his ceaseless optimism, to account for the fate of Romeo and Juliet. Rogers replied that their untimely ends would have been averted if only they had been able to secure the services of a good counsellor. One envisages an encounter group composed entirely of Montagues and Capulets. May's anecdote was curiously apposite. Rogers has turned his mind to just such a contemporary dispute and he told us proudly of the efforts and achievements of a group of counsellors in applying his theories to Northern Ireland.

The overall values and goals of the encounter group movement are unashamedly ambitious. One goal is a spirit of enquiry, that is to say being cautious about making final judgements, being open to new ideas and ways of looking at the world, and being willing to experiment with new ways of behaving. A second goal is expanded consciousness and choice, that is to say a greater awareness of one's self in the world and a greater freedom to choose what one will do and who one will be. A third goal is authenticity in interpersonal relations, namely feeling free to be oneself as opposed to what others would like one to be. A fourth goal is collaboration, that is the ability to work cooperatively with peers, superiors and subordinates in an interdependent rather than authoritarian fashion. Related to this goal is the ability to resolve conflict through rational means which involves a problem-solving approach and a desire to avoid approaches favouring brute force, intimidation or suppression. These are the major values which underpin the human potential movement in general and the encounter group in particular. To be successful, an encounter group must strive to attain five specific objectives, according to Fr Gerard Egan of Loyola University in Chicago and a key figure in the counselling movement in the United States.[9] The first is that all participant concerns must become group concerns. Secondly, participants must accept the fact that their experience is a laboratory experience and that they will be expected to try out new ways of behaving in certain situations arising within the group. Thirdly, the group must establish a cooperative as opposed to a competitive goal structure. Fourthly, the principal focus of the group must be on the here-and-now, that is to say what is happening right now within the group rather than an individual member's past life. Finally, immediacy and specificity are encouraged by using the word 'I', speaking to a particular person, and being concrete and specific in describing another's behaviour.

These values and goals are part and parcel of the post-Rogerian counselling revolution. And a cornerstone of Rogerian theory is the notion of 'experience'. 'The touchstone of validity is my own experience' wrote Rogers:

> No other person's ideas, and none of my own ideas, are as authoritative as my experience. It is to experience that I must return again and again to discover a closer approximation to truth as it is in the process of becoming in me. Neither the Bible nor the prophets – neither Freud nor research – neither the revelations of God nor man – can take precedence over my own direct experience . . . . When an activity feels as though it is valuable or worth doing it is worth doing . . . . I have learned that my total organismic sensing of a situation is more trustworthy than my intellect.[2]

God alone knows what is meant by 'organismic sensing'. We never discovered from Rogers. However, one observer from this side of the water has commented on the contradiction that appears to be involved.

How can one say that 'my total organismic functioning is more trustworthy than my intellect' asks Heaton[10] 'when it is one's intellect that makes the judgement in the first place'? In the Rogerian scheme of things, however, it is not so clear that it is. Intellect and reason, on the relatively rare occasions when Rogers refers to them, seem synonymous with repression and distortion and are portrayed as alien and inhuman phenomena, interfering with the authentic, the 'real' expression of the self.

Rogers' rebellion against the twin institutions of Freudian psychoanalysis and mid-Western Calvinist Christianity continued into the 1970s in the form of a rejection of all corporate institutions. Sin, in so far as it exists, does so through the political parties, the great industrial complexes, the universities and technological colleges, the banks, the oil conglomerates, the judiciary, the bureaucracy, the government. The debacle of Vietnam, the tragi-comedy of Watergate, urban violence – all are attributed to a society which is authority-centred instead of being person-centred. Schools 'are primarily institutions for incarcerating or taking care of the young, to keep them out of the adult world', the universities death-orientated centres, obsessed not by learning and truth but by status and power. Of course there is much in this analysis that is hardly novel. It is Rogers' explanation for the fragmentation of our civilisation that is intriguing, for despite his person-centred protestations, it is not persons in his view who are responsible but impersonal organisations which appear to be accidentally populated by persons.

A similar strategy is employed when it comes to the problem of disease. It has been argued, and indeed repeatedly shown, that however efficacious Rogerian approaches are in helping people who are functioning relatively well to function even better, their efficacy in helping seriously mentally ill people to function at all is highly questionable. In our discussions with Rogers he admitted that the bulk, the overwhelming majority of the people who flock to encounter groups are not mentally ill in the reasonably strict sense of the term yet he seemed reluctant to accept that it might have relatively little to offer to those who are. Instead he embarked on a discussion of psychotic illness which made it abundantly plain that, just as he understands individual evil to be the inevitable reaction to disagreeable social circumstances, so he understands schizophrenia to be a purely psychological response to social stress and an interruption in the psychological growth of the individual. The answer in each case is the same – care, empathy and genuineness and an emphasis on self-actualising and growth.

Rogers seemed surprised by the suggestion that the present state of social disarray might be due more to a lack of critical reflection than an excess of it. We could not help but notice that in our discussions of schizophrenia he appeared totally ignorant of the work of the many social, biological and psychological researchers in Britain and in America who have successfully undermined the notion of a single cause in this most serious of mental illnesses. A lay readership would not necessarily be familiar with such research, but a psychologist of Rogers' stature, prepared to make therapeutic claims concerning this most intractable of conditions, should surely be better read. Of course he knew of Laing (in common with the majority of intelligent laymen) and this appeared to suffice.

This lack of reflection was to be noticeable elsewhere on our journey. People expected us to know of the boundaries which separated Ida Rolf's body therapy from Feldenkrais' massage method, yet were indifferent to and ignorant of developments in the wider medical and psychiatric world. Such ignorance in no way precluded them from making confident assertions concerning the universal usefulness of their particular therapy and the bankruptcy and disintegration of orthodox science and medicine. Nor could such a lamentable state of affairs be attributed entirely to the shortcomings of exposing on a national scale puny minds to half-digested knowledge. *Trahison des clercs* plays an inexorable role. From within the very universities that Rogerian theory vilifies rush supporters to the cause, decrying reason and criticism and throwing themselves wildly into the careering experiential bandwagon. Baruch and Treacher on this side of the Atlantic, Theodore Roszak on the far side – they, and others like them, renege on the values of patient study, the sifting of evidence and hypothetical testing in favour of trusting your gut and going where the mantra leads you.

Rogers is quite happy about where it leads. He exults in the fact that there is a 'radical new budding of persons' in America who may change the fundamental nature of that society. They are the drop-out executives and lapsed clergymen who are forming the counter-culture. They include members of oppressed minorities pushing out from generations of passivity into assertive and active lives. They are open about their sexuality, have a deep concern for 'authenticity', and are dismissive of bourgeois hypocrisy. So far so good, no doubt. In addition, they have a trust in their own experience and a profound distrust of all external authority. 'Neither pope nor judge nor scholar can convince these individuals of anything that is not borne out by personal experience'. So they decide to disobey those laws they regard as unjust and obey those they regard as acceptable. On a minor issue they smoke marijuana, on a major one they refuse to be drafted. Rogers nods approvingly; such views coincide with his mainstream, liberal and intellectual views. These young people are actively self-actualising, have a high regard for self and are in touch with their own and other people's innermost feelings. More important, they 'care'.

The problem arises when their high regard for self takes a direction which does not fit Rogers' clean and hygienic rules for a bloodless revolution. Nowhere in the pages of *Carl Rogers on Personal Power* does even a whiff of tear-gas or an echo of

Baader-Meinhof rhetoric manifest itself. The pages are replete with serious, long-haired preoccupied young Americans struggling desperately to feel feelings, authentic feelings, real feelings, spontaneous feelings through the insidious clamminess of this particular technique while the streets of American cities resound with gunfire and the more pessimistic of their elders batten down the hatches in preparation for the armies of the night. As the cities decay, as the putrefying odour of the Kennedy assassination cover-up is replaced by the invasive stink of Watergate which, in turn, gives way to the murky depths of Chappaquiddick, as yesterday's selfless, dedicated and, no doubt, 'counselled' marchers become today's executives, administrators and compromised legal advisers, Carl Rogers maintains his peculiar brand of cheery optimism and continues to indulge his perky endorsement of man's essential, intrinsic and visceral goodness.

In so far as it represents a counterblast against the mechanistic inanities of the behaviourists and the reductive technologies of the biologists, Rogers' emphasis on personal worth, compassion and altruism is timely and meritorious. But as a political manifesto, a philosophical statement, or a method of treatment for the mentally ill, Rogerian psychotherapy simply will not do. The soapy, sentimental quality of client-centred therapy, which may well explain its ubiquitous appeal, may equally well prove to be its fatal flaw. It is Christian love without the sacrifice or self-denial, personal growth without the struggle and the self-discipline, psychological 'treatment' without any clearly established notion of what is being 'treated' and whether it has any significant effect. It perfectly embodies the American tendency, as Freud saw it 'to shorten study and preparation and to proceed as fast as possible to practical application'. Its anti-intellectualism prophesying with glee the demise of the university as the last mediaeval centre of tradition, privilege and élitism, triumphantly enthrones not reason but instinct in the driving seat of modern man. In its rejection of the mumbo-jumbo, the jargon and the mystification of psychoanalysis and the gloomy, sin-ridden, Jansenism of certain forms of contemporary Christianity, Rogerian psychotherapy does admittedly hit the mark with unerring accuracy. But in its vigorous reaction, its blind and heady endorsement of the 'organismic', it threatens to prove equally disastrous in the long-term. In truth it is a tract and movement for our times. Faced with it and the world in which it flourishes, one is left with the conviction that we will need every shred of Rogers' own personal authenticity and instinctive decency to survive his theory's resolute denial of the dark side of man's soul.

References

1 Rogers, C. R. 1969 *Encounter Groups* p.169 Penguin Books. London
2 Rogers, C. R. 1961 *On Becoming a Person* Houghton Mifflin Company. Boston
3 Storr, A. 1979 *The Art of Psychotherapy* Secker and Warburg/ Heinemann. London
4 Baruch, G. and Treacher, A. 1978 *Psychiatry Observed* Routledge and Kegan Paul. London
5 Luborsky, L., Singer, G. and Luborsky, L. 1975 'Comparative Studies of Psychotherapies' *Archives of General Psychiatry* 32: pp.995-1008
6 Truax, C. B. and Carkhuff, R. R. 1967 *Towards Effective Counselling and Psychotherapy: Training and Practice.* Aldine. Chicago
7 Lieberman, M.A., Yalom, I. D. and Miles, M. B. 1973 *Encounter Groups: First Facts* Basic Books. New York
8 Rogers, C. R. 1978 *Carl Rogers on Personal Power* Constable. London
9 Egan, G. 1970 *Encounter: Group Processes for Interpersonal Growth* Brooks/Cole Publishing Company. Belmont, California
10 Heaton, J. M. 1979 'Theory in Psychotherapy' In: *Philosophical Problems in Psychology* Editor, N. Bolton. Methuen. London

3 Gestalt Therapy and the Holistic Movement

Give away your personal faculties of discernment, of evaluation, of self-reference, and you lose your integrity (your wholeness). Take responsibility for your every thought, your every feeling, your every action.

Fritz Perls. (Quoted
in an Esalen brochure)

A common complaint voiced about contemporary medicine is that it is impersonal and mechanistic. The staggering success of modern technological medicine with its transplants and its dialysis machines, its potent drugs and radiation therapies, its surgical precision and its confident, almost arrogant assumption of ultimate success in the battle against disease has to some extent tempered the resentment that people feel at the dehumanisation and the reductionism inherent in a wholly biological notion of man. But there is a persistent irritation with doctors who only appear at ease with their patients when they have reduced them to the level of defective pieces of machinery. There is, however, a reaction under way, within and outside of medicine, which sees the solution of disease not in terms of treatments such as drugs or surgery, but in terms of healthy behaviour and a more natural way of life.

In a vigorous account of the historical development of concepts of health and illness, René Dubos drew attention to the fact that since classical times there have always been two traditional approaches, compatible yet often, as now, contrasted:

> The myths of *Hygieia* and *Asclepius* symbolise the never-ending oscillation between two different points of view in medicine. For the worshippers of *Hygieia*, health is the natural order of things, a positive attribute to which men are entitled if they govern their lives wisely. According to them, the most important function of medicine is to discover and teach the natural laws which will ensure a man a healthy mind in a healthy body. More sceptical, or wiser in the ways of the world, the followers of *Asclepius* believe that the chief role of the physician is to treat disease, to restore health by correcting any imperfections caused by the accidents of birth or life.[1]

Contemporary medical orthodoxy endorses Asclepius, but there are movements within and outside of medicine, Hygieian in approach, which stress the links between 'natural' living and physical and emotional health and which portray disease and illness as the end-results of the 'unnatural' life-styles of contemporary, and particularly, urban man. The movement has spawned a new word – holism (or sometimes wholism) – which, stripped of its pastoral aura, means treating the individual as a whole person. Where technological medicine posits an omnipotent specialist technician and a passive, ignorant patient, holism emphasises the person rather than the disease, and stresses the importance of the interpersonal relationship between patient and physician and the individual patient's responsibility for initiating and maintaining his or her own health care. In the holistic health movement, *responsibility* is a hallowed word.

If Carl Rogers can be regarded as the father of the Encounter movement, then it is Fritz Perls who should be credited as the creative guru of the holistic movement. The prophet of Now (his is the most ringing endorsement of the need for immediate satisfaction that can be heard amidst the babble of exhortations which make up the new psychotherapy creed), Perls was a Berlin-born analyst who took his first personal analysis with Karen Horney at the Berlin Psychoanalytic Institute not long before Horney split from the Freudian movement. Horney insisted that the relationship between a patient and a psychoanalyst consists of more than a simple repetition of the infant's attitudes towards its parents (the classical Freudian view) and she stressed instead the need for the patient to experience emotionally all so-called 'on-going' feelings. Many psychotherapists, following Horney's view, now pay more attention to the here-and-now aspects of their patients' situations and less to infantile vicissitudes. However, her belief that *feelings* in the actual therapeutic encounter had tended to be overshadowed in orthodox Freudian therapy by intellectualisations and verbalisations, has been taken over and turned into the driving force of the experiential schools of psychology, of which client-centred therapy is one and the Gestalt therapy of Perls is another.

Perls worked with Wilhelm Reich in Germany (Chapter 4), spent the war years in South Africa, then came to America where he established Gestalt therapy during the 1950s. The true founder of Gestalt psychology was not, however, Perls but a nineteenth century German psychologist, Max Wertheimer. (The word 'Gestalt' is also German, meaning form, figure or shape). Wertheimer was fascinated by the phenomenon of perceived movement that in actual fact did not occur at all. For example, if two identical vertical lines appear simultaneously a small distance apart, they are, of course, seen as two stationary lines. However, of one of the lines appears a very short time before the other and slightly displaced to the right or left and, if the time interval is right, one will not see what happens physically nor what takes place in the activation of the retina of the eye, namely first one line and then another appearing in a different location. One sees instead a single line that moves quickly to the right or left. Wertheimer called this the 'phi phenomenon' and it underlies our perception of 'movies' which move only because we perceive movement where there is none, the film consisting, of course, of a strip of successive, slightly different, still shots. Another much quoted example is the vase-face figure shown below. In the figure, there is only one drawing on the paper but it can be seen either as a vase or as two faces turned towards each other. The relation of the parts to the whole in one object is quite different from the relation of the parts to the whole in the other.

It seemed to Wertheimer and a number of like-minded colleagues that traditional psychology had very little to say concerning this fascinating phenomenon, whereby naïve experience and peripheral stimulation do not correspond. The answer that the Gestalt psychologists came up with is that the whole is not simply the sum of the parts that go to make it up. Taking one stationary line and adding to it another stationary line slightly displaced in time and space does not produce a perception of two lines, one appearing before the other, but a perception of one line moving to the right or left.

The late Klaus Conrad, who was Professor of Psychiatry and Neurology at the University of Göttingen, believed that the application of gestalt theory to such diverse phenomena as disorders of speech, delusions and behavioural disturbances was not only productive and illuminating but actually provided a way around one of the major stumbling blocks confronting modern psychiatry.[2] The block, which was initially described by the psychiatrist-turned-philosopher Karl Jaspers, is the sharp distinction drawn between causal and explanatory relationships in psychopathology. Jaspers believed that an abnormal mental phenomenon, say a delusional belief, can be studied in either of two ways. We can try to explain it 'casually' by considering questions of change at the biological or organic level, whether it be some kind of brain enzyme defect or neurotransmitter fault. Alternatively we can try to reduce the psychological phenomenon of the delusion to simpler psychological terms, and, working rather like a historian does, look for psychological relationships. The aim in this second case is to provide some form of so-called 'psychological' understanding of the phenomenon.

These two alternative approaches to 'explaining' abnormal and indeed normal psychological phenomena remain compared and contrasted to this day. In Conrad's own words, 'we can explain scientifically in terms of cerebral physiology, or understand, interpret, propound as an art. Current psychopathology seems to offer us no third way'. He was dissatisfied with such a state of affairs, and insisted that it was as misguided to believe that one has explained an hallucination, once its electrophysiological correlates have been recorded, as it is to believe that one can clarify every problem simply by understanding its archetypal meaning. The third way he proposed was an analysis of psychopathological phenomena in terms of gestalt theory. Conrad defined gestalt as

> anything which stands out from its background as an organised, transposable whole, as a real phenomenon, as an experienced fact.[2]

The psychologist Kurt Lewin applied gestalt theory to the process of understanding interactions within social groups. Such groups can be visualised as units whose properties cannot be predicted from the properties of the individuals who compose them. Fritz Perls took these and related ideas, mixed them with inspirations from existentialism, psychodrama (Chapter 5) and psychoanalysis, and came up with that brand of gestalt therapy which flourishes in the growth centres of the US and within what is termed 'fringe' psychiatry there and in Britain and Western Europe.[3] Gestalt therapy stresses the immediacy of experience in the here and now, focuses on non-verbal expressiveness and describes itself as a philosophy of living in the present rather than in the past or future. As outlined by one of its enthusiasts[4], gestalt therapy is about experience rather than imagination and expression rather than explanation or justification. It stresses the necessity of avoiding the 'should' or the 'oughts' of life in favour of the prior need to take full responsibility for living and surrendering to 'being as one is'.

It is not easy to be sure what modern gestalt therapy amounts to, because most gestalt therapists prefer to indulge their penchant for rhetorical endorsements of the integrated, experiencing man rather than provide descriptions of their techniques. Klaus Conrad, an orthodox psychiatrist, provided a number of examples of how he believed gestalt approaches could be used to provide a fresh understanding of certain normal as well as abnormal mental phenomena. One such phenomenon is the well-recognised one whereby we temporarily are unable to recall a familiar name. It is a normal phenomenon but it is also seen in certain disorders of brain function and there is no firm boundary between the normal and the abnormal variant. Conrad provides an example of the phenomenon and discusses it from a gestalt perspective:

> The writer is discussing Thomas Mann and tries to remember the name of the heroine's second husband (Permaneder) in Mann's novel, *Buddenbrooks*. He thinks 'an Italian name', then 'Pembaur . . . Peano . . . (No, of course not, that's not it at all!)'. His son contradicts him and says, 'It is a typical Bavarian name, something like -inger, I think it has four syllables, and a lot of consonants'. His wife says '. . . . eder', and then, after a pause, 'Permaneder'.[2]

The first point to note, observes Conrad, is that although the missing name eludes identification there is 'something' there. The 'physiognomy' of the something begins to emerge – 'Italian' or 'Bavarian' act as a kind of 'foreshadowing'. Next two false gestalts appear, 'Pembaur' . . . . 'Peano', in both of which the initial letter is correct. The right gestalt is beginning to emerge. The ending of the missing word (-eder) is indeed 'Bavarian' while the quality of its beginning (Perman) is 'Italian'. Both are in fact gestalt qualities of the missing word. What emerges from the analysis, Conrad points out, is that the qualities experienced as 'Bavarian' and 'Italian' are not mistakes nor are they nonsensical but are to a large extent determined by the missing gestalt. With the emergence of the final gestalt the uncertainty which has accompanied the whole process disappears and with it the tension, the feeling of not-quite-rightness which accompanies false gestalts.

> The gestalt comes to us from above, or emerges from the depths; is 'strikes' us, we are illuminated from within. Always it appears to come from another sphere . . . . we are not aware that the final success is the result of an active process; on the contrary, we feel that we are passive participants, even though we may be making considerable efforts. These efforts at times seem almost to disturb the process of discovery, which is often more successful if we think of something else.[2]

There is much speculation concerning the relationship between the so-called 'pre-gestalts' and the unconscious, speculation which is largely unresolved. However, the many possible applications of the theory partly explain its wide appeal. Another example, also provided by Conrad, concerns the phenomenon whereby a deluded patient takes those around him, even strangers, for acquaintances. Whether there is a disturbance in perception, judgement, memory or concept-formation is unclear. For the gestalt theorist, the interesting question is why do these mistakes not occur all the time. Why do we not get people mixed up? After all, every human face is constructed in the same way and the difference can sometimes be hardly measured. To those who are unfamiliar with them, the Chinese often appear all alike. Among our own people, however, we manifest an astonishing ability to distinguish one man from another, even recognising people whom we have only seen once, perhaps, many years ago. However, if the face is seen for a very short period of time, or is presented when there is too little contrast, then mistakes are made. In gestalt terms, there is a particular point at which the undifferentiated stimulus changes and assumes its own particular 'physiognomy' but there is also a transitional zone in which a stranger can be taken as a friend. The reverse process occurs as well whereby the familiar face is no longer recognised. Under emotional stress, a normal person can also make mistakes of identification. Gestalt psychologists have subjected the concept of 'similarity' to intense scrutiny in an attempt to see what aspect it is that accounts for such mistakes of identification, that is to say whether it is some head or mouth movement, some motor habit, facial mannerism or particular posture. Delusional or mistaken identification occurs when one characteristic becomes dominant, the others receding into the background, so that the entire person is embodied in this one gestalt quality.

Gestalt theory emphasises the necessity of breaking down behaviours or feelings into their separate and discrete parts which are in turn analysed in terms of the significance they hold for the person who is involved. Gestalt therapy, as practised by the 'new' psychotherapists bears a somewhat shadowy resemblance to such gestalt psychology but one common facet is this concentration on breaking the whole into its constituents. Various techniques are used very frequently in a group setting. For example, when elements of conflict arise in such a group, the key patient involved may be asked to verbalise the feelings he is bringing to bear on his perception and understanding of his group colleagues. These gestalts are then analysed in fairly traditional ways with role playing and encounter approaches especially favoured. But there are simpler, some might even say, naïve techniques too. For example, when the Gestalt therapist senses that there are unresolved and unexpressed feelings on the part of some individual in the group he may insist that they are expressed and, if the individual has long-standing difficulties in self-expression, the therapist may encourage the playing of a game in which the individual makes a statement and ends it by saying 'And I take responsibility for it'. Where the patient has a fear of offending others, he is instructed to go around the other members of the group expressing his attitudes and feelings frankly to each of them. Similarly, if the patient is excessively prim, prudish or reserved, the therapist may insist that he plays the opposite role, verbalising sexual feelings and attitudes freely.

Gestalt approaches focus on the details of a person's appearance and behaviour. The way the patient talks, breathes, moves, mocks, applauds, approves, rejects, censors, looks for causes and so on may be obvious to him. But, so the argument goes, it is actually the expression of that individual's principal needs, for example to be dominant, good and impressive. 'It is precisely in the obvious that we find his (the patient's) unfinished personality' write Perls and his colleagues in the Bible of the movement, *Gestalt Therapy: Excitement and Growth in the Human Personality*, and they continue:

> only by tackling the obvious, by melting the petrified, by differentiating between blah-blah and real concern, between the obsolete and the creative, can the patient regain the liveliness of the elastic figure/ground relation. In this process, which is the process of growth and maturing, the patient experiences and develops his 'self'.[3]

The terms 'figure' and 'ground' are, of course, derived from the ideas of Gestalt psychology described earlier. The context in which an element appears is called in Gestalt psychology the 'ground' against which the 'figure' stands out. In health, the relation between figure and ground is a process of 'permanent but meaningful emerging and receding'. Attention, concentration, interest, concern, excitement are representative of healthy figure-ground formation whereas confusion, boredom, compulsions, fixations, anxiety and self-consciousness are indicative of figure-ground formation which is believed to be disturbed.

Modern man is seen to pay attention only to those actions which he performs deliberately. According to Perls, he neglects his spontaneous self. Gestalt therapy encourages people to enlarge the area of their awareness by attending to these spontaneous activities – eating, breathing, moving, speaking, posture. The emphasis is on self-awareness because it is this area in which most of us are believed to be handicapped. One is encouraged to concentrate initially on so-called 'external' events – sights, sounds, smells – and then on internal processes – images, physical sensations, muscular tensions, emotions, thoughts. One by one these various processes are to be identified as the individual concentrates as exclusively as possible on each. There is much insistence that modern man lacks an intimate relationship with his own body; we know where our legs are and we can picture them but can we *feel* them? No, we cannot, so there are techniques for concentrating on *feeling* where your legs are, *feeling* the tightness in your chest, *feeling* yourself walking, sitting, standing, lying.

One of the examples provided by Perls concerns the experience of headache. The person complaining of headache is encouraged in gestalt therapy to 'stay' with the pain:

> If he stays with his pains he may find that he has been contracting some muscles or that he feels a numbness. Let us say that he discovers his pains are associated with muscle contractions. Then we will ask him to exaggerate the contracting. He will then see how he can voluntarily create and intensify his own pains. He might then say, as a result of his discoveries up to now, 'It's as if I were screwing up my face to cry'. The therapist might then ask, 'Would you like to cry?'[5]

In this analysis, the cause of the headaches is traced to the individual's 'interruption' of his need to cry by giving himself headaches. At best, the patient may lose his need to cry but even before this stage progress has been made. 'The patient', continues Perls, 'has transformed a partial involvement (headache) into a total involvement (weeping)'. He has changed a psychosomatic symptom into 'an expression of the total self' and through this concentration technique has learned 'how to participate fully in at least one present experience'.

Concentrating on bodily feelings thus sharpens our awareness of our emotions. Another example given is what happens when you concentrate on facial feelings, forehead, eyes, jaw. Concentrating on a particular facial expression (or so it is claimed) enables you to experience the moods usually associated with this expression. So long as one is awake one is aware of something and that something always carries an emotional tone of some sort. And it is a cardinal belief of Gestalt therapy that the extent to which a person becomes aware of this *continuity* of emotional experience greatly determines the extent to which he or she achieves self-realisation – the goal of therapy.

A common feature of the new psychotherapies is that each, in addition to having a guru or leader with whom the movement is closely identified, has a key case, a patient whose psychopathology and/or idiosyncratic response to treatment started the leader down the particular road taken by the therapy in question. Gestalt's 'foundation case' was a young man who came to Perls for help with sexual impotence. In the course of giving Perls the details of his case, the young man described how although his general health was good, he was attending an ear-nose-and-throat specialist for treatment of chronic nasal congestion. This struck Perls forcefully. He remembered that Wilhelm Fliess, the close friend and confidant of Freud during the years of Freud's most basic psychoanalytic discoveries, had argued for existence of a 'reflex neurosis' emanating from the nose encompassing a plethora of physical symptoms including general aches and pains as well as more specific disturbances in the gastric, respiratory, cardiac and reproductive systems.[6] Fliess also argued that such symptoms, whenever of purely nasal origin, could be relieved by anaesthetising with cocaine a certain area inside the nose. Indeed, so impressed was Freud with this theory that he actually permitted Fliess to operate repeatedly upon his own nose and sinuses in the hope that Fliess might be able to cure him of certain neurotic symptoms. Fliess even removed and cauterised part of Freud's nasal turbinate bone.

Needless to say, Perls did not embark on a similarly surgical approach to the sexual problem of his patient. On the contrary, the recollection of Fliess' theory was the signal for Perls to recommend to his young patient that he discontinue all medical treatment immediately.

> During his next session, I requested him to direct his concentration alternately to his nasal sensations and his non-existent genital sensations. And an extraordinary thing happened. The nasal swelling decreased and the tumescence of the penis increased. Now he could both breathe freely and have sexual relations. He had not only interrupted his penis erections and displaced both the sensation and the tumescence to his nose, he had even begun to compartmentalize his symptoms and to pander to his dissociations by having different specialists attend to them. While the ear-nose-and-throat specialist was used to working on dissociated symptoms and local 'causes', the Gestalt approach enabled me to look for the total situation, to examine the structure of the field, to see the problem in its total context and to treat it in a unified way.[5]

Fliess supported his ideas concerning a nasal reflex neurosis by citing, amongst other evidence, the phenomenon of visible swelling of the nasal mucosa during menstruation, the occurrence of occasional nose bleeding during menstruation and pregnancy, and the fact that cocaine applications to the nose could cause accidental abortions.[7] 'Teutonic crackpottery' such ideas may very well be[8] but they are no more eccentric than those of Perls. It is worth noting, incidentally, that Freud was greatly taken with Fliess – he once was moved to call him 'the Kepler of biology'. Some of Freud's apologists are clearly as embarrassed by the uncritical admiration of their hero for Fliess as contemporary analysts are by any attempt to link the apparently bizarre and ersatz notions of the new psychotherapies with the sensible and 'scientific' ideas of more orthodox psychoanalysis.

Perls went to Esalen in the early 1960s and became 'the chief guru'.[5] 'Don't think, feel' and 'Lose your mind and come to your senses' were just two of his many axioms. It was at Esalen that he introduced Gestalt to the human potential devotees who were flocking to Big Sur in search of growth, health and human happiness through encounter. He spent his last days there, the besandalled, white-robed, benign, obese and bearded sage of an alienated, marginal society searching for a star to steer by. There he was joined by other luminaries of the human potential movement including Carl Rogers, Alan Watts, the philosopher who was largley responsible for incorporating ideas from Eastern philosophy into the encounter scene, and Abraham Maslow, an inspirational, charismatic figure whose ideas lie behind the desire for what he termed 'peak experiences', a desire which lies behind much of the enthusiasm for the new therapies. (Chapter 7).

Gestalt promptly steered Esalen into the forefront of the burgeoning holistic health movement. The message became unmistakeable. Without holistic health, we are but hollow men. In July 1977, the Easalen trustees went so far as to outline a general curriculum for health professionals to meet the challenges of the forthcoming decade. Its tone reflects the influence of Perls and the ideas of his Gestalt movement:

1 Caring for your body (e.g. body/sensory awareness, movement, meditation, exercises in jogging, other sports, nutrition and diet, other forms of health care such as massage: Esalen; shiatsu; polarity; rolfing; Feldenkrais; acupuncture; Alexander; homeopathy).

2 Intra/interpersonal awareness (e.g. gestalt, encounter/group process, meditation, 'team building'/organisation development) for day to day living, routine professional contacts, living and dying (being aware of working with death rather than

simply working with disease).

3 Conceptual/metaphysical issues in the field of medical care (e.g. anxiety in illness: positive and negative aspects, dying, perspectives about health, guilt over lack of control over health, malpractice insurance problems and responsibility).[9]

Despite the somewhat mystical aura which surrounds it, the 'wholeness' endorsed in the human potential movement is acceptable enough and indeed perfectly understandable, given the undeniably partial and truncated nature of so much of modern technological medicine. But it is doubtful that the somewhat insistent call for personal responsibility in the areas of health and illness, when stripped of its rhetoric, has quite the substantial content that its supporters claim. There is after all the undeniable fact that people develop illnesses for which they cannot be held responsible and which, despite attempts to forge a link which border on intellectual gymnastics, cannot be ascribed to 'partial Gestalts'. The simplistic application of holistic notions can produce rather dismal results. A twenty-three year-old woman, a few days after a hysterectomy for cancer, cries 'Somehow I did this to myself. I could have prevented this awful development in my life but I didn't. I brought this on myself. It is my fault.' Commenting on this despairing declaration of total responsibility, two psychologists at the University of California express concern at the 'callousness' in any philosophy that can provoke such a sense of abandonment and self-condemnation.[10] They also note with distaste one other feature of the Gestalt message, one it shares with the client-centred approach of Rogers, namely its tendency to focus so exclusively on the individual that it lets society off the hook. If the individual alone is responsible for his or her own well-being, society can continue to encourage us to abuse our bodies and, even worse, can continue to profit from such abuses.

Not that certain of the holistic approaches do not themselves seem more like abuses than therapies. A resource guide, published in 1978 and entitled *Wholistic Dimensions in Healing*,[11] provides details on the smörgåsbord of therapies available. The table of contents lists under the title 'Integrative Medical Systems' such approaches as homoeopathy, naturopathic medicine, chiropractice and applied kinesiology, the last-named based on the idea that 'virtually any disease state . . . is represented by specific muscle weakness patterns . . . Every organ dysfunction is accompanied by a weak muscle . . . and this weakness will be abolished immediately upon ensalivating the appropriate nutritional material'. There is a section on 'Nutrition and Herbs' which includes an exposition of 'Macrobiotics and Oriental Medicine'. This explains how all sickness and all foods can be classified in terms of 'yin and yang' and how foods of one type can be used to treat diseases of the other. In this section, the book's editor, Leslie J. Kaslof describes 'The Use of Whole Plant Substances in Healing' and declares:

> Through plants we re-establish our connection with the environment. Ingested plants touch and awaken aspects of our nature we may have only dreamed existed. Using whole plant substances is like praying – on a biochemical level.[11]

Other chapters cover such diverse and diverting therapeutic methods as 'Aeriontherapy', 'Radiesthesia-Psionic Medicine', 'Astrology' and 'Iridology'. The last named has as its central premise the notion that each organ of the body is represented by an area of the iris, thus permitting the diagnosis of internal ailments.

Many of these unquestionably holistic approaches are on tap at Esalen, 'the Harvard of the Me Decade' as Tom Wolfe mockingly terms it. To sample them come an army of weary businessmen and women, harassed executives of Genral Motors and Chase Manhattan Bank, oppressed housewives caught between the conflicting demands of their roles as mother, worker and wife, opting-out students, starry eyed hedonists and rebellious mid-western puritans. They flood into the Big Sur campus and pay a modest $35 or so a day to loll in the warm mineral baths and luxuriate under a body-oil massage between sessions of 'celebrative awareness' with Jinedra Jain and Katherine Da Silva Jain –

> We can either be saddened by, or just endure, or let be, or we can celebrate the way we manifest ourselves in our lives. In this workshop we shall explore a festive paradigm, examine our barriers, and experience processes to celebrate our emotions, thoughts, sounds, bodies – ourselves, and the Self expressing ourselves.[12]

Or one can get to grips with one's guts, gestaltically speaking in a Gestalt workshop with Pat and Neil Lamper, who in the same issue invite you to:

> Experience your own relating: how to better care for yourself in relationships with those you love. Using gestalt, fantasy, breathing and awareness of body stress, you will work with memories and dreams to re-experience past choices and to bring more energy into the present. We will work on contacting our inner self, our central vigour. [12]

Westerbake Ranch in Sonoma County is where residential workshops are also held in what the brochure invitingly describes as 'an intimate setting' including rustic cabins, home-cooked meals, a sauna and Japanese tub, a large swimming pool and beautiful scenery. There gestalt ranges free and the courses on offer illustrate the extent to which the simple notion of integrating bodily and mental experiences becomes elaborated into procedures, programmes and prescriptions of awesome banality. One summer programme offered Michael Murphy (one of Esalen's co-founders) on running and meditation and Betty Fuller (described in a biographical note as a humanist counsellor, body worker, teacher and consultant in holistic education and communications) fine-tuning 'the instrument of the bodymind' through 'guided imagery, meditation, music, movement, laughter and dance'. Gail Stewart Worth, owner of the Berkeley Massage Studio, hosted a weekend of movement, body meditation, relaxation and massage in which the first invitation was 'to make yourself at home – in your own body' and the second 'to touch, rock and rub each other with ease'. Should we have decided that we were already quite at home in our own bodies and just wanted 'to give ourselves permission to have fun, be silly and take risks, to experience reality and change', then Jasmine Nash and the San Francisco Dancers' Workshop Associates would have been just the job and 290 dollars for the five days seems a snip at the price, given that Jasmine and her friends threw in meditation and massage and 'low energy Black dance with live conga drums'.

This is all a long way from Gestalt psychology and the notion of wholeness being greater than the sum of the parts. Another way in which Esalen is currently exploring 'wholeness' is its attempt to create a balanced community or extended family in Big Sur. A moving spirit behind this particular approach is one of the co-directors, Janet Lederman. She identifies herself as an artist and teacher and is author of *Anger and the Rocking Chair* which she describes as 'a poetic account' of gestalt learning processes. Esalen, she asserts was once totally dominated by men; the women were allowed to be passive recipients of the wisdom of such male luminaries as Fritz Perls, Abraham Maslow and Aldous Huxley but children were not even seen, let alone heard.

Now there is a special section of Esalen reserved for children, 'the Gazebo', where adults, in the words of the characteristically po-faced and sonorous brochure, 'can come to learn about and with children'. Examination of the enlightened new approach to pre-school education reveals nothing apart from nudity which could not be found in a moderately progressive nursery school in the UK – sand and water play, climbing frames, paint. But 'in the spirit of the Universe, the Gazebo is ever changing' (microchip play next year perhaps?) and the goals and purposes include the reasonable, if elusive target, of a world environment that is healthy for all children. It should be said at this point that gestalt therapists have a tendency to declare goals of universal acceptibility (such as health, world peace and clean lungs) with such a wide-eyed and breath-taking spirit of pioneering as to suggest that the rest of us are hell-bent on arteriosclerotic dementia, nuclear armageddon and fetid respiratory systems as desirable ends in themselves.

Three weeks before our own arrival in Esalen a baby had been born, an event of even greater significance than we could have dreamt from the effulgent expression on the face of Ms Lederman. For this infant's portrait was to appear in the next Esalen prospectus alongside that of seventy-four-year-old biologist, Gregory Bateson, who since his arrival at Esalen the previous year had been tagged the 'resident patriarch' by the 'faculty members'. The message, lest we refugees from a diseased and disintegrating world missed it, was spelled out for us – the seven ages of man, were encapsulated within such a joint portrait. Esalen had found a role for two formerly forgotten and redundant groups, the very young and the very old.

Gregory Bateson was then a great, shaggy bear of a man, whose slow, often halting delivery contained enough of the traces and the timbre of an English accent to remind one that however long he might have lived in North America he was still unmistakeably an Anglo-Saxon academic. A world-famous anthropologist, he entered and remained in the US at the outbreak of World War II, married Margaret Mead (they later divorced in 1950) and from 1972 was a visiting professor at the University of California at Santa Cruz. One of the most remarkable scientific thinkers of his time (he was one of the first people to apply cybernetic and systems theory to the social sciences), here he was in Esalen surrounded by people for whom the whole edifice of scientific research and practice appeared to represent a brain-damaged and partially blinded leviathan, rampaging around in a wildly destructive fashion. It seemed clear to us why Esalen wanted Bateson. His stature conferred a certain aura on this university of feelings and his potential as guru and elderly patriarch seemed irresistible. But why was Bateson at Esalen? His answer to this question was that for his purposes Esalen was a congenial place to be. He was dying of cancer (though he was having therapy from an Eastern healer who was convinced that it was the tumour that was dying) and he felt happier surrounded by the easy and acceptable intimacy and emotional 'hanging-out' of the Esalen habitués than by his more cerebral, emotionally withdrawn academic fellows at the University of California. Bateson acknowledged that the search for therapy was in fact a search for a philosophy and accepted with a certain degree of helpless resignation that whereas the questions asked at Esalen and other American growth centres were often the right ones, the answers were almost always incongruous, inappropriate and inept. But his was a sympathetic dismissal – 'they know many things are wrong', he said of the earnest and intense seekers after holistic health at that time attending an evening of mantra, music and meditation while we talked in Bateson's cabin, 'but it is very difficult to put one's finger on what's wrong in one's own civilisation.'

The endless self-examination amused rather than disconcerted him. ('Britain is very much frightened of self-examination' was one of his few comments on the state of his birthplace.) For Bateson could see underlying the fripperies and excesses and inanities of Gestalt therapy an understandable impulse, which was a reaction against an excessive Western emphasis on intelléct at the expense of emotion. His tolerance, too, seemed founded on an awareness of the inadequacy of modern science to cope with the problems, philosophical, psychological, epistemological, inherent in the mind-body problem. If modern, established, orthodox science has manoeuvred itself into a cul-de-sac of reductionism, he seemed to be saying to us, then do not be too hard on where the unorthodox have ended up. In an 'Afterword' to a collection of essays on his thinking, Bateson wrote two years before his death:

It may comfort those who find the matter hard to understand if I tell them that I have driven myself over the years, into a 'place' where conventional dualistic statements, of mind-body relations – the conventional dualisms of Darwinism, psychoanalysis and theology – are absolutely unintelligible to me. It is becoming as difficult for me to understand dualists as it is for them to under-stand me. And I fear that it's not going to become easier, except by those being slowly exercised in the art of thinking along those pathways that seem to me to be 'straight'.[13]

Bateson is here talking about his complicated idea on evolution, cybernetics, species difference. But, for our purposes, the important point to note is his rejection, nay indifference, to a dualist notion of man with all its associated notions of mental and physical events existing separately, only affecting each other along particular points of contact. What his monistic view is, is difficult to comprehend and in the brief time we were at Esalen we saw precious little evidence that the participants in the university of feelings were over-anxious to obtain any illumination from the master. 'Resident patriarch' he may well have been to Janet Lederman but for most of the Esalen students he was a famous old man who held somewhat complicated ideas on existence and had a stubborn and old-fashioned devo-tion to the importance of words.

Yet the wholesale spreading of 'holism' (like an uncontrolled nuclear reaction was how an editorial in the resolutely orthodox *Journal of the American Medical Association* described it)[14] with its advocacy of touching, talking and trotting as the panacea for almost every human ailment from haemorrhoids to ulcers, arth-ritis to manic-depression, has not been contained within the United States. Britain may indeed be afraid of intense self-scrutiny but the fear has not deterred Gestalt from making a landing here and setting up shop. In the vanguard was Quaesitor, a London-based growth organisation which was set up in 1969 'to introduce, experience and develop new ideas in creative group work in human relations and personal growth'. Among its offerings were Rogerian encounter therapy, body massage, transactional analysis, psychodrama, eastern medita-

tive approaches and gestalt. In its hey-day, the list of introductory groups, day-time workshops, weekend workshops, intensive groups, professional and training groups read just like its
American counterpart, which may well be due to a rather sizeable American contingent of therapists amongst the overall
staff. The blurbs describing the particular characteristics of
courses exuded the same air of chummy intimacy and friendly
affection as its American counterpart though there was perhaps
a trace more information for the less experienced and emotionally naïve' British consumer. For example, one course offered
plain 'Gestalt' which it bluntly described as 'here and now . . .
you and I . . . what is, rather than what "ought to be" ' and
continued, 'Let's take time through work with ourselves and
each other, to discover and explore our way in the world. And,
if you choose, experiment with new ways of expressing yourself'. However, moving away from the introductory course to
one for the initiated, then it is like being back again at Big Sur,
though in this case, the course was in Kilburn and December!

Gestalt Dreams and Guided Fantasy
Bring your dreams, they are signposts along your path. And
bring your adventurous spirit for journeying into the mysterious
interior. As a group we will share our creative energy, so that
through a new awareness, we are awakened to greater vitality,
perhaps to deeper joys. (If you cannot remember your dreams,
bring yourself. We may find some secret, yet important dreams
lurking just under the surface).[15]

That last bracketed injunction, delivered straight to the reader, a
neat personal touch, is authentically transatlantic, in its insistence, a trifle urgent admittedly, on the fact that everyone can
avail themselves of the offered package, even those poor
benighted souls who somehow in this post-Freudian era still
cannot get it together to dredge up even the most minuscule
vision for discussion and working through.

The dewy enthusiasm and Madison Avenue proselytising are
only some of the features of the new psychotherapies which
embarrass the older, more sedate and orthodox practitioners of
psychoanalysis. They are offended, horrified even by the
somewhat seamy undertones to the growth movement, the tales
of nude encounter groups, of group 'grope-ins' in hot tubs and
the proliferation of 'touchie-feelie' techniques masquerading

under the respectable umbrella of 'therapy'. But some of their distaste can be traced back to an embarrassment similar to that shown by parents whose children make rude comments in public or, even worse, say and do in public what they, their parents, communicate in veiled and elliptical ways in private. After all, the ideas and the techniques of movements such as Gestalt may seem a trifle ridiculous but perhaps no more ridiculous than the psychoanalytical ideas from which they descend. Fritz Perls is described by Judd Marmor, a contemporary and main-stream psychoanalyst who writes critically about the human potential movement, as an 'ex-psychoanalyst'[16] although it is difficult to know quite what an ex-psychoanalyst is. It is easier, however, to understand why Marmor uses the term. The fact that Perls was an analyst at all is embarrassing and that he was a dedicated disciple of Horney and Georg Groddeck, two contemporaries and colleagues of Freud and influential figures in the development of psychoanalytical ideas relating to so-called 'psychosomatic medicine' well-nigh humiliating. Analysing impotence back to a reflex nasal neurosis may seem bizarre but is it any more bizarre than attributing neurosis itself to the male child's desire to have intercourse with his mother or the female child's anxiety to have a penis? Psychoanalytic critics speak disparagingly of the new movements as 'pseudo-scientific cults' but such denigration only emphasises the necessity of being able to distinguish the pseudo from the scientific. But as the more shrewd and mature of orthodox psychoanalysts realise, it is not easy. Jules Masserman, himself a prominent and respected American psychoanalyst, has told how, invited to address a group of physicians, he presented them with a fanciful yet detailed parody of psychodynamic formulations and interpretations centred on the ingrowing toenail. He used, in the manner of experienced psychoanalysts, imprecise terms and hypotheses of an untestable kind and, in Aubrey Lewis' account, 'his exposition read like a grossly far-fetched exercise in free-wheeling interpretations, in terms of libido, catharsis, regression and sexual symbolism.'[17] Nonetheless, to Masserman's extreme surprise, the address was received enthusiastically and members of his audience later congratulated him on the 'analytical perspicacity' with which he had devised the specific dynamic formula for the cause and possible treatment of that hitherto unexplored psychosomatic disorder – ingrowing toenail.

The Gestalt analysis of bodily posture is no less scientific than the Freudian analysis of linguistic slips of the tongue which isn't to say that either have any claims to being scientific at all. In the last analysis, what determines the acceptability and the standing of a theory, be it Sigmund Freud's notion of the oedipal complex, Wilhelm Fliess' 'discovery' of the nasal neurosis of Fritz Perls' idiosyncratic concept of the gestalt is its susceptibility to being tested and surviving. To date, in this respect, there is more uniting the new with the old psychotherapies than dividing them.

References

1 Dubos, R. 1960 *Mirage of Health* Allen and Unwin. London
2 Conrad, K. 1952 'Gestalt Analysis in Psychiatry'. Translated by Marshall, H. In: *Themes and Variations in European Psychiatry* Editors, S. Hirsch and M. Shepherd. John Wright. Bristol
3 Perls, F., Hefferline, R. F. and Goodman, P. 1972 *Gestalt Therapy: Excitement and Growth in the Human Personality* Souvenir Press. London
4 Naranjo, C. 1971 'Contributions of Gestalt Therapy In, *Ways of Growth* Editors, H. Otto and J. Mann. Pocket Books. New York
5 Perls, F. 1973 *The Gestalt Approach and Eyewitness to Therapy* Bantam Books. New York
6 Fliess, W. 1893 'Die Nasale Reflexneurose' *Verhandlungen des Kongresses fur Innere Medizin* pp.384-394 J. F. Bergmann. Wiesbaden
7 Sulloway, F. 1979 *The Unknown Freud: Psychoanalysis as Psychobiology*
8 Gardner, M. 1966 'Freud's Friend Wilhelm Fliess and His Theory of Male and Female Life Cycles' *Scientific American* 215: pp.108-112
9 *The Esalen Catalogue* April-June 1978 p.7 Esalen Institute. Big Sur
10 Shapiro, J. and Shapiro, D. H. 1979 'The Psychology of Responsibility. Some second thoughts on Holistic Medicine' *New England Journal of Medicine* 301, 4, pp.211-

212

11 *Wholistic Dimensions and Healing: A Resource Guide* Editor, L. J. Kaslof. Doubleday. New York

12 *The Esalen Catalogue* July-October 1978 Esalen Institute. Big Sur

13 Bateson, G. 1978 In: *About Bateson* Editor, J. Brockman p.236 Wildwood House. London

14 'Holistic Health or Holistic Hoax?' Editorial *Journal of the American Medical Association* 241, 11, p.1156

15 *Quaesitor* Winter Programme 1976/77 London

16 Marmor, J. 1980 'Recent Trends in Psychotherapy' *American Journal of Psychiatry* 137, 4, pp.409-416

17 Lewis, A. 1966 'Analysing the Analyst' *Times Literary Supplement* 3346: pp.317-319

4 The Body Therapies

If you think about it for a minute, you realise that the mind and the body are one, that nothing that goes on anywhere in the body can fail to affect every other thing in the body. When you see that, it really does not make any sense that all of people's distress can be dealt with mentally. The fact is that people are distressed by their relationships with each other, they are distressed by the kinds of things they have to do at work, the food they have to eat, their lack of physical activity; you have to work on everything; you have to deal with every aspect of the person's life which is not healthful.

Claude Steiner, holistic therapist
and transactional analyst.

In Britain, a common complaint voiced by people about their doctors is that they do not have enough time to listen to their difficulties and anxieties. Doctors appear only interested in physical symptoms and tend to treat emotional problems with tranquillisers, sedatives, anti-depressants, when what the patients want to do more than anything else is to *talk*. In parts of affluent America, on the other hand, a lot of people do have the opportunity to talk, sometimes interminably, and, disappointingly, it doesn't always make that much difference.

Now, some of the newer therapists, disenchanted with the shortcomings of 'talking' per se, and influenced by the holistic ideas of Gestalt and related theories, are turning back for the answer to man's emotional and psychological problems to – the body. Jogging, which one might be forgiven for believing is just an approach to keeping physically fit, has been elevated to a form of holistic therapy while natural foods, herbal remedies, fluid balance, skin cultivation, formerly seen almost entirely as providing physical benefits are now regarded as having an all-round effect on mental as well as physical health. In therapy groups, deep breathing and physical contact between the members are also regarded as beneficial. Claude Steiner a therapist whose eclectic approach embraces Transactional Analysis (Chapter 6) as well as holism, uses both.

What I do is to get together with a group of people, and we don't talk – we use a lot of massage and touching and holding. People will hold each other. I may give some instructions that have to do with relaxation and focussing on the particular body experience of the moment, and I will stimulate people into breathing deeply and going inward on their physical experience, which is facilitated by their deep breathing. This will put people in an emotional state which often is explosive. Every so often a person in a 'body work' experience will say: 'That changed my life'. It's like the Christian experience of being born again, only this has nothing to do with Christianity; it has something to do with a very strong emotion that has been held back for a long time.

Here we encounter the idea of 'body work', a term which to the uninitiated, evokes car mechanics rather than therapy. But treatments, particularly psychiatric treatments come in fashions and it is safe to say that 'body work' is currently enjoying a boom in that fertile womb of the talking therapies, California.

The news-stands and supermarkets offer brochures advertising workshops on such attractions as deep massage, the Feldenkrais method of mind-brain synthesis and Jack Rosenberg's 'system' approach – ('The inner body is a non-verbal archetyal experience and the body is the vehicle where that experience takes place in this reality. This session will be a review of the process Dr Rosenberg uses to combine his approach to body therapy, psychotherapy and higher consciousness'). Throughout these brochures and the 'body' movement in general, the name of one of Freud's earliest pupils keeps recurring like some seminal motif. It is the name of Wilhelm Reich.

Not even the most ardent supporter of Freud would deny that the first psychoanalysts numbered amongst their ranks some of the most complicated, cranky and, in a number of instances, highly disturbed individuals existing outside the confines of a mental asylum. Paul Roazen, who in his book *Freud and his Followers* is at pains to dismiss the legendary accusation about psychoanalysis ('it either drove people mad or sent them to their death'), nonetheless provides systematic evidence of the troubling fact that so many of the early analysts killed themselves or came otherwise to a bad end.[1] Paul Federn, Freud's longest-standing pupil at the time the Nazis entered Vienna, shot himself while sitting in his own analysts's chair. Wilhelm Stekel, one-time patient of Freud, then disciple, became paranoid and killed himself. Victor Rausk shot and hanged himself while

Herbert Silberer, an early member of the Vienna group, took criticism badly and killed himself in a most horrible way, hanging himself on a set of window bars, leaving a flashlight shining on his face as he strangled so his wife could see him when she came home. One of Freud's women disciples, Ruth Mack Brunswick, became a drug addict. There were many others whose lives and deaths stand in sharp contrast to the maturity and health that were believed to spring from analysis. But, in many ways, the life and death of Wilhelm Reich, the father of today's 'body work' remains the oddest of them all.

He was born in Austria in 1897, received his medical degree in 1922 from the University of Vienna Medical School, became a protégé of Freud and over the next eight years rose rapidly in psychoanalytic circles. He was prominent both as a teacher and an organiser in various psychoanalytical and political organisations. A Marxist, he was in Roazen's words, 'one of the few analysts of his time capable of building bridges between psychoanalysis and social science'. Freud, however, held him at arm's length, refusing to analyse him and leaving him instead to other, experienced analysts around at that time. From 1924 to 1930 he was the director of the Seminar for Psychoanalytic Therapy, and was responsible for systematising some of the technical developments in analysis. In 1928 he joined the Austrian Communist Party and two years later moved to Berlin where he formed the German Association for Proletarian Sexual Politics whose aims included the abolition of laws against abortion and homosexuality and the dissemination of birth control information. In 1933 he was expelled from the Communist Party and the following year was likewise expelled, or, perhaps more accurately, 'edged out' of the International Psychoanalytical Association. While in Berlin, he served in the same communist cell as Arthur Koestler who recalled Reich in his contribution to *God that Failed*. Koestler wrote 'a Freudian Marxist; inspired by Malinowski, he had just published a book called *The Function of the Orgasm* in which he expounded the theory that the sexual frustration of the Proletariat caused a thwarting of its political consciousness; only through a full, uninhibited release of the sexual urge could the working class realise its revolutionary potentialities and historic mission'.[2] Reich, however, was unable to convince his comrades of the importance of his views and his expulsion from the Party followed Moscow's branding of his writings as 'un-Marxist rubbish'. His expulsion from the International Psychoanalytical Association has been linked to anxieties lest an association between Marxism and psychoanalysis embarrass the latter movement at a time when fascism was on the rise.

In 1933 Reich wrote a book attacking German fascism as the sadistic expression of sex-repressed neurotics,[3] an action which did not endear him to the Nazis. He fled, via Scandinavia, to the United States in 1938 and spent the remainder of his life there. He died, a certified psychiatric patient, in November 1957.

Reich, and his legacy today in the 'body' movement, can best be understood in the light of Freud's theories concerning mental energy. Freud was not especially clear concerning his notion of mental energy but he did tend to equate it with erotic energy or 'libido'. His initial theories are described in his *Project for a Scientific Psychology*, written in 1895 and published posthumously and indicate that he hoped they would approximate to the way the brain, as a biological organ, works. The extent to which Freud spoke metaphorically when he spoke of mental energy is not clear but one man, Wilhelm Reich, believed in the objective reality of such energy and elaborated a remarkable, some might say fantastic, explanation of its origins and effects.

For, although in the popular mind, it is Freud who began the process of tracing all human unhappiness back to the question of sex, it is Reich who saw the enterprise through to its conclusion. For him, neurosis involved a lack of 'orgastic potency', the latter being defined as 'the capacity for surrender to the flow of biological energy without any inhibition, the capacity for complete discharge of all damned-up sexual excitement through involuntary pleasurable contractions of the body'. Charles Rycroft, the British analyst, points out that Reich's theories of personality and sexuality constitute a sweeping indictment of the sexual life of modern man that is reminiscent of D. H. Lawrence, combining as they do 'an intense almost mystical belief in the prime importance of sex with a puritanical insistence that it should always be treated with high if not dead seriousness.'[4]

According to Reich, only the orgasm, and the use of its energy, which he called orgone energy, enables a person, and thereby society, to free himself and reintegrate his mind and his body. He maintained that the primary biological needs and impulses of the average human being have been suppressed for thousands of years and the bases for these theories are provided in *The Invasion of Compulsory Sex-Morality* which he published in 1931.[5]

It is customary for contemporary psychoanalysts writing about Reich to divide his life into two phases, the first extending up to the early 1930s during which his Marxist and psychoanalytical ideas, while unconventional, were as Rycroft delicately puts it, 'clearly related to time and place' and a second phase, in which his ideas took a highly idiosyncratic and private course and his followers were restricted to a relative handful of ex-patients. Not everyone, however, accepts such a simple division. Martin Gardner, for example, in his highly entertaining and irreverent *Fads and Fallacies in the Name of Science*[6], points out with asperity that psychoanalysis is still in such a confused and pioneer state that writings by 'incompetent theorists' are easily camouflaged by technical jargon and a sprinkling of sound ideas borrowed from others. Only when the analyst turns, as Reich turned, to biology, physics and astronomy, where there is a solid core of verifiable knowledge, does eccentric thinking become easier to detect.

Gardner has a point. Reich's theory of orgasm, has its roots in Freudian theories. Freud himself divided the neuroses into two groups; the so-called actual neuroses, which were the direct, physiological result of present-day disturbances of sexual function; and psycho-neuroses, which were complicated, psychological consequences of past disturbances. The distinction between the two is questionable and for our purposes unimportant. What is important is that Reich took the view that an actual neurosis formed the core of every psycho-neurosis and that it was the inability of neurotic individuals to discharge sexual energy completely and with satisfaction during orgasm which led to a damming up of sexual energy which fed the psychoneurosis. However, it should not be thought that any kind of discharge of sexual energy would protect mental health. True orgastic potency, as said earlier, involved, in addition to the mechanical capacities for successful intercourse, 'the capacity for surrender to the flow of biological energy without any inhibition' and 'the capacity for complete discharge of all dammed-up sexual excitement through involuntary pleasurable contractions of the body'. He was convinced that all neurotics and most so-called civilised men and women lack 'orgastic potency' and he believed that in addition to providing the fuel for persistent neuroses the undischarged sexual energy became experienced as anxiety. Once again, it is a case of Reich taking his master too literally. Freud's original theory of anxiety was that it was undischarged libido simply 'converted' into anxiety. He modified this view in the 1920s, (the extent to which he retained it is a subject of great controversy amongst orthodox analysts), but Reich clung on to the idea of an intimate, physiological connection between libido and anxiety. Indeed, he strengthened the connection by scrapping the notion of 'conversion' and maintaining instead that anxiety is quite simply sexual discharge occurring through the cardiovascular system. That is to say, whereas sexual pleasure is libidinal energy experienced through the genitals, anxiety is libidinal energy experienced through the cardiac and diaphragmatic regions of the body. Another outlet for undischarged libidinal energy was sadism. 'Every kind of destructive action by itself', he wrote, 'is the reaction of the organism to the denial of the gratification of a vital need, especially the sexual.' Reich's views on the link between sexuality and aggression formed the basis of the 1960s revolutionary slogan, Make Love Not War, and indeed were celebrated in a much-praised film of that period, WR – Mysteries of the Organism.

Gradually his notion of sexual energy became transmuted into orgone energy, the élan vital or life force made accessible and useful. Its characteristics were delineated with remarkable matter-of-factness. It was blue – hence the blueness of oceans, lakes and sky. The 'heat waves' seen shimmering on hot days above pavements and mountain tops were not heat at all but orgone energy. All the phenomena attributed by physicists to 'static electricity' were according to Reich merely manifestations of orgone energy – lightning, radio interference, sunspot-induced electric disturbances and so on. In the body, orgone energy became accumulated in the sexual parts during coitus and during orgasm flowed back throughout the remainder of the body. By breathing, the body charged its red blood cells with orgone energy and Reich claimed to be able to detect, by the way of the microscope, the blue glimmer of red corpuscles as they absorbed orgone. In 1947 he measured orgone energy with a Geiger counter and subsequently declared that the unit of living matter was not the cell but a smaller vesicle or 'bion' which consisted of a membrane surrounding a liquid which pulsated continually with orgone energy. Bions were believed to propagate like bacteria which led many of Reich's critics to suspect that bions were bacteria!

In 1940, he developed a therapeutic box, technically called an Orgone Energy Accumulator, consisting of a structure resembling a phone booth, made of sheet iron on the inside and organic material, such as wood, on the outside. His theory was that orgone energy was attracted by the organic substance on the outside and passed on to the metal which then radiated it inward. Since the metal reflected orgone, the box acquired an abnormally high concentration of orgone energy. Patients came to the Orgone Institute, in the main suffering from cancer, to use the accumulators and for blood tests. In Reich's book, *The Cancer Biopathy*[7], the workings of the accumulators are described. By sitting inside, lightly clothed, the patient charged his body with orgone energy, felt first by a prickling warm sensation, accompanied by reddening of the face and a rise in body temperature. After having absorbed as much energy as was required, there would be slight feelings of nausea and dizziness. Reich even developed an 'orgone energy accumulator blanket' for people who were bedridden and there were also tiny orgone boxes, called 'shooters', for application to local areas.

It is not only orgone therapy but also a type of treatment related to it, termed 'character analysis', which links Reich to the 'body therapists' of the present time. Once again, Reich's initial formulations derived from Freud's notion that a person's character, that is his habitual, stereotyped attitudes and responses to situations, might represent a defence against threat. Reich, however, in the view of many analysts, developed such an idea in a genuinely imaginative way. According to Rycroft, he was the first analyst to appreciate that it might be better to treat patients by analysing their character than by analysing their dreams or their free associations. Rycroft continues:

> Even when he was a conventional analyst he took the view that it was a waste of time listening to a patient's free associations or interpreting his dreams unless the analyst had previously made him aware of, say, submissiveness or rudeness towards the analyst and had succeeded in getting him to understand why he found it necessary to relate to him in such a stereotyped way. Only after this had been made clear to the patient could the

patient, in Reich's view, become at ease and spontaneous with his analyst and open up sincerely to him in a way that made his free associations valid communications.[4]

However, Reich soon decided that character was the essential defence and that civilised western man was imprisoned in a character-armour which prevented him from expressing his immediate and spontaneous feelings and in particular from experiencing orgasm. This character-armour, according to Reich, is not just a psychological defence but is expressed through physical means. Reich believed that every neurosis was linked to muscular armour, seen, most vividly in such physical features as a furrowed brow, hunched shoulders, tense neck muscles, tight anus, stooped posture and restricted chest and diaphragmatic movement. Reich and his followers laid great emphasis on the need for the patient to understand the cause of his muscular tensions and they elaborated certain technical procedures to enable him to obtain relief. For example, tightness in the jaw muscles, related to an unconscious desire to bite someone, would be relieved by the provision of a towel on which the patient would be instructed to bite. Another important approach involved attention to breathing. A key Reichian belief was that no neurotic was capable of exhaling deeply and evenly, owing to abdominal tension. So the patient must overcome his inhibition against breathing out properly, often with the therapist assisting by applying pressure on the abdomen. As the breathing therapy advances, so a new phenomenon appears whereby the patient has an involuntary need to move his pelvis. 'A dead pelvis' according to Reich, is a rigidity due to 'pleasure anxiety', in turn rooted in childhood punishments for bedwetting, masturbation etc. Such rigidity prevents the neurotic from moving his pelvis naturally during sex and also causes lumbago and haemorrhoids. The forward movement, alleged to occur spontaneously in breathing therapy, is an instinctive motion equivalent to the motion made by the hips during coitus. (A voluntary effort to move the hips during coitus was considered by Reich to be neurotic).

Reich became increasingly convinced that he had stumbled on the secret of life. He was puzzled by Einstein's apparent indifference (he had told the physicist of the energy difference inside and outside the orgone energy accumulator and, according to Reich's wife, Einstein had said enigmatically that if it were true it would be a 'bomb'!). He was incensed by more active scientific critics, particularly those who derided his claims to treat cancer, and eventually published *Listen Little Man!*, a vituperative attack on the critics of orgone research[8] which, in its polarisation of society into the little men referred to in the title and the 'specious worthies' who manipulate, enslave and exploit in the name of politics, religion, and education, exudes that remarkable mixture of naïvety, paranoia and pungency which twenty years later characterised many of the more polemical writings of the radical movement in the United States and elsewhere. It also exudes a remarkable grandiosity most notably in its final panegyric with its poignantly prophetic note:

> Whatever you have done to me or will do to me in the future, whether you glorify me as a genius or put me in a mental institution, whether you adore me as a saviour or hang me as a spy, sooner or later necessity will force you to comprehend that *I have discovered the laws of the living* (Reich's italics) and handed you the tool with which to govern your life, with a conscious goal, as heretofore you were able only to govern machines. I have been a faithful engineer of your organism.[8]

Reading the book one detects signs of the persecutory notions, which were to flower flamboyantly in the last few years of his life. That Reich was a highly suspicious man is confirmed by his wife Ilse in an otherwise unrevealing book on her husband. She describes how when she came back from a trip to England in 1947 she was put through 'a third-degree questioning as to everyone I had seen' and she almost had to take an oath of fidelity before his jealous suspicions could be put to rest. Ilse, in the same passage, draws attention to Reich's double standards on sexual fidelity, and the fact that while he always preached that sexual behaviour could not be judged by moral standards but only by standards of health and sickness, 'he was not entirely free of moral judgements of sexuality'. His following a double standard in regard to sexual behaviour of wife and husband was one contradiction while another was his attitude towards homosexuality. He never knowingly accepted a homosexual for treatment and his wife recalls how Reich, on learning that a referred patient was a homosexual, refused to treat him saying, 'I don't want to deal with such filth.'

By the beginning of the 1950s, Reich was obsessed with using orgone energy to heal radiation sickness, neutralise the effects of the atom bomb and eventually neutralise mankind against nuclear radiation. Shortly afterwards he sustained a number of heart attacks, became increasingly suspicious of his wife's fidelity and began to have even wilder ideas about orgone which involved cosmic phenomena, outer space, weather conditions, drought and rainmaking. He believed that the US Airforce and the President himself were aware of the importance of his work and he would point to planes and jets flying routinely over his institute saying they were watching and protecting him. In 1954 when the Food and Drug Administration sought and obtained an injunction against his work, he became convinced that the communists had infiltrated the FDA. The legal action spiralled into a charge of criminal contempt of court and during the hearing Reich repeatedly stated that he could not mention several facts in his defence because to mention them in public might be against the national interest. Never the possessor of a sense of humour (few if any of the gurus of the new psychotherapies have been exactly a barrel of laughs), Reich now seriously maintained that the earth was being attacked from outer space and that only with the help of his orgone theories could mankind be saved from this menace. His wife, in her biography, notes rather pathetically that 'a number of Reich's former friends and co-workers were then and still are convinced that even those points . . . . were completely rational and supported by facts'.[9]

Throughout the court action, which lasted until 1956, Reich remained convinced that he was the victim of an elaborate conspiracy. In a letter to his great admirer and friend, A. S. Neill (the founder of Summerhill School), he referred to the role of the US manufacturers of drugs in the witch-hunt and added:

> There is lots of information to the effect that (they) were in collusion with and incited by Russian Red Fascists. These, i.e. Stalin, were the teachers in method of both the Hitlers and the McCarthys. Once the whole thing will be over, you will know the whole truth . . . .[9]

Even so, once the whole thing was over Reich ended up with a prison sentence of two years. After ten days in a routine penitentiary Reich underwent a psychiatric examination and was transferred to Lewisburg which at that time was the only federal penitentiary with psychiatric treatment facilities. He never availed himself of the treatment, however, and the psychiatrists decided to declare Reich sane and legally competent because, according to Reich's wife, the psychiatrists did not feel that much would be gained by reopening the entire case for reasons of insanity nor did they feel that a man of Reich's standing should be made to suffer from the label of legal insanity. His wife greeted this decision with relief although she notes with irritation that this decision has since been used by some of Reich's friends and co-workers as support for their claim that all his decisions and views were perfectly sane.

Reich was by no means the only analyst who laid particular emphasis on the relationship between body and mind. Georg Groddeck (1866-1934), who is sometimes called the father of psychosomatic medicine, held quite extraordinary and idosyncratic views about the psychological basis of much organic disease (for example, he argued that a woman who is childless 'grows a compensatory uterine tumour'), and in his first letter to Freud, he outlined his conception of organic illness and suggested that:

> the distinction between body and mind is only verbal and not essential, that body and mind are one unit, that they contain an It, a force which lives us while we believe we are living.[10]

For Groddeck, the It is a force which manifests itself in the thoughts and emotions of man, his organic and mental illnesses, and in the external appearance of man and he drew attention to the fact that Freud's concept of the unconscious had to be widened in order to allow the psychoanalytic examination of physical illness. Freud's concept of the Id was derived from Groddeck's It although it is clear from Groddeck that he felt they had little in common. The It is not the unconscious, is not the Id, it is not theEgo. It is 'this infinitely mysterious entity', which permeates all human life', 'exists before the formation of the brain', 'is man himself in all his vital manifestations'.

Groddeck was particularly interested in the relationship between the effects of massage and of psychotherapy. He was certain that massage, however it is carried out, not only has a psychological impact on the patient but it has diagnostic implications for the masseur. The sense of touch is heightened, vision is sharpened and 'the patient's changing expressions reveal hidden secrets of his soul' that otherwise would not come to the knowledge of the observer. Groddeck believed that unconscious impulses and deeply buried character traits betray themselves in involuntary movements, while an acute sense of hearing on the part of the masseur will enable him to follow specific and highly revelatory changes in breathing. Oddly, it was a masseur's sense of smell that Groddeck regarded as the prize diagnostic skill and he declared that 'no one who gives massage can avoid noticing remarkable changes of smell', changes which he indicated enigmatically reveal changes in the course of the disease being treated but, perhaps wisely, he refrained from being any more specific.

Ideas such as those elaborated by Reich and Groddeck are to be found at the core of a veritable miscellany of new approaches in psychotherapy ranging from body therapies such as Rolfing to psychodrama and primal therapy (Chapter 5). Before we went to interview Ida Rolf and see the therapy in practice, we talked to Dr Stanley Keleman, a San Franciso-based therapist who endorses many of the views and values of the 'body' school and is a follower of the approach known as *Bioenergetics*. The founder of bioenergetics, Dr Alexander Lowen, was a psychiatrist-psychoanalyst who split from the group of disciples surrounding Wilhelm Reich in 1954 to form Bioenergetic Analysis. Keleman himself is a powerfully built man with modest consulting rooms in Berkeley. Suspicious at first, he seemed to find the idea that a psychiatrist might want to find out what the body therapists are all about so unlikely that the interview must have some more sinister purpose. The fact that Sally Thompson represented the BBC, a much more respectable institution than British psychiatry, understandably reassured him! He gradually relaxed and talked quite freely of his ideas. Straightaway it became clear that Reich's orgone and Groddeck's It were alive and well but were living under the newly assumed name of energy. Keleman was very quick to dismiss any simplistic idea that the energy that he and other body therapists had in mind, might be related to the nervous energy studied by neurophysiologists and other orthodox scientific researchers. But what, we asked him, is this 'energy' of which Rolfers, bioenergetic analysts and the other hundred and one psychotherapeutic masseurs speak? Keleman's answer left us unenlightened.

When the egg and the sperm come together [he said], and the

embryological pathway begins to be laid down we are dealing with as far as we can tell an invisible field. We know there's something there. There's a sort of excitatory pattern that we can detect . . . . but we cannot see it. It's a sort of excitatory field which begins to lay down pathways of tissue.

The situation became not much clearer when Keleman described the therapeutic implications of the notions of energy, fields, etc.

The Alpha and the Omega of bioenergetics includes the analysis or the observation of what we feel is the excitatory or energetic economy of this person. How does he regulate himself and his energies seeking gratification? Can he take a lot of excitement or does he retreat from it? Does he show a cyclic movement in which he's more excited than at other times? Does he shy away from basic sexual or loving experiences? The way he regulates his excitatory or instinctual life is of great concern to us because that is how the personality is formed. Personality we call character. So we are interested in what is the shape of the organism. What does it look like? What are its chronic holding patterns and what is the chronic pattern or the consistent pattern that the person uses to regulate his own excitatory or sexual levels?

The patient's character is analysed using psychoanalytic notions of resistance and defence and bioenergetic notions of excitation, field and tissue alteration. Keleman provided as an example a person who appears to have a retracted pelvis. 'One could say from looking at it, its tone is kind of apathetic and fearfully pulled back.' Such persons are demonstrating that

they want to get away from their genitals, or from the excitement they feel coming from a male or a female. So that here we have an inhibition of movement, an inhibition of excitement and we could tie it back to a defence against sexuality or tie it back into incest or guilt or the fearfulness (of living) in a very paradoxical family that tells you that sex is bad and stay away.

The new techniques described by Keleman involve getting the patient to *feel* by kicking or stretching or breathing. Much emphasis and value is placed on the therapeutic benefits to be derived from breathing in a bioenergetically approved way. A patient with difficulties in expressing anger is encouraged to kick the bed or to strike it in such a way as to 'make the person immediately feel the inhibition to his own movement which would be the same as the inhibition to his own emotional qualities'. If the person is afraid to hit out he will contract his shoulder muscles and will 'feel' the stiffness in his shoulder and if he feels the stiffness in his shoulder then he might just feel the anger and his fear of his anger. Then there are the opportunities for unravelling the 'historical meaning' of the fear for the patient. During the actual body therapy the person may realise that as a child whenever his father approached him he, the patient, would hold his breath and pull his shoulders up. Or perhaps it was whenever his mother tried to discipline him that he would bite his lips and stiffen his jaw. It is the feeling of the inhibition of the movement or the feeling of the fear of the emotion, felt during the physical part of the therapy, which brings with it the historical context.

Much is made in these therapies of the power of muscle or tissue manipulation to evoke memories of infantile or childhood traumas because it is this therapeutic power which allegedly distinguishes the myriad of post-Reichian therapists from the physiotherapists, chiropractors, osteopaths and other more orthodox body manipulators who practise within the ambit of more orthodox medicine. Here is Keleman describing his approach to a fifty-five-year-old man (described incidentally as 'elderly'!) who was finding it difficult to cry over the death of his father.

> I asked him to take off his shirt and I looked at him. I saw that his chest and his neck were held in a chronic inspiratory position, held up high and his neck was locked rigid though he did not feel that and I said 'do you realise that you cannot breathe out?' He was a physician actually and he said 'No, I think I can breathe out'. I said 'Well you can't'. I put my hand on his chest and put some mild pressure on it and he felt that in fact he did not breathe out. So with some mild pressure I got him to exhale more and more and he began to feel the stiffness more and more that he could not let down in his neck and his chest. Then he began softly to sob and I let him sob, the relaxing of his chest did that, and he had very specific memories of not being allowed to ask his father a lot of things.

The recognition of his childhood fear of his father led the physician to break down and really cry. Keleman's analysis was that the patient was prevented by his fear from mourning properly, yet buried his fear which was only expressed through the distorted chest and neck posture uncovered in therapy. Keleman added that the physician had previously suffered from several attacks of pericarditis (inflammation of the tissue covering the heart) and that, as a result of his therapeutic experience, 'he saw now the relationship there might be between his pericarditis and his inhibited respiratory expiration'.

This particular case, we were assured, did not warrant full-scale character analysis. The symptomatic relief obtained from the therapy would be enough and there would not be a need in his case to delve deep into his attitudes to, say, sexuality or his competitiveness with his father or his relationship with his mother. However, in so far as Keleman discussed each character analysis, it sounded more or less like a résumé of the sort of psychotherapeutic exploration which any psychotherapist, lay or medical, amateur or professional, with a smattering of Freud and the post-Freudians, might indulge in.

Keleman's other particular idosyncrasy (if to practise bioenergetics can be termed an idiosyncrasy) is his psychotherapeutic interest in death. He believes that practically all fearfulness, all social inhibitions, all phobias are accompanied, indeed are riddled with the fear of death. What people are really saying when they complain of being frightened sexually or frightened of academic failure or frightened of going on-stage is that they are frightened of annihilation, being struck down, the end. Living a biological life, which apparently is what bioenergetics is all about, is not living a hedonistic life or a materialistic life or a narcissistic life, but is living a life in which one recognises that one is going to die. The great dilemma for psychotherapy and for the Western world, according to Keleman, is what is dying about? Such a portentous statement may seem strikingly indifferent to the fact that coming to terms with death is by no means a parochial problem restricted to what Keleman calls 'the Western world' but before we could put that particular objection we were back with Reich, and the fact that until he mounted his assault in the mid-thirties, orthodox psychotherapy appeared to be profoundly neglectful of the body. Now we have to redefine psychotherapy so as to make clear its task of helping the organism in its totality and in its ability to think, feel and act. Asked for an example of how a restored balance between mind and body might present in practice, Keleman looked non-plussed but then embarked on a discussion of the resistance by young Americans to the Vietnam draft, a resistance which he believed was due in part to their recognition of the fact that their bodies, their physical organisms did not belong to the state.

It seems a long way from Reich and his orgone boxes to draft resistance and the Vietnam War but we became accustomed to this kind of semantic gymnastics during our explorations of the new therapies. Few exponents see their utility in a limited light. Some are perhaps fuelled by a desire for publicity or money or both; others, genuinely dazzled by the apparent simplicity of things, have no difficulty whatsoever in making comparisons between incomparable phenomena and arriving at meretricious but highly attractive conclusions.

Perhaps she sensed this scepticism in my posture, but when eventually we tracked down Dr Ida Rolf, the founder of Rolfing, to her small house in New Jersey, she pugnaciously refused to make claims for her therapy over and above its usefulness in correcting chronic postural abnormalities. When I, and subsequently Sally (after I had been irritably dismissed as a cynic) put to her that the Rolfing session we had witnessed being directed by one of her disciples, Michael Salveson, in Berkeley seemed to amount to more than the merely physical she somewhat huffily retorted that Salveson did not learn such an approach from her. So what is Rolfing according to the physiologist-turned-body therapist who 'discovered' it? Is it not just a rather muscular form of massage? Certainly not, Ida Rolf replied with some heat.

Massage is an entirely different thing with an entirely different object, an entirely different rhythm, and entirely different approach. Massage is random compared with Rolfing – Rolfing is a very ordered, organised, patterned arrangement that you are producing. The internal parts of the body are being moved, the soft tissues are being moved to a new place. As a result of the tissues moving, the hard tissues move to a new place. As a result of the new place, the energy work is more able to travel the body.

What all this means is understood, if understood it can be, by examining a number of key concepts at the heart of Rolfing. Rolfers are interested in the way in which the body arranges itself in space and the extent to which this arrangement accommodates itself to the influence of gravity. The notion that the body must be aligned with gravity or 'grounded' as the technical terms puts it, appears to be crucial, as Ida Rolf explained it.

People [she said,] do not recognise the fact that a man is a field and he is living in a larger field. You are an energy field and you are living in a much larger energy field over which you have very little control; if your field is supported by the larger field, you will be in good health for many a day, and if not, the bigger field breaks you down every time. I talk about the Peanuts cartoon where Linus is going along and Lucy has just fallen down and Lucy gets up crying. Linus is meditating and says: 'For thousands of years there have been little girls and for thousands of years there have been sidewalks and for thousands of years little girls have been falling on the sidewalk and the sidewalk always wins and this is the story of gravity.' Gravity is the big field, it always wins and there is only one thing you can do about it: you can organise the small field so that the gravity field reinforces it and does not break it down, and that is all you can do. That is what rolfing does.

Dr Rolf talked a great deal about energy fields, tissue movement, space and gravity. She did so with the enthusiasm and rigidity of one who clearly believed that what she was saying was both innovative and revolutionary. In fact, not for the first time did I find myself hearing the thoughts and ideas of fifty years ago propounded as earth-shatteringly novel. Most of what she and her fellow-rolfers are on about has been said before, and, it has to be said, a good deal more comprehensibly. Take Georg Groddeck's lecture to a psychotherapeutic congress in Dresden in 1931:

The exigencies of life are such that the four extremities, the legs even more than the arms, hang downwards almost the whole day long. The only effect usually noticed is that the influence of gravity sets up small disturbances of the blood-circulation which have little importance in view of the strength of the heart-beat. But other fluids are circulating in the body . . . . it is remarkable that this other type of circulation hardly appears in medical theory or practice. The fact remains that certain lower parts of the adult body always contains an excess of fluid . . . . chief of these parts are the feet, the hands and the joints . . . . The water-logging . . . . is at once revealed to the masseur . . . . usually it needs only a slight pressure to establish this fact . . . . A great part, a very great part of our unconscious mental energy is used up merely in warding off pain from these water-logged places . . . . All things considered, we may perhaps be allowed to contend that massage and psychotherapy can be usefully employed together.[10]

While Dr Rolf was disclaiming any connection betwee. methods and psychotherapy, over in Berkeley, Michael Sa. son, leader of a six week seminar for trainee rolfers, wa instructing his students not only in the manipulative techniques of rolfing, but also in how to deal with 'discharge', the release of pent-up emotions similar to those experienced by Stanley Keleman's 'elderly' patient mentioned earlier. In the course of this seminar we ourselves witnessed a Rolfing sesion in which the client, a young woman in her twenties, appeared to be experiencing something other than mere relief of physical disorders in her foot, namely an emotional high which one would be unlikely to observe in the physiotherapy department of the average hospital.

But Salveson too denies that abreaction or catharsis (Chapter 5) is one of the aims of rolfing.

> I think one of the forks in the road that rolfing has taken, [he said] occurs when we approach some understanding of the concepts of order and form. From the point of view of a rolfer, a large part of what may be viewed as abreaction or discharge may be a function of imbalance. The biological system becomes more stable as it approaches higher levels of order and that stability will manifest itself in an openness and a freedom of expression, a fluidity of feeling or a circulation of energy whichever metaphor we choose to use. But there will be that freedom of flow without the necessity for discharge.

The order and flow of which he speaks is produced in ten sessions each lasting an hour to an hour and a half.

> I would begin with the tips of my fingers, occasionally with my knuckles, occasionally with my elbow, systematically, on a superficial level to begin with and then on ever deepening levels, to look to those areas that had thickened or shortened themselves and that in that thickening are now acting to hold you in your present configuration. I would then selectively go and release those areas and in the releasing begin to re-establish the continuity of connected tissue.

Salveson's manipulation of the girl's foot was gentle and accompanied by quiet explanations of what he was doing, sometimes for her benefit, sometimes for the students'. But later we talked to a British university lecturer, Tudor Parfitt, who had undergone a series of rolfing sessions while living in the United States. His sessions, he told us, were extremely violent. Indeed, was partly the fact that they were so painful that made them 'valuable' for him, for, as he observed, until the therapy he had never before had the experience of extreme pain. The rolfer was a man of about sixteen stone and at one point he used his elbow underneath his client's armpit with such vigour that Parfitt actually fainted with the pain. Parfitt's own words on this are of some interest: 'There were two people in the room who encouraged me to hold in with the pain and not to try and avoid it but to experience it and go through it rather around it, to use the jargon, and when the thing was over I felt terrific.' Parfitt only had time to have three sessions. Prior to taking the plane from Los Angeles back to Toronto (where he was working at the time) he discovered he could not walk! He telephoned his rolfer who said that clearly the therapy would have to continue and he should complete the course of ten sessions. Parfitt, however, was quite unable to stay and was carried on to his aeroplane on a stretcher. After some injections in his knee he was able to walk again and there were no repercussions. But in spite of his somewhat worrying experience, Tudor Parfitt speaks of his partial rolfing with some appreciation:

> Certainly, for the first few days I felt terribly well co-ordinated. It was really quite extraordinary. I had no way of explaining it. I used to be quite a serious runner when I was at school and university but I do not think I have ever had quite that sense of physical well-being, though it was somewhat shortlived.

In spite of that personal testimony, the temptation to dismiss Rolfing as just energetic physiotherapy with a bit of talking therapy thrown in is difficult to resist. The entire body movement with its seemingly endless talk of rectifying the mind/body split sometimes seems to amount to little more than saying that headaches can be due to tension and tension can be due to headaches and we already know that by courtesy of those television diagrams provided by the well-known makers of a best-selling analgesic. The advocates of body therapy however will have little truck with such scepticism. Indeed, sometimes they become almost mystical when describing its qualities.

> What has happened recently [Claude Steiner told us] is that we have rediscovered something that people have known for centuries, which is that certain people's hands applied under certain circumstances, in not very dramatic or spectacular ways, have a

very healing effect. The most obvious example of that would be when someone is very unhappy and despondent, a simple caress, a brotherly caress can be a very soothing experience. The fact is that the human hand when attached to the human heart is capable of creating tremendous change in people's well-being.

It says something for the high degree of seriousness which sur rounds all this theorising, that the vision of the human hand attached to the human heart was conjured up without the slightest glimmer of a smile. Indeed Steiner describes his own qualities as a therapist in terms which would not seem out of place in a modern translation of the New Testament.

> I am a human being that is able to soothe and heal other people, with his interest, and his love and his attention and his know-ledge, and it is this relationship that makes the difference. It is not the physical contact with a particular part of the body, it is the energy, and the loving, nurturing energy that comes from me that comes through and has an effect on the other person.

Holistic theorists like Steiner make much of the importance of diet and herbs, while making clear their hostility to much of what is currently prescribed in the form of drug therapy by more orthodox medical professionals. It seems necessary for them to emphasise the differences between what they practise and the medicine practised by ordinary doctors, yet for all the trium-phant arrogance of people who believe that they have stumbled on a truth that has eluded the majority of their fellow human beings, the concept of holistic health is as old as Hippocrates. What the Californian therapists like Steiner have done, and they have done it with characteristic verve, brashness and gusto, is to brighten up the old concept by clothing it with strikingly vivid language.

> There is a new sentence, a new phrase that is being used around here, 'living in place', which has to do with being aware of the effect of what you do has on you. If you drink a cup of coffee and you recognise what it does to you, then you are living in place; if you go out and take a walk and breathe in the clean air and you are aware of what it does to you, then you are living in place.

To help you 'live in place' there is no end to the therapists and the therapies available. Cyra McFadden, the novelist, lives in Marin County, just outside San Francisco and she told us about just a few of the holistic goodies available in her neighbourhood.

We have here the Holistic Health and Nutrition Center which dispenses quantities of vitamin pills instead of Valium, which has a reflexologist who diagnoses and treats all sorts of things through examination and palpitation of the foot; iridologists who examine the irises of your eyes and prescribe from there; acupuncturists – and whatever value there is to acupuncture is being dissipated by this tendency to embrace it wholeheartedly, without examination, so that people now wear acupuncture staples in their ear lobes to reduce excess weight.

Wearing them in your mouth might be more effective but doubtless less holistic. Intoxicated by what they see as a revolutionary view of man, the body therapists according to McFadden do not shrink from endorsing California's claim to be the harbinger of a new civilisation.

There are certainly Marin gurus who have told us that this is the new Athens, that we are evolving here in Marin County, once again, a perfect fusion of mind and body. The whole person who is sensitive, in touch with his own world, has reached a state of enormous emotional evolution. He is, of course, also marvellously fit and strong physically because of diet and of jogging and of embracing physical well-being in general. What falls by the wayside here is the rational mind. We have repudiated intellect as Athens did not, in a rather flamboyant fashion.

But in spite of the activities of its lunatic fringe, many of the basic tenets of the holistic movement are worthy of consideration. In May 1978, the American Medical Holistic Association was founded for physicians and the following year, at the American Medical Association's Winter Meeting at Las Vegas, three hours of prime time on continuing medical education was devoted to a discourse on the subject. It is not easy to quarrel with holistic medicine's avowed philosophy of complete personal fulfilment, however unlikely it is ever to be attained. It is a message that, as an editorial in the Journal of the American Medical Association remarked somewhat acidly, is as old as the Bible and as American as apple pie – personal growth through self-actualisation and maximum functioning of mind, body and spirit. Its proponents may indeed be a curious assortment of faith healers, chiropractors, clergymen, masseurs and PhDs along with others without visible signs of qualifications, but the idea they champion has been at the core of Western medicine for far longer than they themselves appear to realise.

After all, Britain's much-maligned general practice system itself is based on a holistic notion of health and the last two decades have seen a steady stream of research and clinical reports emanating from that quarter testifying to the complex interaction of physical, psychological and social factors in the genesis of conditions which present to GPs. (It may not be too fanciful to suggest that present American interest in the British primary health care system owes something to the realisation that providing a genuinely holistic medical service on a national basis demands a more basic and frontline system of care.[11])

It is also interesting to reflect that despite the existence of some body therapies which appear to be little else but opportunities for overt sexual exploration and experimentation, overall these are the approaches which can justifiably claim to be re-establishing albeit in an often highly idiosyncratic fashion, a neglected Freudian theory. In their emphasis on the importance of sexuality they are, at the final moments of the twentieth century, merely echoing what the Master vigorously enunciated at the beginning. Scarcely were the sexual theories of Freud elaborated than revision began. Adler was the first to go having critically expressed tentative reservations about Freud's libido theory as early as 1908. By 1911 he had finally departed, convinced that the neuroses did not arise from sexual maladjustments but as compensations for inferior and inadequate psychological and physical attributes. The following year it was Jung's turn to baulk at Freud's insistence on such crucial sexual ideas as the incest taboo and the Oedipus complex. His Fordham Lectures in New York were received 'favourably', he told Freud in a letter of typical modesty, and everywhere he was met with 'great interest'.[12] Freud commented bitterly in his *On the History of the Psychoanalytic Movement* that Jung's American reception 'was nothing to boast of, and the more he sacrificed of the hard-won truths of psychoanalysis the more would he see resistances vanishing'.[13] One of the 'hard-won truths' was the notion of sexuality as the very centre-post of neurosis. Jung himself was perfectly straightforward about it, declaring in the self-same letter to Freud, and sounding for all the world like a shrewd politician tailoring a message to a critical audience, that 'my version of psychoanalysis won over many people who until now had been put off by the problem of sexuality in neurosis'. Karen Horney was another of the many who likewise were 'put off'. Her attempted revision in

1937 emphasised the significance of cultural factors and depre-
cated the importance attributed by Freud to infantile sexuality.
This steady retreat from the most daring of all Freud's proposi-
tions was confronted by one man, Wilhelm Reich, who took the
Master's message and would not allow it to be diluted even by
the Master himself. Reich scorned these latter-day Thomas Bowd-
lers and he insisted, most notably in an interview with the
psychoanalyst Dr Kurt Eissler in 1952, that whatever his public
hesitations and modifications Freud 'never gave up the sexual
theory, the libido theory'. Poor Reich would have none of the
heretics who declared that the notion of libidinous energy was
metaphorical, tautological or merely a prop for the imagination.
He despised these attempts to water down the unpalatable truths
of psychoanalysis in order to soothe the ruffled feelings of a puritanical American culture. Sexuality meant genital sexuality,
energy meant orgasmicenergy and all attempts to make sex less
sexual were attempts to meet the needs of a sick society.

Now, in Reich's name, the belief in sexual energy as the
mainspring of health and neurosis has resurfaced. The embarrassment that it provokes within the orthodox psychoanalytic
camp is akin to the uneasiness experienced by affluent
bourgeois Christians suddenly confronted by Christ's injunction to sell all and follow him.

References

1 Roazen, P. 1976 *Freud and his Followers* Allen Lane. London
2 Koestler, A. 1950 *God that Failed: Six Studies in Communism* Ed:
   Richard H. S. Crossman Hamish Hamilton. London
3 Reich, W. 1933 *The Mass Psychology of Fascism* English translation 1972. Souvenir Press. London
4 Rycroft, C. *Reich* 1971 Fontana Modern Masters. London
5 Reich, W. 1931 *The Invasion of Compulsory Sex Morality* English
   Translation 1972. Souvenir Press. London
6 Gardner, M. 1957 *Fads and Fallacies in the name of Science* Dover
   Publications. New York
7 Reich, W. 1948 *The Cancer Biopathy* Orgone Institute Press.
   New York
8 Reich, W. 1948 *Listen Little Man* 1st British Edition 1972.
   Souvenir Press. London

9 Ollendorf Reich, I. 1969 *Wilhelm Reich* St Martin's Press. New York

10 Groddeck, G. 1947 *The Meaning of Illness* Selected Psychoanalytic Writings. Hogarth Press. London

11 Williams, P. and Clare, A. W. 1979 *Psychological Disorders in Genral Practice* Academic Press. London and New York

12 *The Freud–Jung Letters* 1974 Editor, William McGuire. The Hogarth Press and Routledge & Kegan Paul. London

13 Freud, S. 1957 *On the History of the Psychoanalytic Movement. The Standard Edition of the Complete Psychological Works of Sigmund Freud* Vol 14, The Hogarth Press. London

5 The Therapeutic Theatre

What the aesthetic drama has done for deities like Dionysus, Brahma or Jehovah and the representative characters like Hamlet, Macbeth or Oedipus, the psychodrama can do for every man. In the therapeutic theatre an anonymous average man becomes something approaching a work of art – not only for others but for himself. A tiny, insignificant existence is here elevated to a level of dignity and respect . . . The world in which we all live is imperfect but in the therapeutic theatre a little person can rise above our everyday world. Here his ego becomes an aesthetic prototype – he becomes representative of mankind.

J. L. Moreno[1]

One of the oldest ideas enshrined within the modern talking therapies, is that which envisages as the cause of mental disorder some traumatic event which lies buried in the patient's subconscious waiting to be revealed. Cures performed among primitive peoples by medicine men and shamans reveal how literally such an idea can be taken. The cause of the disturbance was often attributed to the actual presence in the body of a harmful foreign substance, such as a bone, a pebble or even a small animal and the medicine man achieved a cure by 'extracting' from the body of his patient such a disease-object. Modern commentators tend to dismiss such procedures as quackery and deception, yet there is little doubt that such manipulations are often successful and this despite the fact that in many cases the patient seems well aware of the implausibility of the therapist's claim that the object did actually exist within the patient's body and was the cause of all the trouble.

A development of this idea is healing through the re-enactment of the initial traumatic event. Ellenberger[2] describes a number of examples amongst the Pomo, an Indian tribe from California, and the Navaho Indians. In one case a patient was taken ill after hunting in the mountains. The medicine man guessed that he had seen a water monster at a spring, made a model of the monster and showed it to the patient. The latter was seized with fear and started to attack the people around him and eventually collapsed. The medicine man then made him perspire, bathed him, refreshed him and then explained what had happened. The man promptly recovered. In another case, a woman who had been frightened during the night became ill. A 'psychotherapist' assumed that she must have seen a ghost, rapidly disguised himself accordingly and, with the help of her father, frightened the patient after which he reassured her and explained the whole business. Next day, she recovered.

While there are elements of modern behavioural techniques contained in these examples, it is probable that today some of these treatments would be classified as psychodrama. At the heart of psychodramatic approaches is the idea of *catharsis* or emotional purging; it was the 'carthartic method', developed by Breuer and Freud in the late 1800s which served as the precursor of Freudian psychoanalysis. The theory underlying this method was that neurosis developed as a product of psychological traumas evoking terror, anxiety, shame or physical pain, if there had not been an adequate discharge of emotion at the time they occurred. As a result of being left undischarged, emotion was then so bound up that it could only be discharged subversively in the form of symptoms. In order to achieve a cure, the psychoanalyst, like the primitive medicine man, had to revive the buried memory and translate the repressed emotion into words. The therapist had to persuade the patient to relive the traumatic event with an appropriate degree of emotion. The patient's resistance to breaking down and reliving the trauma had to be undermined in order to achieve the required degree of emotional release or abreaction. In this model, neurosis was envisaged as a splitting of consciousness between memory and emotion, the cure residing in the healing of this split.

Classical psychoanalysis presents the story of Anna O as the prototype for the cathartic theory of neurosis. The lady in question having been abreacted in a highly dramatic fashion by the neurologist, Josef Breuer in the early 1880s. The case excited much discussion amongst the devotees of Viennese salons coinciding as it did with the publication of a book on the Aristotelian theory of catharsis by Jacob Bernays, the uncle of Freud's future wife. Anna O was an attractive, strong-willed and intelligent lady who had a highly dramatic illness characterised by paralyses, eyesight disturbances, disorganisation of speech and the development of an alternative personality. Under hypnosis she gradually recovered, primarily by being encouraged to relive the memories associated with the development of each of her unusual symptoms. Similar cases has been described at the beginning of the nineteenth century but had lapsed, as had interest in the entire phenomenon, so that the re-emergence of cathartic ideas was greeted by Freud and his contemporaries as an exciting new discovery.

Indeed, it is difficult to avoid the conclusion that it is the fate of the theory of catharsis to be rediscovered periodically and promulgated vigorously as the most momentous and original of advances. In this chapter, two modern variations on the eternal theme, each apparently very different yet possessing striking and fundamental similarities, are described. Each eloquently testifies to the flamboyant quality of the theory and the practice in this area. Given the highly charged atmosphere of the whole field of hypnosis, suggestibility, emotional discharge, 'acting-out' and abreaction, the Rogerian emphasis on the crucial therapeutic significance of the qualities and the personality of the therapist never seemed more appropriate. In the case of Jacob Moreno, the inventer of psychodrama, the cathartic theory found a most charismatic and theatrical man by whom to be rediscovered.

There is some confusion, appropriate in the case of a self-proclaimed genius, about the location of Jacob Moreno's birth. According to Ira Greenberg,[3] he was born in Vienna in 1892. Legend has it that he was born in a boat on the Black Sea. Then again it is claimed that he was born in Bucharest, youngest of the six children of a prosperous Rumanian businessman who shortly afterwards moved to Vienna. Moreno grew up in that city and trained in medicine and subsequently in psychiatry. The idea of drama as therapy evolved from a theatrical experiment launched by Moreno shortly after the end of World War I. He called it the Theatre of Spontaneity and initially, at any rate, he intended it to be simply entertainment. Professional actors, taking their cues from the audience and from current events, would improvise the plot, the action and the dialogue. According to Kobler[4] one of the first actors hired was a footloose former bank clerk named Peter Lorre. The origin of psychodrama as therapy is, by tradition, related to two individuals involved in this theatrical innovation, named George and Barbara. Barbara was a young actress with the company who tended to portray gentle, frail and wistful women onstage. She was married to George, a playwright and close friend of the young Moreno.

Now George revealed to Moreno that Barbara, off-stage and at home, was a temperamental and irascible shrew whose viciousness and hostility were playing havoc with their marriage. Moreno suggested that Barbara broaden her onstage range and persuaded her to play more unsympathetic roles: disagreeable and violent characters, petty criminals and street prostitutes. This she proceeded to do and with such skill that it disturbed her fellow-performers who felt she should cease lest in some way she suffer psychological harm. In fact, the change of roles had quite the opposite effect. The more she played such parts onstage, the more she became reasonable, sweet-tempered and relaxed offstage. After a few months the marriage recovered. It was from this spontaneous and auspicious beginning that Moreno went on to develop the whole range of dramatic techniques and theatrical tricks which collectively he entitled psychodrama. By 1923 he had illustrated another quality possessed by most of the protagonists of the talking therapies, namely an awesome ability to write books, nine of them having appeared by this time and all devoted to his theories! Around this time he is said to have met Freud and he seized the opportunity to tell the great man after hearing him lecture at Vienna's Neuropsychiatric Institute, 'You reduce people's dreams, I expand them.' 'Good', replied Freud, 'I wish you well.'

Moreno found the orthodox theatre too stifling and he was irritated by the whole procedure whereby actors were given lines to memorise written by others, portrayed characters they were not themselves and performed cut off from their audience in darkness. He introduced an open stage in the centre of a room with the audience all around, invited actors and audience to portray their own dramatic situations and, in the words of one commentator, he perceived what he had created

> as a form of dramatic religion, a theatre to call forth the spontaneously creative self and learn with God what it means to be a creator. This became the therapeutic theatre to heal the distresses and conflicts of the inner life by allowing the patient to act them out in the face-to-face encounter of psychodrama.[5]

Moreno moved to the United States in 1925 and he continued to combine private practice and psychodrama. He founded the Moreno Institute in New York City, which had Friday night psychodramas open to the public, and later, in 1934, the Moreno

Institute at Beacon Hill in upstate New York where professionals and non-professionals from all over the world came to learn his methods. Moreno died in 1974 but the Moreno Institutes continue under the benign supervision of his widow, Dutch-born Zerka Moreno, herself a psychodrama practitioner.

By all accounts, not meeting Jacob Moreno before he died deprived us of an experience to remember. When the freelance writer, John Kobler, met him to write a piece on psychodrama for the *Saturday Evening Post*[4], he was at once struck by the 'verve and flamboyance of the master showman' combined with 'the roguish charm of a Viennese *bon vivant*'. Massive, broadshouldered, wearing his hair in 'the Bohemian artist's style of yesteryear', Moreno exuded charisma. The sociologist, Lewis Yablonsky, was struck by his eyes. Yablonsky felt Moreno could read his mind and possessed mystical qualities, 'an intellectual giant', he called him, who has contributed more to 'the possible salvation of our civilisation' than any other contemporary figure.[6]

Zerka Moreno met her future husband at Beacon in 1941 soon after she arrived in the States from Europe. She had gone there with her older sister who was mentally ill and needed help urgently. She too was instantly enthralled by his physical magnetism.

> He had a romantic air, [she told us, when we met]. He had a white suit, a blue shirt, a blue tie and he had these flowing manes – he could have been a musician, he had something Beethovenesque about him. He had this massive head, extremely impressive, very electrical personality and slightly exophthalmic eyes. You had the feeling when he looked at you that he looked through you, but he saw you . . . . What struck me was that I knew instantly that this man was a great genius and I was never likely to see his like again.

It seems clear from these accounts that Moreno possessed all the charismatic qualities which make dramatic, and indeed therapeutic, impact. They were qualities which stood him in considerable stead in his role as psychodrama's first director. The elements that make up a psychodrama session are the *director* or *therapist*, the *protagonist* or central subject of the psychodrama, the so-called *auxiliary egos*, the *audience* and the *state*. The protagonist is the group member who becomes the focus of the session and whose life provides the situations which are re-enacted. Auxiliary egos are other group members or trained assistants to the director who play roles in the protagonist's life. The audience may be patients or professional workers or even a family, or they may be people off the street as occurred during the days when Moreno was working in New York City. After what is called a warm-up session in which the participants get to know each other a little, an incident, memory, traumatic event or whatever is chosen and the protagonist takes the centre of the stage. For example, the protagonist may complain that he has great difficulty coping with a difficult boss or an intractable marital partner. Or he may complain of feeling troubled by a childhood memory or recurrent pattern of unproductive behaviour. Psychodrama uses a number of fundamental elements in its theory and a plentiful array of therapeutic techniques with which to handle such case material.

At the heart of the theory is the concept of *spontaneity*. Moreno defined it as the response a person makes which contains some degree of adequacy to a new situation or novelty to an old one. It is the amount of spontaneity which an individual can display in various situations which determines his degree of mental health and this level can be raised through psychodramatic therapy. Indeed, Moreno was so certain of the importance of this idea that in *Who Shall Survive?*, published in 1934[7], he concluded that man's spontaneity is a resource that he has never used beyond the most rudimentary stage and that his survival, no less, is bound up with his ability to break out of his rigid personality moulds and break the chains that constrict his psyche. In the psychodramatic 'situation' (another key-word in the theory) man can develop his spontaneity most effectively. The natural barriers of time, place and states of existence (even the dead can walk the psychodrama stage) are obliterated so that everything onstage occurs in the 'here and now'. There is no past, no future, no geographical distance. The protagonist works out his problems by relating to the auxiliary egos, who play the roles of absent people involved in his problems and fears, summoned from time past and present and whence they rest. 'Tele' is said to occur when there is a high degree of spontaneity demonstrated between two or more individuals in a psychodramatic situation. Moreno called it 'a feeling of individuals into one another, the cement which holds groups together'.[8] As early as 1914, he provided this rather more graphic definition, which in its starkness, conveys a little of what Rogers talks about in his more prosaic notion of empathy.

> A meeting of two: eye to eye, face to face. And when you are near I will tear your eyes out and place them instead of mine, and you will tear my eyes out and will place them instead of yours, and then I will look at you with your eyes and you will look at me with mine.[9]

'Catharsis' and 'insight' are the end results of the inter-relationship of spontaneity and tele that takes place in the psychodramatic situation and emerge from the efforts of all the participants. It is insight, the sudden perception and under-standing produced by the therapy, which is the ultimate objec-tive. The protagonist acquires a new perspective on his predi-cament and with it new solutions. In such an optimistic therapy there are few doubts that insight leads directly to altered behaviour, and its emergence on stage is the signal for congratu-lations and displays of emotion normally reserved for the scor-ing of a goal in professional football or the birth of a new baby!

The various techniques employed in psychodrama are best described as they are employed in practice. Zerka Moreno told us of her sessions with the master when she brought her sister to Beacon. By her own account, her sister was gravely ill. Just before war broke out she had been in the Maudsley Hospital in London where Aubrey Lewis pronounced her to be suffering from a chronic and untreatable psychosis. By the time the two sisters arrived at Beacon, Zerka was finding it difficult to cope and Moreno was presented with a psychodrama situation in which there were two co-protagonists. One of the first tech-niques Moreno used with them, and it is said to be one of the most effective techniques for generating the tele phenomenon, was *role reversal*. The sick sister became Zerka. Zerka became the sick sister. Role reversal involves the protagonist and one of the auxiliary egos switching roles. This technique enables the pro-tagonist to see himself from outside. More particularly, he is also able to see himself from the standpoint of the person rep-resented by the auxiliary ego, be it his spouse, parent, employer or anyone intimately involved with his problems and predica-ments. In the case of Zerka and her sister, the role reversal enabled her sister to understand the impossibility of the demands she was placing on Zerka, while Zerka obtained an insight into her sister's terror at being left alone and isolated.

Another technique is the use of the *double*, whereby a second person stands with the protagonist and at moments when the protagonist finds it too difficult emotionally to speak or to capture his feelings with words, he will suggest some words. The protagonist can then assess and decide whether the proffered words fit his feelings or not. Another technique is the *substitute role* in which the protagonist plays not himself but somebody else, somebody who is especially important or close to him in some way, possibly a parent. Another is the *mirror technique*, which like role reversal, enables the protagonist to obtain some notion of how other people see him. When the director feels this technique is required, the protagonist stands aside or sits in the audience and an auxiliary ego chosen by the director assumes his role and involves himself with the other auxiliary egos in a psychodramatic interaction which enables the protagonist to see for himself what he looks like to others.

Props may be used such as the *auxiliary chair*. The chair may be high (an ordinary chair placed on a box or the patient standing on a normal-sized chair) thereby providing the patient-protagonist with the power or the feeling of power which he needs, or feels he needs, to enable him to deal effectively with people who are important in his life but who overwhelm him in everyday situations. Or the chair may be empty. In the empty chair technique, the protagonist acts out situations by imagining his antagonist seated in an empty chair placed on the stage. The protagonist interacts with this phantom participant; indeed, he may even reverse roles and interact with this absent person, playing the role the way he would envisage the absent person would play it. This is a psychodrama technique much used in Gestalt therapy although as Ira A. Greenberg, the founder and executive director of the Psychodrama Center in Los Angeles, points out with that touch of irritation often manifested by those who believe that sufficient credit is not being given to their master, many Gestalt therapists appear unaware that it was invented by Moreno and attribute it erroneously to Perls.[3]

Another intriguing technique, and one which enables the protagonist to live out his fantasies in the psychodrama situation, is the *magic shop*. The protagonist is confronted by the magic shopkeeper, played by an auxiliary ego or even by the director, who offers him anything in the world that the protagonist may want, such as wealth, health, happiness, love, material possessions, talent, intelligence or whatever takes his fancy. In return, however, the shopkeeper demands as payment something that the protagonist may also value such as his prestige, love or professional attributes. The shopkeeper's skill lies in his ability to identify what it is in the protagonist that keeps him from normally getting what he wants and then to ask for it as the price of the requested item. The protagonist is placed in a situation in which he obtains a dramatic insight into what it is he really wants out of life and what he is or is not prepared to change to get it. As a result of the magic shop confrontation, he may be able to resolve his conflict or, as often occurs, he may remain in a state of indecision. Either way, he is seen to have learned something of value about himself as a result of the visit.

As is the case in so many of the newer, more spontaneous alternative talking therapies, psychodrama sets itself up selfconsciously as an alternative theory to classical psychoanalysis. For the 'Moreneans', as the early exponents of psychodrama called themselves, the concepts of Freudian analysis required profound re-evaluation or, in some instances, needed to be discarded altogether. As Zerka Moreno once put it:

> For id, ego and super-ego, we have substituted creativity, spontaneity and the cultural conserves; for psychoanalysis, group psychotherapy; for free association, the role; for the couch, the stage or open action space; for interpretation, the warming-up process and psychodrama and for verbal communication, the set.[10]

The first psychodramatic stage was built by Moreno at the Moreno Institute in Beacon in 1934 and it still stands and functions there today. It is a three-level series of concentric platforms, above which there is a balcony (which can be used in fantasy portrayals) in the setting of an eighty-five-seat theatre. There is a multicoloured lighting panel which is used to help establish the mood of the various dramatic interactions taking place onstage – red for anger, blue for introspection etc. There is no curtain, scenery or props except for some chairs scattered around the stage. The Institute is about sixty miles north of New York City, in high, green-banked hills bordering the sluggish Hudson River. It is situated in thirty acres of land and, in addition to the theatre, consists of four buildings which can accommodate over thirty participants and twelve staff.

Our arrival at Beacon House coincided with a teaching session involving approximately eight students led by an experienced psychodrama teacher. We were both invited to participate in the situation which involved, as the protagonist, a somewhat intense, humourless but forthcoming young Swedish psychologist. The predicament he had chosen to explore involved the death of his aunt when he himself was quite young. For reasons which emerged during the psychodrama, the young boy was not permitted by his father to attend the aunt's funeral. His father, according to this Swedish protagonist, was fundamentally a weak man who himself lived in the shadow of an authoritarian, strong-willed figure, the protagonist's grandfather. Various psychodramatic techniques were exploited to re-enact scenes from the Swede's childhood and Sally was cast as one of his sisters and I as his pathetic and inept father. The *situation* reached its climax with the dead aunt being summoned back from the next world so that the protagonist could express directly to her his feelings of loss and melancholy and his bitter regret and resentment over his enforced absence from her funeral.

The director on this occasion, Don Miller, had worked with Jacob Moreno and orchestrated these particular proceedings with enormous gusto and flair. A dynamic, extroverted character, Miller never allowed the pace to flag, quickly switching the mood and tempo by adopting first one psychodramatic technique, then another. He also demonstrated a particular technique which I had not associated with psychodrama before, although I had seen it used in certain kinds of family therapy in Britain. Miller called it the protagonist's 'Social atom'. (I had troubles with Don Miller's accent and originally understood him to name the technique 'Social Adam' but when this appeared in *The Listener* an irate member of the Moreno Institute staff wrote complaining of this 'translantic gaffe' and saw it as symptomatic of my ignorance of Moreno's contribution to sociology and especially his development of sociometry!) In the circumstances perhaps Don Miller should explain the concept himself:

> My social atom would be my father, my mother, my grandmother, my brothers and sisters, maybe a special teacher that I encountered a great deal in my early life. In psychodrama we might say 'show me your social atom' and the protagonist would

introduce one after another of these significant persons. In meeting these significant persons we are obviously also meeting the protagonist and, if something is amiss, if something is in conflict, we can often work through the conflict by working on the social atom.

In living out the hitherto unexpressed emotion, the repressed trauma and the buried guilt, the protagonist it is hoped, will repair the damage of the past, unravel its complicated extension into the present and obtain a fresh understanding not merely of the person he is but of the processes which have made him that person. Did the Swedish protagonist obtain relief from his session with us? Apparently so, for in the emotional scenes which followed the psychodrama he insisted to all of us that he had. Did it matter? That seemed to be a more difficult question to answer. After all the memory of his aunt and the sad circumstances of her death had not actually led to the development of symptoms and certainly not to symptoms of the dramatic intensity and quality of Breuer's Anna O, or Pierre Janet's even more dramatic case history of Marie.* But then again this was a training session for prospective psychodramatists and so dramatic psychopathology was hardly to be expected.

One was struck, however, by the extent to which the psychodramatic situation had to rely on the protagonist's version of the scene being enacted. If the protagonist did not think that the auxiliary ego playing his sister or his mother or his aunt was getting it right then the action was halted and alternatives explored. In the session we attended I felt that there was rather a bias towards interpreting the events of the Swede's childhood

---

*Marie was a nineteen-year-old who just prior to her menstrual period would become gloomy and violent and the moment her periods began would become delirious and manifest dramatic bodily contortions for up to forty-eight hours. Janet unravelled the cause by getting the girl to re-enact the experience of her first period when she was thirteen. So upset had she been by the unexpected appearance of her first period that she tried successfully to stop it by immersing herself in a bath of ice cold water. She developed violent shivering and delirium as a consequence but her periods did not return for five years. On their return, she developed the symptoms for which Janet successfully treated her. On the basis of this case and a number of similar ones, Janet formulated his idea of 'psychological automatism', an idea on which Freud and others were to draw some twenty years later in their theories of the conscious and the unconscious mind.

through the eyes of the Swedish protagonist himself. However, Don Miller disagreed:

> It may seem [he said] that we got all our information from the protagonist; as a matter of fact we didn't. We got a lot of information out of our experience, and out of the situations which he created in the psychodrama. The situation produces expectations in our minds about what is likely to be the case; so he gives us the raw material and we process it.

I am still not sure that this is so. A powerful protagonist or director should have little trouble imposing his view of the 'situation'. The techniques of psychodrama lend themselves to exploitation by any extroverted charismatic performer with but an ounce of dramatic expertise about him. In fact the accounts of Moreno's own appearance: his presence, his physique, his eyes, testify to the enormous influence he exerted over others and the ability he displayed in persuading others to accept his views and his interpretations.

In therapy after therapy, from est to primal therapy, TA to Gestalt, one encounters the difficulty of distinguishing between faith in the therapist and evidence that the therapy actually works, that is to say that it produces in the final analysis what it promises. Faith is often born out of intense emotional involvement; evidence emerges from a somewhat more detached, analytical scrutiny.

As we proceed through these therapies we can see that each in some way embodies a particular value and contributes a special notion to the overall language and system of our self-assessment culture. Gestalt provided holism, Rogerian psychotherapy authenticity. Psychodrama's central credo is *spontaneity*. Moreno was drawn to the philosophy of Bergson in his attempts to derive an acceptable and adequate concept of what he termed 'the moment of being'. He had been dissatisfied with Nietzsche's preoccupation with creativity and spontaneity linked to creative writers, artists, musicians and political supermen. Bergson came closer with his idea that time itself, being ceaseless change, is totally creative. We only have to plunge into immediate experience in order to participate in the great life-stream of creativity. In 1940 Moreno drew attention to the way in which the notion of spontaneity, of man providing a genuine, sincere and truthful expression of his thoughts and wishes, had become elevated into a prized social and cultural value.[1] He was aware and critical of the tendency, apparent even in his time, to ally spontaneity more closely with emotion and action than with thought and rest. As he noted, this bias almost certainly developed because of the assumption that a person cannot really *feel* something without at the same time *being spontaneous* and that thinking gets in the way of spontaneity. Such a view is widespread today in the contempt for so-called 'head-tripping' and in the contrary emphasis on suspending one's critical faculties and trusting one's 'gut feelings'. Moreno saw in the opportunities for developing spontaneity one of the major riches of psychodrama. He did not seem to visualise the possibility that people might become so adept at playing roles, and not merely on the psychodrama stage at Beacon House, that the problem of achieving true spontaneity would actually become more rather than less acute. Everywhere we went in our odyssey we met people trying to be spontaneous, 'heavily into' getting their heads together, 'getting centred' so that they could be authentic. It was difficult not to conclude that the very emphasis on the immediacy of personal reaction in American society, the daily injunctions to say what you really feel at virtually every opportunity, the earnest examinations carried out into the state of the psyche with a view to establishing precisely where it stood with regard to everything from the state of the US presidency to the social virtues of deodorants had exhausted individual spontaneity; that a too-intense desire for spontaneity had made it more elusive than ever. Like the person who for ever seeks true love, the over-zealous pursuer of spontaneity ends up perpetually wondering whether what he feels is really spontaneous or is he merely feeling that he should be feeling what he feels . . . .

However, against these criticisms have to be set the achievements of the technique. It has given rise to a variety of role-playing 'exercises' which are used widely in industry, education and other fields. Moreno was a pioneer and his influence is to be found in a variety of educational and psychiatric terms such as 'play techniques', 'release therapy', 'play therapy' etc. But in common with virtually all pioneers in the realm of psychotherapy, Moreno believed that his ideas had a general relevance for the human condition and the future of man and were not limited to the clinic or the school. He was also something of a mystic and towards the end of his life his speculations on the religious meaning and implications of his work took on a quality reminiscent of some of Reich's more grandiose notions of omnipotence. (See Chapter 8).

One person for whom psychodrama is far from the earth-shattering breakthrough in understanding that the Moreneans claim, is Arthur Janov. Janov himself claims to be a pioneer of mental exploration and believes that his discovery of the existence of 'primal pain' ranks with Freud's discovery of the unconscious. Psychodrama, for all its pretensions, is just an 'as if' game. While it does have a limited use in loosening up a group in conventional therapy, essentially all it does, in Janov's opinion, is 'to offer one more unreal role for a person to portray when he has been acting the role of himself for many years'.[11] Janov is even more critical of the idea that by acting out his feelings in the psychodrama, an individual will be able to function more effectively in the real world. For Janov, psychodrama is just acting and acting is what most of us do pretty well as it is.

Going through elaborate dramatic re-enactments or engaging in little intellectual self-explorations, just strengthens our defences. It keeps us from the *pain* and in doing that it merely reinforces the very cause of all our problems. For until we feel the pain we are doomed forever to crawl through life, neurotic, stunted and numb. The rest of us may wonder from time to time whether this or that therapeutic approach might not have something to offer. Janov is engagingly dismissive. 'Until the Pain is felt', he observes, characteristically spelling the portentous word with a capital P, 'any one thing will be as ineffective as another – whether it be psychodrama, dream analysis, sensitivity training, meditation or psychoanalysis'.[11] The way to feel the Pain is through Primal therapy.

Primal therapy, as practised in the Primal Institutes of Los Angeles and New York and as expounded in a veritable stream of books including *The Primal Scream*, *The Primal Revolution*, *Primal Man* and *The Feeling Child*, is Arthur Janov's brainchild. He had worked in the United States for seventeen years as a psychologist and a psychiatric social worker before making a 'discovery' which was to change his life and, he insisted, 'the nature of psychotherapy as it is now known'. What changed Janov was a sound – 'an eerie scream welling up from the depths of a young man lying on the floor during a therapy session'.[11] The young man in question, called Danny Wilson by Janov, was a quiet, withdrawn student who, during a therapy session, talked of a theatrical act he had seen which involved a character striding around a stage in diapers, drinking milk, and shouting 'Mommy, Daddy, Mommy, Daddy' at the top of his voice before ending the act by vomiting and passing paper bags out to an audience exhorting them to do the same. Janov, for some reason, persuaded Danny to call out 'Mommy, Daddy' which led to him writhing around the floor, screeching, gasping and moaning before releasing 'a piercing, deathlike scream' that rattled the walls of Janov's office and, if he is to be believed, brought the walls of orthodox psychotherapy tumbling down around us. What happened baffled Janov for some time, well actually for some months until, several similar episodes later, Janov put together his explanatory theory. The scream he saw as 'the product of central and universal pains which reside in all neurotics'. These pains he terms 'Primal Pains' because they constitute the earliest, infantile traumas on which later pains are built. Such pains 'exist' at all times in 'every neurotic' but often they are not consciously felt because in some way they are diffused throughout the entire organism and are manifested in physical distress of various kinds and in 'the distorted way we behave'. That last 'we' makes plain what Janov elsewhere makes little effort to conceal, namely that by his definition we are all 'neurotic', we are all locked into our primal pain pool and we are all accordingly sick.

Primal therapy is the only way that such pains can be eradicated. In Janov's modest opinion, his view is nothing short of revolutionary because 'it involves overthrowing the neurotic system by forceful upheaval'. All neuroses stem from the same specific cause, according to Janov, and therefore they respond to the same specific treatment. Most of us survive without primal therapy by building up defences, by developing artificial, public, false selves, by becoming neurotically preoccupied with power, material goods, sensual experiences or by retreating into full-blown dependency. The healthiest people are those with no defences. Anything that builds a stronger defence system deepens the degree of neurosis. So after Primal therapy what is life like?

There is a state of being quite different from what we have

conceived: a tensionless, defence-free life in which one is completely one's own self and experiences deep feelings and internal unity. This is the state of being that can be achieved through Primal therapy. People become themselves and *stay* themselves. This does not mean that post-Primal patients will never again be upset or unhappy. What it does mean is that, despite what they may undergo, they will confront their problems realistically in the present. They no longer cover reality with pretence: they do not suffer from chronic, inexplicable tension or fears. [11]

According to Janov, neurosis begins with a failure to meet Primal needs. Like Freud, he anchors the origins of psychological distress in the earliest infant experiences, but whereas Freud identified at least some of the trouble as originating within the infant as part of insatiable id-derived impulses, Janov's theory makes no secret of who are the villains of the piece – parents. The case histories which adorn his prolific texts consist entirely of individuals screaming about parental neglect, parental brutality, parental indifference. 'Mommy, why don't you love me? Please love me', moans one woman. A man screams repetitively for 'Mommy and Daddy' and each time brings up the 'sickness' of wanting them in the form of 'heavy, gluey saliva/mucus'. Each case history testifies to the central tenet of the theory; neurosis is pain and pain results from unmet infantile needs; the need to be fed, kept warm and dry, to grow and develop at the correct pace, to be held and stimulated. If he is unable to persuade his parents to satisfy the particular need, the infant experiences continuous pain until eventually he 'shuts off' the pain by shutting off the need. This separation of self from need produces a split which then bedevils the individual throughout his life in the form of substitute needs and symbolic needs. A common example is that of the infant who, deprived of the maternal breast, becomes a chronic smoker in adult life. Indeed, most of Janov's examples of adult neuroses reflecting infantile trauma can be traced directly back to Freud's theories concerning infant psychological development. The difference, however, is less to do with theory than with therapy.

For Primal therapy is another of those new therapies which reject psychoanalysis and analytically-derived psychotherapy because they encourage people to talk about their problems, their pain, without providing them with the means to relive them. In classic psychoanalysis, you may be taken back into early childhood there to confront the classic triad, Mother, Father, Child, the great oedipal conflict and the tumultuous stirrings of the great war between id, ego and superego but it will all be done through the medium of dispassionate, detached, talk. In Psychodrama the personnel of those early confrontafions can be summoned up and the conflicts replayed to arrive at a more acceptable result. But in Primal therapy, the individual *returns* to the scenes of his childhood or even infancy and relives the horror, the humiliations, the deprivations, in short the pain, which in its various sublimated forms has dogged him through his life, distorting his emotional growth and stunting even his physical development.

The Primal Institutes make a great deal of being in the business of therapy for genuinely sick people and reject the idea that like est or certain forms of encounter therapy for instance they are involved in the self-growth industry. Primalling is a serious business and according to Vivian Janov, Arthur Janov's wife and a co-director of the Los Angeles Primal Institute, it is rare for someone to apply 'who does not feel the burden of his past'. When an unsuitable individual does apply he is not accepted, but as Primal therapy is not cheap (6,600 dollars for a course spread over about a year, the whole sum to be paid in advance) one criterion of unsuitability might well be lack of funds. Perhaps anyway it could be assumed that anyone prepared to spend this sort of money on having a few Primals, must by definition be in pain.

The Los Angeles Primal Institute is situated at 620 North Almont Drive. Visitors are screened on arrival by a distinctly unfriendly receptionist who sits in a booth behind what we were told was bullet proof glass. The rooms which open off the reception area are all locked and the silence is broken only by the rattling of keys as solemn young men and women (patients? therapists?) pass to and fro. On the bright June day we visited the Institute, Vivian Janov's room, furnished in heavy dark wood with thick lush carpeting, was lit dimly by a single lamp.

To this Institute comes the intending Primaller. For his $6,600 he gets a three week intensive course with his own full-time therapist and the opportunity to achieve a Primal in private, followed by seventy-five group sessions, each three hours in length, in which he Primals with other participants who have also negotiated the intensive sessions. During the three week intensive course, the therapist will guide him back to the origins of the pain that he has come to experience. To become whole again, declares Janov, it is necessary to feel the split and 'scream out' the connection that will unify the person once more. The prize, therefore, held out to the participant who has come to LA clutching his dollars and bereft of family, friends or anyone to call an acquaintance, is the primal, defined by Janov as the experience of the Pain. But it takes time, which in this paragon of the brief therapies, means a couple of days. Before that there are pre-Primals, moments of physical anguish, emotional tension and discharge, as the patient experiences more and more the fears, passions and terrors of early troubles. But then comes the big one. The individual is tense, gasping for breath, his throat tight, his chest constricted. He wants to gag and retch. He starts to thrash around, moaning and gesticulating. Words come with difficulty. All the time his therapist encourages him to spit it out, let it come, regurgitate it.

> Finally, out it will come: a scream – 'Daddy, be nice!' 'Mommy help!' – or just the word 'hate': 'I hate you, I hate you.' This is the Primal scream. It comes out in shuddering gasps, pushed out by the force of years of suppressions and denials of that feeling.[11]

Not everyone actually screams. Many utter a more restrained cry, moan or whimper. The point is to experience the pain. How you express it is your own business. But that there is pain to express, that there is agony there to ooze like pus from an over-ripe boil is the one cardinal principle of the entire theatrical extravaganza. Everything is taken as evidence of this truth. Stuttering is 'graphic evidence' of the conflict between the real self, suppressed through traumatic experiences, and the false, defence-laden self which negotiates 'reality'. Homosexuality is the result of boys being brought up by neurotic women, the consequence of being forced to act an image instead of being what they want to be. Headaches are real! Primal pains, cancer the consequence of repressed feelings.

Nor should it be thought that the pain referred to so constantly by the Janovs is the consequence of extreme deprivation of infantile needs. True, their case histories are replete with accounts of bellicose fathers, footloose mothers, sadistic drunkenness, authoritarian cold-blooded tyrants and emotionally inadequate misfits. But it is also clear that less flamboyant examples of parental failure can produce emotional mayhem. Parental embarrassment over sex, excessive shushing of childish exuberance, a childhood accident – the trivial and the portentous all can and apparently do wield awesome deterministic influences. One twenty-seven-year-old reminisces about his childhood and recalls being hit by a swing. The memory flooded back and with it the pain – not the pain of the swing but the pain that Mommy was not there. The reason he forgot about the swing was that he could not bring himself to recall how lonely and frightened he had been. Janov, characteristically, ends this account with the following comment:

> When he became ready to face the fact that his mother, whom he imagined to be loving, really didn't care about him and never had, his memory of the swing became conscious, total and real.[10]

In actual fact, no evidence other than the frenzied memories dredged up by the patient is offered to support the diagnosis of a rejecting and unloving mother. The mother herself was never seen and no attempt is made to check the young man's description of life as a child with any third party account. Nor is there any attempt to interpret his difficulty remembering the incident in any way other than that which fits Primal theory. Not surprisingly, parents are on a hiding to nothing in Primal therapy and it can sometimes take bizarre turns. The most bizarre is the view of the birth process itself as being a major cause of adult neurosis. In an appendix to *The Feeling Child*[12] there is a photograph purporting to be of bruises on the leg of a forty-eight-year-old woman who had been 'reliving' in a Primal session being held upside down and 'spanked' by the doctor just after birth. The doctor, the text informs us, was very rough and apparently left an imprint of the fingers of his left hand around the infant's leg. The text adds that the woman's family confirms the bruising at birth but neglects to tell us how such information was obtained. But the message is clear. 'The body is a memory bank', according to Janov, 'which preserves all of its experiences' forgetting nothing while the conscious mind struggles to recall its earliest experiences.

According to Mrs Janov, it was many years before she and Arthur would believe that people could actually re-experience their birth but after a while it became impossible to ignore the evidence of their own eyes. (It actually didn't take that long. *The*

Primal Scream came out in America in 1971. *The Feeling Child* with its account of 'Birth Primals' was published in 1973. Two years, even in LA, is not a long time!) It may be cynical to recall that Janov, for all his self-proclaimed genius, was not working in a vacuum. In France, Frederick Leboyer was insisting that modern methods of delivery, including bright lights, the emphasis on sterility, and the inhospitality of modern obstetrical delivery rooms, caused traumatic effects in the newborn, while in Britain, R. D. Laing was musing on the possibility that many of us are suffering lasting effects from our umbilical cords being cut too soon. Earlier than both of these radical critics, Wilhelm Reich provided a highly emotive critique of the 'inhuman but routine separation of birth'.[13]

Janov's insistence on being a pioneer, the discoverer of the cause of all neurosis, is a classic example of historical amnesia from which, if Gore Vidal is right, Americans are prone to suffer more than most. Despite his stout defence of the originality of primal theory, there is no convincing evidence, behavioural or physiological, that so-called 'Primals' differ from hysterical episodes or cathartic abreactions, phenomena which have an elaborate history and a pedigree which includes some of the most significant names in the history of psychopathology including Mesmer, Charcot, Bernheim, Janet and Freud himself. As for his ideas on birth trauma, they are the most obviously second-hand of the lot. As Roazen points out, as early as 1908 Freud himself was speculating about the act of birth as a source of anxiety, an idea which was taken up by his close friend and colleague Otto Rank, and developed into a full-scale theory of neuroses in a book entitled *The Trauma of Birth* and published in 1923. During the early 1920s, Rank, who had been born of humble origins in Vienna in 1884, occupied an exceptional place in Freud's private and professional life. Indeed, when the manuscript of the book was completed it was presented to Freud on his birthday on 6 May 1923. Ernest Jones (Freud's biographer and colleague) quoted Freud as observing some time later that 'he didn't know whether sixty-six or thirty-three per cent of it is true, but in any case it is the most important progress since the discovery of psychoanalysis'.[14]

According to Rank, two sets of strivings resulted from the trauma of birth. The first is the impulse to return to the womb in order to re-experience prenatal security. The second reflects an intense desire for a less traumatic rebirth or separation from a material object so as to achieve mature independence. The first striving stimulates the growth of dependent, infantile, clinging relationships while the second appears as a 'will' to grow, to achieve and to separate from confining relationships. The life of individuals is governed by these contradictory impulses to unite and to separate. Rank went on to develop his notion of 'separation anxiety' which, in his view, manifests itself as a 'life fear' whereby the person recognises creative capabilities within himself which threaten to separate him from others, thereby giving rise to fears of having to survive as an isolated individual. In contrast, the 'death fear' manifests itself by a terror of losing one's individuality and being swallowed up by others.

Such ideas, in less dramatic form, have been exploited by analysts such as Winnicott, Bowlby and Fairbairn and have had a substantial impact on the way early mother-child relationships have been interpreted. Janov himself pays no more than a passing acknowledgement to Rank and it is true that there is little evidence that Rank made much use of such ideas in his own analytic practice. Like the other designated heir-apparent, Jung, Rank eventually broke with Freud and after several trips to the United States, where he trained and influenced some of the most dominant of that country's first generation of analysts, he ended up in Paris where he became a friend and confidant of a number of artists and writers, among them Henry Miller and Anaïs Nin. Eventually, Rank came to regard neurosis not as an illness but as a failed work of art and the neurotic as one to be treated as a failed artist. He became disenchanted with science and psychoanalysis and turned to intuition as the means to the answers. In Rank can be found much of what these days is regarded as truly innovative in psychotherapy – the notion of the traumatic effects of an unsatisfactory birth and the notion that neurosis and creativity are different sides of the same coin. Yet again, the so-called 'new therapies' are merely old psychological models done up in new and transparent clothing.

Janov may have to insist on the novelty of his ideas, and push this claim in a series of books, because he is in California where therapy is business and survival is linked with novelty and the publicity it generates. Janov is also fiercely protective about his creation. A Primal therapy centre in Northern Ireland which incidentally had earned a certain degree of hostility from the locals and its members the title 'the screamers'[15] was denounced by Dr Janov who insisted that he had never heard of them and that untrained Primal therapists could be 'exceedingly dangerous'. Training in Primal therapy takes years, he assured readers of the Irish *Sunday World* and for untrained individuals to practise it would be potentially disastrous. However, doubts have been expressed about the rigour of the training of his own therapists. Janov's daughter was reportedly administering therapy while still in her teens[16] while other therapists in 1972 included a Hollywood actor, a grocery store owner and a New York stage actress, none of whom had any psychological training prior to becoming Primal patients.

In so far as Janov has described the qualities of a therapist there is the familiar Utopian grandeur enveloping the outline. A Primal therapist cannot have any defences. He must permit 'bone-chilling Pain' to erupt in patients. He must be sensitive and perceptive, i.e. he must have felt all his Pains. He will be feeling and thus will know when someone else is not. He needs to have an appreciation of scientific methodology and 'know what evidence consists of'. This last qualification reflects the recurrent insistence throughout Janov's writings that he has arrived at the answer to man's neuroses *scientifically*. What does he mean? Scientific truth, he declares, ultimately rests on predictability – Primal therapy cures. It is no use, he adds, sententiously, just piling up case upon case to 'prove' therapeutic efficacy. It must be scientifically established.

All very fine and, given that Janov made these declarations back in 1971, there has clearly been time to establish the efficacy of Primal therapy scientifically. In fact, Janov relies entirely on piling anecdote upon anecdote to verify the 'truth' of his theory. And the claims are remarkable. Primal therapy makes breasts, hands and feet grow bigger. Males grow beards where before was pristine skin. The senses are heightened – one woman noticed her husband's body odour for the first time after she primalled. Menstrual periods become regular, frigid women become sexually voracious, tennis players play shots hitherto beyond their powers. There are dramatic changes of habit too. An opera fan becomes a Rock freak. A baseball addict no longer loses sleep over who wins the pennant. The only scientific reference throughout this impressive testimony consists of a footnote to the work of Hans Selye on hormones and stress, the connection being clear to Janov but being somewhat tenuous to any reader familiar with that particular area of research.

Whereas psychotherapy and psychiatric treatment in general tends to use as one of its measures of effect, a return by the sick patient to a premorbid level of social and personal functioning, Primal therapy makes a virtue out of a decline in functioning. Probation officers can no longer work. Psychologists take up menial unskilled work. Marriage counsellors give up. In each case Primal therapy opens their eyes to the pointlessness of their former work. A television producer gives up his 'hack job' in order to write 'a more meaningful personal statement'.

Such information is relatively worthless when it comes to any attempt at evaluation. If it were put forward as a justification of the efficacy of drugs or behaviour therapy it would be laughed out of court. But Janov clearly believes that it will suffice though he does admit that 'a great deal of follow-up research' is needed. The fact that it has yet to materialise has not affected his belief that he has stumbled on the one theory of neurosis that makes all other theories invalid. His writing teems with psychologists who have achieved nothing, child counsellors whose work with children was utterly fruitless, marital therapists who got nowhere until they Primalled. Janov is every bit as cavalier about his use of the notion of neurosis as he is about marshalling evidence showing how his therapy conquers it. The neurotic 'spends a lifetime doing unreal things', has a personal stake in the denial of truth, delights in the struggle and not the result, is preoccupied with the desire for perfection. The normal person, in contrast, is 'defence-free, tensionless, non-struggling'. The normal does not feel lonely. The normal is straight. The normal is stable, can accept his age, is able to enjoy himself. The normal is healthy. He doesn't need to bother doctors because 'there is no pull toward being unreal, no symbolic system to keep the body restless and fatigued'.

Given that his theory blames all on parents, it is hardly surprising that Janov has written a primer as a guideline for those currently floundering with their offspring. *The Feeling Child*[12] is dedicated to the world's largest oppressed minority, children. The book neatly illustrates the primal therapist's love of scientific method and respect for scientific evidence. From beginning to end (and it is 286 pages long), it consists of a remarkable series of unsubstantiated yet striking claims concerning the pathological effects of parenthood, the traumatic impact of birth, the disastrous effects on adult personality of caesarean deliveries, (the clinching evidence for the last is that Primals in people born this way 'lack the fluid rhythms of the usual birth contractions'!) Premature deliveries are due to unconscious maternal desires to be rid of the baby, delayed births due to equally unconscious desires to hang on. Neurotic women have children for the 'wrong' reasons, e.g. a desire to leave some part of themselves living on after they themselves have died. Accidental pregnancies are impossible in Primal women, many of whom 'feel' when ovulation begins within them.

Throughout the book is the simple message – Let Children Be. It is a staggeringly simple and quite beguiling message, replete with echoes of the 1960s. Janov disdains to consider anything as complex as a parent-child interaction. Children, in his model, are passive, non-responsible and the helpless recipients of whatever their parents dish out. Nor is there any reference to the possibility that parental indulgence could produce problems in later adult life or inconsistency. In so far as any scientific literature is quoted, it is a hotch-potch of ill-digested and often irrelevant references to endocrinology, neurology and outdated behavioural research. Footnotes abound instructing the inquiring reader how he can read 'an excellent discussion' on the hormones of the hypothalamus or 'a technical discussion' of the diagnosis of neuroblastomas. But any references to such renowned workers in the field of child and family development as Jean Piaget, John Bowlby, Michael Rutter or Lee Robins is notable by its absence.

Whatever his faults Janov cannot be accused of trying to hide them. He has written prolifically in an age of universal literacy. His books have been widely read and are, by all accounts, best-sellers. It does appear that the need to cling to a simple, unqualified, dogmatic theory outweighs whatever critical awareness that Janov's readers possess. Of course it may be that critical awareness is the one quality that they do not possess, particularly when it comes to evaluating the pot-pourri of potted physiology, speculative behavioural theory and scraps of child psychology which Janov puts together.

References

1 Moreno, J. L. 1940 'Mental Catharsis and the Psychodrama' *Sociometry*

2 Ellenberger, H. F. 1970 *The Discovery of the Unconscious* Allen Lane. London

3 Greenberg, I. A. 1974 'Moreno: Psychodrama and the Group Process' In: *Psychodrama* Editor, Ira A. Greenberg. Souvenir Press

4 Kobler, J. 1962 'The Theater That Heals Men's Minds' *Saturday Evening Post* 235: pp.70-73

5 Johnson, P. E. 1959 'Interpersonal Psychology of Religion' In: *Psychodrama* Ibid

6 Yablonsky, L. 1974 'A Brief View of Moreno' In: *Psychodrama* Ibid

7 Moreno, J. L. 1934 *Who Shall Survive?* Nervous and Mental Publishing Co. Washington, D.C.

8 Moreno, J. L. 1945 *Group Psychotherapy: A Symposium* Beacon House, Inc. Beacon. NY.

9 Moreno, J. L. 1914 *Einladung Zu Einer Begegnung* R. Thimmas Erbe. Vienna

10 Moreno, Z. T. 1970 'Moreneans, The Heretics of Yesterday are the Orthodoxy of Today' *Group Psychotherapy* Ibid

11 Janov, A. 1973 *The Primal Scream* Sphere Books. London

12 Janov, A. 1977 *The Feeling Child* Sphere Books. London

13 Reich, W. 1954 *Listen Little Man* Souvenir Press, 1972. London

14 Jones, E. 1953 *The Life and Work of Sigmund Freud* Vol.III, p.59 Basic Books. N.Y.

15 Manning, M. 1976 'Screaming for Help?' Community Care 15 December p.13-14

16 Rosen, R. D. 1978 *Psychobabble* Wildwood House. London

6 A Game Therapists Play

Transactional Analysis is a new way to talk about behavior, a new way to sort yourself out, a new way to figure out what's really going on between you and your boss, your wife, your husband, your children, the teacher, the salesman, or your club president.

TA Sales Brochure

Barely had America welcomed the Viennese sage to her shores than the process he feared and predicted began. The process that is of shortening 'study and preparation' and proceeding as fast as possible to 'practical application'. Of all the many dilutions and adaptations of psychoanalytical psychotherapy, one movement more than any other appears to have mastered the mass-marketing of Freudian ideas, wrapping the commodity in catchy, gritty, abrasive sales jargon, and in the process actually daring to inject a tincture of humour into the whole solemn arena of psychological problems. True the humour is often somewhat heartless, but there is without doubt, an engaging quality about TA or transactional analysis and that is something singularly lacking in most of the other so-called 'new' psychotherapies.

As with all the others, so it is with TA – it is the brain-child of one man, a Canadian psychoanalyst, trained in the classic Freudian manner, namely Dr Eric Berne. Berne, now dead, graduated from McGill Medical School in Montreal, worked for some time at Yale University, studied at the New York Psychoanalytic Institute and spent some time in the US Army during the war before wending his way, like so many psychoanalysts before and since to the lush, therapeutic pastures of sunny California. In San Francisco's Mount Zion Hospital, Berne taught young psychiatrists group therapeutic approaches and what he was to term 'a unified system of individual and social psychiatry'. He was fascinated by general systems theory and believed that the structural analysis of human relationships would provide a more general and sound theory than orthodox psychoanalysis. In 1961 Berne published *Transactional Analysis in Psychotherapy*[1] in which he laid out, in some detail, the principles of his approach to interpersonal relationships but few outside the specialised field of psychiatry and psychotherapy ever read it. The book which made Eric Berne an international name and placed him at the top of the bestselling lists was *Games People Play* published in 1964 in the United States.[2]

As with Moreno and psychodrama and Janov and Primal therapy, Berne's theories began with a case. As we have seen, all new therapies begin with some classic case which, by virtue of its striking simplicity and the shining nugget of truth at its core, sums up for the most naïve as well as the most cultivated of minds the essential, splendid, remorseless truth of all that is to follow. In the case of transactional analysis, it all began with Mr Segundo. (In fact, in Berne's account there is also a Mrs Primus who had trouble with hallucinations but for some unexplained reason Mr Segundo takes precedence in the historical account of the birth of TA).

Mr Segundo told Berne the following story. An eight-year-old boy, vacationing at a ranch in his cowboy suit, helped the hired man unsaddle a horse. When they were finished, the hired man said: 'Thanks, cowpoke', to which his assistant answered: 'I'm not really a cowpoke, I'm just a little boy.' Mr Segundo then remarked: 'That's just the way I feel. I'm not really a lawyer, I'm just a little boy.' Mr Segundo was a highly successful lawyer but behaved for much of the time just like a small boy. When not performing his adult role in court, he would retire to a holiday hut in the mountains, which was stocked with whisky, guns and pornographic pictures, there to indulge himself in childish fantasies. Later in therapy, Mr Segundo introduced a new aspect of himself into the situation. That is to say, although most of his attitudes, feelings and behaviour could be categorised into so-called Adult and Child categories, there were certain residual states which fitted neither. 'These states', Berne noted, 'lacked the autonomous quality of both Adult and Child'. They appeared to have been introduced from outside and there was an imitative quality about them. For example, there was Mr Segundo's contradictory attitude towards money. The Child was penurious and miserly and would gleefully steal chewing gum and small items from drugstores just as he had done as a small boy while the Adult handled large sums with the shrewdness of a banker and was willing and able to spend money to make money. But another side of him indulged in fantasies of giving all his money away for pious and philanthropic reasons. His background was benevolent and charitable and he did indeed give large sums to charity (in Berne's theory very much as his father had before him.) This third side became categorised as the Parent.

The Child, Adult and Parent are what Berne termed *ego states*. By ego state he meant a coherent system of feelings related to a given subject (a phenomenological definition) and a set of coherent behaviour patterns (an operational definition). Drawing on the ideas of psychoanalytical theorists such as Paul Federn and Eduardo Weiss, Berne argued that each adult person contains within him three distinct ego states which are actually experienced. In support, he pointed to William Penfield's experiments involving direct stimulation of the brain, experiments which appeared to show that within the human brain were located experiences derived from different stages of development which could be called up by stimulation and which the conscious individual could recognise as being derived from these different stages. Experiments with drugs such as LSD provided similar insights and Berne was led to postulate the three pragmatic absolutes of transactional analysis (that is to say conditions to which so far no exceptions have been found). These are:

1 That every grown-up individual was once a child.
2 That every human being with sufficient functioning brain tissue is capable of testing out and arriving at some operational notion of reality.
3 That every individual who survives into adult life has had either functioning parents or someone *in loco parentis*.

There are three corresponding hypotheses which, simply stated, are that the relics of childhood survive into later life as complete states, that the testing of reality is a function of each discrete ego state and not an isolated, intellectual capacity, and that the individual decision-making process can be taken over by the complete ego state of some outside individual, most notably a parental figure.

According to Eric Berne, the principles of transactional analysis can be grasped in ten weeks and after a year of supervision 'an otherwise well-qualified clinician or research worker can become quite adept in theory and practice'. This represents quite an advance over the theory and practice from which the whole package derives, psychoanalysis. To become adept at psychoanalytical theory and practice can involve up to two years of daily one-hour trainee analytical sessions and even then one would be regarded as a very green and immature psychoanalytical novice.

Not that Berne completely reneged on the theoretical jargon on which he had been breast-fed at the New York Psychoanalytical Institute. He did refer to the Child in us all as 'Archaeopsychic relics', the Adult as our 'neopsychic functioning' and the Parental influence as 'Exteropsychic functioning' but for once his disciples opted for simplicity and Child, Parent and Adult have stuck ever since. Applying these three ego states to everyday activities and feelings is an ever-engrossing source of amusement for many. Berne's first example concerns a news story about embezzling. The Child in us reacts with excitement, identifying by way of his own fantasies with various aspects of the story. The Adult expresses his interest more matter-of-factly, speculating on how it was done, how the embezzlers were caught and so on while the Parent provides a judgemental, moral response to the whole affair. 'In the language of transactional analysis', declared Berne, 'the fault-finding Parent plays Blemish, the Adult plays Accountant, and the Child wants to play Cops and Robbers'.

Transactional analysis is full of games but before discussing these it is worth looking at some of the other notions that are part and parcel of the approach. One important idea is that each ego state can emerge to the exclusion of the other two. For example, some adult individuals persistently engage in childlike activity; they are immature in their emotional responses, demand instant gratification and attention, are exhibitionistic and histrionic and manipulate others by being intermittently seductive and belligerent. The constant Adult is the funless, objective scientist or diagnostician; the constant Parent, to Berne's mind, is many a virtuous clergyman. A related idea is that of *contamination* between the ego states. An example would be where someone would advance as a reasonable and reasoned proposition what turned out to be in fact a Parental prejudice or a Childish need. Some individuals are capable of either stubbornly persisting with one or other ego state or of shifting rapidly and opportunistically from one state to another. There are, in short, people who are slow to start or to stop playing, thinking or moralising and there are those who are able to switch rapidly and efficiently from one of these activities to another and back again as their situation demands.

In structural terms, a 'happy' or 'normal' person is one in whom important aspects of the Parent, the Adult and the Child are all syntonic with each other. Berne quotes the example of a young doctor, contented with his work, but who had marital problems. His father was also a doctor much respected by his mother so that the young man's Parent ego state approved of his career. His Adult was satisfied because he was interested and competent in his speciality while his Child's 'sexual curiosity was well sublimated and well gratified in his practice' (a whiff there of good old Freudian explanations of the appeal of medicine!) Hence Parent, Child and Adult all respected each other and derived satisfaction from his profession. Away from his work, however, he was not so happy. 'The moral' observes Berne, 'is that one can define a happy person but no one can be happy all the time.' Quite so.

Nor, indeed, need one be a doctor to be happy. One might be quite happy as a concentration camp commandant or a professional criminal. One can, as Werner Erhard says (see Chap. 7) be perfect in one's nastiness and, according to Berne, one can be happy too. So bringing up one's children so that they will be 'happy' is not a sufficient ambition, structurally speaking.

There are particular demeanours appropriate to the three ego states. That of the Parent is stern, paternal, upright, a warning finger is extended, there is a gracious mothering flexion of the neck. The Adult demeanour is one of thoughtful concentration, often with pursed lips or slightly flared nostrils. The Child is indicated by a certain coy inclination of the head, cuteness and the fixed brow of sulkiness. There are appropriate 'voices' too, and vocabularies. Typical Parental words are naughty, disgraceful, ridiculous, childish, low, vulgar and many of their synonyms. Curses, expletives and epithets are the common utterances of the Child while verbs and substantives, referring as they do without prejudice, exaggeration or distortion to objective reality, are essentially Adult. Certain words, however, can be employed by any ego state. Good, for instance, with a capital G is Parental, applied realistically and in a defensible fashion is Adult and denoting instinctual gratification is Child.

In summary, therefore, there are three ego states denoted in transactional analysis. Each has its own pattern of organised behaviour, is capable of adapting its responses to the immediate social situation, can modify responses as a result of natural growth and previous experiences and can mediate the phenomena of experience. The Parental ego state is a set of attitudes, feelings and behaviour derived from and resembling those of a parental figure. The behaviours associated with it consist of voices, gestures, vocabularies, demeanours and other characteristics of a recognisably parental kind. The Parental set of patterns can often be elicited in response to child-like behaviour on the part of someone else in the immediate environment. The Parental ego state is exhibited in two forms – the prejudicial Parent, manifested as a set of apparently arbitrary, irrational attitudes, usually prohibitive in nature and the nurturing Parent, usually manifested as sympathy for another individual. The Adult ego state is characterised by a set of feelings, behaviours and attitudes which are adapted to current reality, is organised, rational and intelligent and is founded on a constant testing of external reality as experienced by the individual. Again, there are appropriate demeanours, voices, vocabularies and gestures associated with this ego state. The Child ego state is a set of feelings, attitudes and behaviours which are remnants and relics of the individual's own childhood. There are two forms – the adapted Child, manifested by behaviour which is inferentially under the influence of the Parent, such as compliance, submission, withdrawal or acquiescence, and the natural Child, manifested by autonomous forms of behaviour such as rebellion or self-indulgence.

These ego states form the theoretical framework within which TA works. The basic aim of transactional analysis is the mastery of internal conflicts so that the Adult can maintain control of the personality during stressful moments. In Berne's view, it is best done in therapy groups. The TA group usually devotes the first two or three sessions to such preliminary matters as the introduction of the participants to each other and the introduction of them all to the theories of TA itself. Then therapy proceeds and by therapy is meant the analysis of transactions, pastimes and games.

According to Berne, human beings need stimulation. Intolerance of boredom or isolation gives rise to the concept of *stimulus-hunger* particularly for the kinds of stimuli offered by physical intimacy. In *Games People Play* Berne sums up this notion in the colloquialism: 'If you are not stroked, your spinal cord will shrivel up.' Once we have ceased being infants, we are confronted for the rest of our lives by the dilemma that whereas we are forever baulked by social, psychological and biological forces in our adult life we strive perpetually to re-attain our infantile levels of physical intimacy. As adults we transform such stimulus-hunger to a greater or lesser extent into a so-called recognition-hunger. We strive for recognition rather than intimacy. The urge may vary in its intensity – the movie actor may require hundreds of 'strokes' from his anonymous admirers whereas the scientific researcher may remain content with one 'stroke' a year from a highly respected master. Because while stroking may be used as a general term for intimate physical contact, it is also used in TA to denote any act implying recognition of another's presence. For these reasons, a stroke is regarded as the basic unit of social action. An exchange of strokes constitutes a *transaction* which is the unit of social intercourse and it is these transactions which form the subject matter of transactional analysis in groups.

A cardinal belief of TA is, that as far as the human organism is concerned, any social intercourse is better than no social intercourse at all. Accordingly, we carefully structure our time by what Berne terms *programming*. Material programming arises from the vicissitudes of life; social programming involves simple and elaborate greeting rituals (the gestures and small-talk which characterise everyday transient interactions) and pastimes individual programming occurs when people become less guarded, more intimate and more involved with each other. Pastimes usually take the form of semi-ritualistic discussion of such commonplace subjects as the weather, possessions, current events or family matters. Many groups, therapeutic and otherwise, never get beyond the pastime stage and confine themselves to playing variations of 'Small Talk' such as 'General Motor' (comparing cars) and 'Who Won?' (both 'Man Talk'), 'Grocery', 'Kitchen' and 'Wardrobe' (all 'Lady Talk'). Berne is endlessly fertile when it comes to applying pithy descriptions or name tags to these pastimes; there is 'How to' (go about doing something or other), 'How much' (does it cost?), 'Ever Been?' (to some exotic location city or tourist attraction), 'Do you know' (so-and-so?) and 'What became of' (good old Joe?).

In individual programming, definite and more elaborate patterns of interaction tend to appear and these too are amenable to sorting and classification. Such sequences of interaction, which in contrast to pastimes are based more on individual than on social programming, are called *games*. Now it is important at the outset to realise that Berne does not imply by his use of words like game and pastime that the participants are fooling about or are not serious.

> The essential point of social play in humans is not that the emotions are spurious but that they are regulated. This is revealed when sanctions are imposed on an illegitimate emotional display. Thus play may be deadly serious or even fatally serious but the social consequences are only serious if the rules are abrogated.[1]

Nonetheless, Berne does seem to want to have his cake and eat it for, his protestations of seriousness notwithstanding, he plainly regards pastimes and games as 'substitutes for the real living of real intimacy'.[2] It is difficult to avoid feeling that the gritty, somewhat pitiless terms he applies to various interpersonal games such as 'Wooden Leg' and 'Lush' suggest a somewhat derisive and even contemptuous attitude towards the individuals who 'play' them.

Not that Berne believed that only patients play games. Everyone plays games, even psychiatrists. Indeed the game 'Psychiatry' is one form of adult activity which in its projective form is known as 'Here's what you're doing' and in its introjective form as 'Why do I do this?', both popular games in the lives of participants in the growth movement. Transactional analysis itself even spawns a game for its more intellectual devotees entitled 'Which part of me (Adult, Parent, Child?) said that?' – although apparently this game burns out as the participants realise that they are wasting time.

Perhaps the commonest game played between spouses is the one colloquially termed 'If it weren't for you'. Berne described it in *Games People Play* and when we went to see one of Berne's closest disciples, the psychologist Claude Steiner, in Ukiah, California, he also used it as an example of a typical Bernean game. It is a game much played by couples who are locked into each other in a mutually destructive way, who are isolated from others and who are not having a very satisfactory life. The game is that one blames the other for the dismal state of affairs. 'If it weren't for you,' says the husband, 'if I didn't have to support you and if I didn't have to take care of the children and if I didn't have to work so hard, I would be a concert pianist, or a great surgeon, or a happy man.' Conversely she can be 'into' the same thing. 'If I wasn't washing dishes all day long, I would be a literary critic or telecaster or whatever.' Any conversation which might develop between these two, and which might begin as an attempt by them to relate in a positive and loving way, soon degenerates into 'If it weren't for you' and this can be played several times a week or by regular players, several times a day. There are other games such as 'Why don't you, Yes but' which is a game in which one person keeps making suggestions while the other refutes them one by one. 'Why don't you take up a hobby?' suggests the sympathetic GP to the bored housewife. 'Yes but,' she replies, 'I'm too tired after tidying up all day'. 'Well, why don't you get some help?' persists her doctor intending only to be helpful. 'Yes but I would then have to reorganise my daily routine and that would mean even more pressure on me', and so on. There's the game 'Kick me' where one person keeps making the same mistakes in his life over and over again and others put him down repeatedly. According to TA that is the way the individual concerned has learned to get his 'strokes', the fact that they are purely negative strokes doesn't matter; negative strokes are better than no strokes at all.

Certain games appear to recur throughout the individual's lifetime and seem to be segments of larger, more complex sets of transactions called by Berne 'scripts'.[1] A common pathological script is that based on the 'rescue fantasy' of a woman who marries one alcoholic after another. The script calls for some form of magical cure of the husband. When this is not forthcoming, there is a divorce and the woman starts all over again. Berne attributes the origin of the script to the fact that many such women had alcoholic fathers, and that the adult rescue operation is founded on earlier child desires for father to be sober, reliable and kind.

While the theoretical content of transactional analysis is heavily psychoanalytical in origin, in practice it is ruggedly reality-based. Freud is the name most mentioned if TA exponents care to mention anyone from the past, but here as with many other contemporary psychotherapists, one wonders if they have identified the correct ancestor. That the child has a feeling of inferiority which compels him or her to strive for superiority, that man is a social being and his interactions with not just his parents but his siblings, relatives and others form the subject-matter of life and therapy, that neurosis is a trick or 'game' played by the individual to enable him to escape fulfilling his duties to his dependants and the community, these are the sort of ideas that belong more properly to the theories of Alfred Adler than to Sigmund Freud.

Like Freud, Adler was a Viennese Jew. One of the master's chosen disciples, he broke from Freud in the first of the major disaffections which marred the early years of the psychoanalytical school. Where Freud has been portrayed by his followers as an aristocrat of the mind, with characteristics similar to those of Schiller and Goethe, Adler has been portrayed as a little petty bourgeois, (a 'pygmy' was Freud's derisive comment) who reduced the subtlety and complexity of psychoanalysis to plain commonsense. Where Freud laid such emphasis on unconscious processes and the libido, Adler seemed more excited by the role of conscious processes and the activities not of the primitive and largely unconscious but the reality-based and largely conscious ego.

For Adler, the most important drive in man is his striving for superiority. As a diseased heart's musculature will enlarge and hypertrophy in an attempt to compensate for the damage, so individuals struggle to compensate for the intrinsic powerlessness and vulnerability of infantile life. History is full of examples. Demosthenes stammered, the grandiose Kaiser Wilhelm II had a withered arm, Napoleon was notoriously small. Factors other than such organic ones as inferior physique, deformity or defective bodily function, also contribute to lowered self-esteem and hence to a vigorous struggle for control and assertion. The deprived, brutalised or spoilt child is likely to develop strong feelings of inferiority. Indeed, even in the most satisfactory of circumstances, the normal child must feel small and helpless. In order to compensate for inferiority feelings, each child develops in the early years of his life his own particular strategy for dealing with the vicissitudes and ramifications of his situation. In the light of this experience, he goes on to form the attitudes and behaviour patterns which Adler called 'life styles' but which have more than a passing similarity to Berne's notion of life scripts.[3]

According to Adler there are three possible outcomes of the individual's strivings for superiority and his efforts to overcome his feelings of inferiority. The first is *successful compensation* whereby the striving leads to competent and harmonious adjustment to what Adler regarded as the three challenges of life, namely society, work and sex. Secondly, there is *overcompensation*, when the striving becomes excessive and leads to pathological degrees of maladjustment such as the overweaning little man, the weakling turned mafioso, the painter-decorator turned megalomaniac Hitler. Finally, there is the *retreat into illness*; for Adler, every neurosis could be understood as an attempt to free the self from feelings of inferiority in order to acquire the feeling of superiority.

Most commentators on the Adler-Freud dispute comment on the ordinariness of the former versus the impressive and imposing stature of the latter. Adler was an unassuming little man with a small moustache who lived in a bourgeois residential area of Vienna, held informal meetings in cafés, gave informal courses to school-teachers, wrote his books in a prosaic and rather plain form and earnestly promoted a rational, socially oriented psychology with immediate practical implications. Freud, in contrast, lived in the best residential quarter, had an impressive art collection, held a university title, gave academic lectures, was a master of German prose and founded a depth psychology which he classed as the science which would unlock the secret of man's soul. To one historian at least these discrepancies help to explain why Freud's legacy is well known, respected and constantly acknowledged, whereas Adler, whose writings influenced a whole series of analysts, including Fromm, Horney and Harry Stack-Sullivan, is all but forgotten.[4]

Certainly, throughout all our travels into the land of the new therapies, we never once heard the name of Adler mentioned. Yet the transactional analysts' preoccupation with the activities of the so-called Adult (ego), his view of early childhood as a time when the individual is taught what games to play and how to play them, and learns the procedures, rituals and pastimes appropriate to his position, strongly resemble ideas originally formulated by Adler.

Berne himself was in no doubt that orthodox Freudian theorists had failed to provide a satisfactory analysis of the dynamics of interpersonal relationships:

Theories of internal individual psychodynamics have so far not been able to solve satisfactorily the problems of human relationships. These are transactional situations which call for a theory of social dynamics that cannot be derived solely from considerations of individual motivations.[2]

The similarity between Adlerian theory and transactional analysis is even more striking when the public image of TA, as expressed through its considerable publicity and advertising machine, is scrutinised. One of Berne's most enthusiastic followers is psychiatrist Tom Harris, author of 'I'm OK, You're OK', a bestseller which diluted the *Games People Play* distillation of Berne's original theories still further so that now they could be understood by every devotee of the airport lounge book store. His simple yet clearly appealing TA philosophy was quoted by M. L. Gross in his book *The Psychological Study*.

Right from birth, life is pretty rugged. The child almost immediately develops 'not OK' feelings. My own experience leads me to conclude that this 'not OK' position exists in the early portions of childhood in ninety-five to ninety-six percent of the population. Later in life the 'not OK'-ness is seen in feelings of inferiority and inadequacy, with a loss of self-esteem from disappointment.[5]

In fact, as Claude Steiner has pointed out, this view is diametrically opposed to Berne's view that we are born princes and the civilising process turns us all into frogs. Such a disagreement, however, between two of the late Dr Berne's most influential followers, has not prevented TA from being widely popularised outside the relatively narrow field of psychiatry. In the United States it is being used by business organisations as a technique to help employees deal with difficult customers. One example, quoted by Steiner[6], concerns the purchase by Off Track Betting, a turf accountancy firm in the US, of the TACT system (Transactional Analysis for Customer Treatment) from American Airlines. The airline had originally developed TACT from the theories found in Harris' 'I'm OK – You're OK'. In the Off Track Betting training course, the sellers and cashiers are taught to recognise what state a horseplayer or punter is in and to react with the appropriate ego state of their own. A *New York Times* report revealed how the approach works in practice:

For example, a customer who yells and threatens to punch the employee or stick a hand through the window would be in a child ego state. A customer behaving like a 'parent' would be authoritative and demanding, likely to make sweeping statements. In the adult ego state, the decision-making part of the triad, the person would be calm and rational.

'We try to swing the behaviour on to an adult level' said Erika Van Acker, director of training at OTB. 'But sometimes you have to play a different role. If an angry customer is coming from a heavy child ego state the clerk might want to go into a heavy parent ego state. He might say something like 'This kind of behaviour isn't tolerated here'.[7]

The answer, of course, is a 'stroke'. 'Usually', says Miss Van Acker, 'all an irate customer needs is a stroke. Just be nice to them and they calm down.' A neat example this of how being polite, behaving rationally and coping with stress in a civilised manner needs the elaborate endorsement of a psychotherapy package to give it respectability.

Steiner, however, is worried about another aspect of the growing use of TA. He points out that the approach was invented by Berne for use as a contractual therapeutic technique and that he was suspicious of and hostile to one-sided situations, such as occur often in industry, in which one person or institution holds all the cards. Transactional analysis was designed as a two-way, co-operative, contractual process, and, declares Steiner with some heat, 'its one-sided use as a tool for behaviour control is an abuse of its potency, similar to slipping a customer a sedative in a coke so that he'll buy a used car.'

Steiner has a point, though it is difficult to be totally sympathetic with his view of Berne as the austere professional shunning the market-place and Harris as the smart operator, swamping the market with an emasculated version of the TA truth. Berne himself 'happily' took his ideas to the top of the book charts in North America and not only with *Games People Play*. His follow-up book, *What Do You Say After You Say Hello?*, shows little signs of having been put together with the two-sided contractual therapeutic situation in mind. Indeed, in the preface to that book, Berne expresses approval of the fact that his theories are being tested 'in many different fields' including industry, education and politics and while he declares that the book is primarily for professional psychotherapists he clearly hopes that non-professionals will read it too.[8] The numbers who subsequently bought the book suggest that his hope was not in vain.

Steiner expressed the fear, in 1974, that in five years' time 'transactional analysis is going to be completely discredited' because of misuse. There is some evidence that after a period of immense enthusiasm the approach is having to give way to even more pugnacious and effervescent packages such as est. Steiner blames the decline on the fact that in marketing TA, people like Tom and Amy Harris removed 'the profound and radical perspective' within it. But, with the best will in the world, it is difficult to see quite what is so profound or radical about TA. Indeed, behind all the froth and the packaging, it seems to amount to nothing more than a rather zippy and punchy *description* of the ways some people interact with each other some of the time. Indeed, to judge by Berne's writings on the matter, the provision of a description seems sufficient. Whether change occurs or not seems little better than chance. That is to say, when people are shown the games that they play they may change – or they may not. For example, in *Games People Play* he describes the game of 'Harried'.[2] It is a game played by many housewives and well-known to many psychiatrists. The game itself is simple. The housewife who plays it takes on all the many and varied roles of being a housewife (mistress, mother, nurse, cook, hostess, decorator, diplomat) and *takes them all on together*. So, all within the same twenty-four hours, she agrees to hold a supper-party, take the children to the dentist, redecorate the bathroom, make a crème caramel, weed the garden and take the dog to the vet. Some time in the middle of the afternoon she collapses and the recriminations of her husband and the lamentations of her children add to her guilt and misery. After this has occurred on numerous occasions, her marriage is in jeopardy, her children are confused, her nerves are shattered and she is a likely candidate for the analyst's couch or a bed in the local psychiatric clinic.

To compound the problem, she has almost certainly married a man who tends to criticise her for not being as efficient as his own mother. But having found a suitable partner with whom she can settle into the game of 'Harried' she will not readily give it up whatever its unfortunate consequences. If they do come to a psychiatrist it is either because the husband wants something to be done about his wife (i.e. he wants her to be turned into his mother) or the wife seeks an ally in her struggle to cope with her husband.

The description of the case provided by Berne is characteristically humorous and tart. The solution, however, is less convincing. Indeed, it is clear from Berne's rather pessimistic conclusion that, in this instance at least, TA can diagnose better than it can treat. The psychiatrist is locked into an interaction with five protagonists – the wife's Parent and Child and her husband's Parent, Adult and Child – with only the wife's Adult to count as an ally. 'If he (the psychiatrist) quails', concludes Berne ruefully (and my quailing began half-way through the diagnostic résumé), 'he can take the easy way out and offer his patient on the altar of the divorce court, which is equivalent to saying "I surrender – let's you and him fight" '. A rather pale and timid outcome given the energetic and colourful diagnosis.

I don't hold it against transactional analysis that it has little to offer such pathological marital relationships but not all Dr Berne's successors are as honest as he is, and nowhere in the voluminous literature which pours out in the form of folders, pamphlets, advertising blurbs, and course syllabuses, is there much trace of humility concerning the theory's potential.

A case in point is the application of transactional analysis to the understanding and treatment of alcoholism. The transactional analyst according to Claude Steiner, 'considers alcoholism the end result, or effect of "alcoholic" behaviour'.[9] Alcoholics are people who wilfully engage in repetitive, interpersonal behaviour sequences which involve alcohol and have what Steiner refers to as 'an interpersonal pay-off' as the covert motive. According to the TA view, there are three distinct types of such games. In all three games, the alcoholic operates from a position exemplified by the statement: 'I am no good and you are OK (ha, ha).' In all three, the alcoholic deliberately places himself in a position of being disapproved of, puts those who do the disapproving into a position of appearing blameless and virtuous while at the same time so contriving the situation as to ensure that not only are they not virtuous and blameless but they are foolish and at least partly responsible for his plight.

The specific thesis of the first or *Aggressive* game is 'you're good, I'm bad (try and stop me)'. The colloquial name for the game is 'Drunk and Proud of it' or 'D & P'). In this game there is the alcoholic and a player who alternates between being a persecutor and a 'patsy'. The alcoholic is intent on getting persecuting Parents so angry that they show their impotence and their foolishness. Often played by salesmen and business executives with their wives, the aim of the game here is to punish the wife for her dominating and possessive attitude.

> Under the influence of alcohol the D & P player can engage in extracurricular activities with his secretary, can lose large sums of money at the poker table, and stay out with the boys until all hours of the night, with complete impunity. When his wife reproaches him the morning after, he apologises, saying 'Boy, I feel terrible about this, honey, I'll try to be good from now on.'[9]

The wife is either forced to persist in the role of Persecutor or she can accept the apology thereby leaving herself open to being a Patsy. Such alcoholics rarely come for treatment and are only seen by psychiatrists if the wife eventually threatens to break up the marriage. Even then, the D & P alcoholic has no interest in treatment and will turn any unsuspecting therapist into the same roles of persecutor and patsy given even half a chance. The childhood prototype of the D & P game is 'Try and Stop Me' characterised by repetitive messing over food, telling obvious lies and getting parents angry over trivia.

The second game, *Psychosocial Self-Damage*, is played in response to a lack of 'strokes' and is usually played with a partner who is unable to give, or has difficulty giving strokes. As a consequence, the alcoholic's persistent drinking is of some advantage to his partner since as long as it continues, the partner's emotional inadequacy will not be exposed. The colloquial name for this game is '*Lush*'. Because the Lush player reacts to strokes, he is given to intermittent cessation of drinking and he also often makes considerable progress when therapy begins. However, because the therapist's strokes do not replace the needed strokes from the partner, the temporary progress is quickly cut off. The aim of therapy is the facilitation of 'a mutual stroking relationship' involving the two partners and involving too an intense examination of their sex life together. If the partner does not participate in treatment, no progress will be made and, short of divorce, there is no way that the Lush player can hope to overcome his script. Even then, he may well marry another 'non-stroker' and the whole game will start again.

Unlike D & P, Lush involves a lot of people and many of those who come into contact with the Lush player, in addition to his spouse, will assume the various roles of Persecutor, Patsy or Rescuer. The childhood prototype is getting attention by hurting oneself, making messes, etc.

The third game, *Tissue Self-Destruction*, is part of an intensely self-destructive life script. The thesis is 'I am sick (try and avoid that), you're well (Ha, ha).' In this game, colloquially referred to as *'Wino'*, the alcoholic obtains strokes by making himself ill. He may wind up in a soup kitchen where he will be fed, a jail where he will be sheltered, or in a clinic where he will be given medical and nursing care. In either case he pays a physical price in order that others may take care of him. But his real 'pay off' is a confirmation of the position 'I'm not OK, you are OK (Ha, ha)'. This on a deeper level in fact means quite the reverse, (I'm OK, you're not OK') because to the alcoholic, people only care for him when he is ill; when he is well he believes they don't give a damn so the fault is not really in him, but in them.

The childhood prototype of this game is crying and getting fed, playing sick and getting medicine etc. In giving Winos various 'treatments', many therapists are insufficiently tough-minded and by providing strokes are in effect adjusting the noose around the condemned man's neck rather than actually helping him to opt out of the terrible game altogether.

These then are the games that alcoholics play. In response, the transactional analyst refuses to play. Insisting that alcoholics can be cured and that he expects to succeed with those patients interested in changing their lives, he thereby exploits three powerful therapeutic factors. The first two, according to Steiner, are directly related to the conviction about the transactional basis for alcoholism. By refusing to participate in the alcoholic's game, the TA therapist leaves the patient devoid of any incentive to play. Secondly, he places the responsibility on the patient 'where it belongs'. Thirdly, he inculcates 'positive expectancy and hope'. If therapists expect their alcoholic patients to be chronically ill then chronically ill they will be. If, on the other hand, they expect them to get better, then better they surely will be.

Claude Steiner's *Games Alcoholics Play*[10] has been called 'the most effective scientific psychotherapeutic approach to date in the treatment of the alcoholic', a testimony which might have carried more weight had it not been made by Dr Eric Berne, a not altogether unbiased observer. In fact, of the forty-four references to the alcoholism literature quoted by Steiner, not one refers to a study of the efficacy of this 'scientific' approach and to date such claims remain unsubstantiated. When we put aside the pungent prose, the snappy titles and the effulgent endorsements what does the whole business amount to? That people get certain satisfactions from indulging in socially unacceptable behaviour? Well, as Steiner himself admits, Adler said as much, and did so much more economically, when he remarked that 'every problem child, every neurotic, every drunkard, or sexual pervert is making the proper movements to achieve the position of superiority'.[4] That those who try to help others often find themselves caught up in the role of colluder ('Patsy') or disapprover ('Persecutor')? This is one of the planks which underpin the professional notion of 'detachment' and which, ironically, comes under such fire these days from those, like Steiner, who enthusiastically endorse a more committed, a more involved and a more open therapeutic exchange between therapist and patient.

But the real problem comes when we examine more closely the assumption on which the whole elaborate theory rests. In the case of the TA review of alcoholism, it is the argument that the alcoholic 'wilfully plays the various games of alcoholism with a covert motive', that he is 'crooked' and employs a duplicity that is 'difficult to detect'. Indeed, these comments led one critic to accuse Steiner of suggesting that 'the alcoholic is consciously engaged in a game of deception with malevolent intent'[11], which would be to ignore much that is known about the nature of so-called neurotic behaviour. The basic problem with Berne's exposition on neurosis in general, and Steiner's analysis of alcoholism in particular, is that man is portrayed throughout as entirely autonomous with a well-developed capacity for volition and a marked sense of purpose. In the case of alcoholism this is taken to the extreme of ignoring the fact that what is involved in the whole process, in addition to the Patsies, the Persecutors, the Rescuers and the players themselves, is *alchohol*, that most potent, addictive and psychotropic of universal intoxicants. A testable hypothesis of Steiner's TA faith is that an alcoholic would stop playing the alcoholic game were he to be marooned on a desert island alone with a crate of Scotch, the game depending for play on the presence of at least one other person. Short of hearing the testimony of an alcoholic Robinson Crusoe, as another alcohol expert pointed out[12], we cannot prove or disprove the claim but it is worth noting that few experts, in commenting on Steiner's article, were very sanguine about it.

Steiner's argument makes much of the fact (in his view) that any notion of alcoholism which does not place the cause of the condition directly at the feet of the alcoholic, saps him of responsibility and thereby gravely compromises his ability to change his behaviour. It is a very contemporary criticism of the so-called 'disease model' and transactional analysts have taken the lead in the assault being made on traditional notions of disease not merely in the field of alcoholism but vis-à-vis many psychiatric disorders, such as schizophrenia and manic-depressive illness. However, this is to confuse aetiology and responsibility. Blaming addicts for their addiction is not a new and shattering theoretical and therapeutic break-through, but a position with a long, though not necessarily very respected or respectable tradition. It has not, on the whole, been found to be helpful largely because it tends to ignore the fact that man, and particularly drugged or psychologically dependent man, does not invariably make free and unfettered choices.

This problem is partly the consequence of the curious mixture of psychoanalytical theory and sociological thought that makes up Berne's TA. Transactional analysis, from the viewpoint of the sociologist, involves the analysis of roles and interpersonal relations and makes no assumptions whatsoever concerning the psychological state of the participants. It merely *describes* the actual actions and the consequences. In so far as TA does this it is a fertile generator of hypotheses and an entertaining game in its own right. However, Berne and Steiner both interpret the participants' intra-psychic feelings and attitudes while dealing only with his interpersonal behaviour. For example Steiner's discussion of 'pay-offs' only considers interpersonal pay-offs and totally ignores any question of an intra-psychic pay-off, despite the fact for instance that there is considerable evidence to the effect that many alcoholics do drink for drink's psychological (and physical) effects.

It may be a trifle fanciful to speculate on the blatantly commercial and economic flavour to the language and the ideas of transactional analysis. Yet with all the talk of 'transactions' and 'pay-offs', and the merciless exposition of interpersonal exploitation existing side-by-side with a vigorous exaltation of the possibilities of individual growth, it is not perhaps so surprising that TA has become a business in its own right.

Business or no, transactional analysis cannot escape the inexorable thrust which propels every new therapy into a creed of salvation. Reichian massage, Moreno's psychodrama, Rogerian psychotherapy – they each began as a relatively circumscribed approach to helping the mentally distressed and ill and ended up as a programme for living, a philosophical statement and a religious message. Steiner's irritation with Harris is not just because the latter overturned Berne's optimistic 'I'm OK, You're OK' statement about the human condition but because the replacement 'I'm Not OK, You're OK', which Harris claims is the infant's initial position is too close to the religious notion of original sin for Steiner's comfort. And true enough, Harris does devote the latter half of his book[13], which is supposed to be about TA, to such problems as America's fear of Red China, the student revolt and the nature of religious experience. On the way we learn that the United Nations 'has survived many crossed transactions', and that religious may be 'a unique combinations of Child (feeling of intimacy), and Adult (a reflection on ultimacy) with the total exclusion of the Parent'. The book ends with Harris reminating on the fact that man, after negotiating the darkness of war, pestilence and hatred, may through the insights of TA be on the threshold of a new dawn and the day when he can fulfil his existence 'to the fullest of human spiritual capabilities'.

Once more the circle is complete. Once more an idea is grasped, turned into a therapy, from a therapy into a cult and from a cult into a creed for humanity. At no state has its actual worth ever been seriously evaluated. The fact that it sells a million paperbacks and makes a few temporary reputations is evidence enough of its truth. It is difficult to avoid the conclusion that transactional analysis like the other arrows in the therapeutic quiver is potentially useful if aimed at the right target but it is certainly no match for targets such as the meaning of life, the purpose of existence or even the nature of pain.

But the boundary between therapy and philosophy of life is now really giving way in our passage through the new psychotherapies and in the next chapter it finally collapses with the most extraordinary yet, we would argue, predictable consequences.

References

1 Berne, E. 1961 *Transactional Analysis in Psychotherapy* Grove Press. New York
2 Berne, E. 1964 *Games People Play* Grove Press. New York
3 *The Individual Psychology of Alfred Adler* 1956 Editors, H. L. Ansbacher and R. R. Ansbacher. Basic Books. New York
4 Ellenberger, H. F. 1970 *The Discovery of the Unconscious* Allen Lane. London
5 Harris, T. A. 1978 Quoted in *Psychological Society* M. L. Gross. Simon and Schuster. New York.
6 Steiner, C. M. 1974 *Scripts People Live* Bantam Books. New York
7 *New York Times* 21 March 1973 'OTB Placating Losers with an Ego Triple'
8 Berne, E. 1972 *What Do You Say After You Say Hello?* Grove Press. New York
9 Steiner, C. M. 1969 'The Alcoholic Game' *Quarterly Journal for the Study of Alcoholism* 30: pp.920-928
10 Steiner, C. M. 1971 *Games Alcoholics Play* Grove Press. New York
11 Pattison, E. M. 1969 'Comment on "The Alcoholic Game"' *Quarterly Journal for the Study of Alcoholism* 30: pp.953-956
12 Edwards, G. 1969 'Comment on "The Alcoholic Game"' Ibid 30: pp.948-951
13 Harris, T. A. 1969 *I'm OK, You're OK* Harper & Row. New York

7 The 350 Dollar Poke in the Ribs

If you don't take it out into the world, you didn't get it in the first place. What I got clear about was that it would require an organisation – and a particular kind of organisation – to take the experience of transformation out into society.

Werner Erhard[1]

One of the major criticisms of classical psychoanalysis is that it is immensely time-consuming. Not surprisingly, the newer and more unorthodox psychotherapies drew attention to the fact that they were far less demanding in terms of time (and money) and yet were every bit as effective. Inevitably, competition led to some remarkable claims so that now there is a human potential movement which claims to 'transform' the mental health of those who engage in it in just sixty hours! Erhard Seminar Training, or est as it is more popularly known, is one of the fastest growing as well as ostensibly one of the fastest working 'enlightenment' movements in the United States. Created in 1971, its graduates, as those who have taken the est training are called, now number upward of a quarter of a million world wide. There are centres in twenty-four American cities, three in Canada, one in London and one in Bombay. In London, three thousand people took the training (which currently costs £172 including VAT) in the three years following its arrival in November 1977.

The creator, driving force and absolute master of the multi-million dollar business is Werner Erhard. The story of where he came from and where he is going has been often told. The man himself is the subject of a eulogistic and improbable biography by the philosopher William Warren Bartley III, whose previous claims to fame were scholarly and lucid analyses of the work of Karl Popper and the influence of the Vienna School Reform movement on the middle period of Ludwig Wittgenstein's life and work.[2]

Erhard was born as Jack Rosenberg in Philadelphia in 1935. A second-hand car salesman and business executive, he left his wife and their four children in 1960 and changed his name, first from Jack Rosenberg to Jack Frost, and then, somewhat more imaginatively, to his present one, a compound formed as a result of his reading a magazine article on the two men who 'transformed' Germany: Werner von Braun and Chancellor Erhard. The 'new' man headed towards the West Coast where he worked for the sales department of a magazine. By the late sixties, he was vice-president of Parents' Magazine's Cultural Institute which sold encyclopaedias.[3]

But before that, some time in the early sixties, Erhard had had what he describes as a 'peak experience'. What precisely this experience was he is unwilling to reveal ('there are experiences which can't be captured in words') but it lasted about three months. 'That', he says, 'got me dedicated to the whole issue of transformation, because it was very clear to me that it really wasn't worth living the old way, that whatever I had been experiencing during that three months was not even comparable to life ordinarily and I decided to dedicate my life to getting that experience back again.'

The method he chose was studying what he calls 'disciplines'. 'I studied all of the ones I can think of and most of the ones anyone can think of. I either read about them or practised them or had them done to me or learnt to do them with other people.' According to Bartley he immersed himself in hypnosis, mind-over-matter experimentation, psychic control of pain and bleeding and telepathy as well as the various manifestations of the human potential movement such as gestalt and encounter training. He studied Zen, under the supervision of Alan Watts (the Western guru who has popularised Eastern philosophy), before becoming a very successful instructor in Mind Dynamics, a pseudo-spiritual enterprise started by an Englishman named Alexander Everett. Like hundreds of thousands of other Americans, Erhard fell for a time under the spell of the Dale Carnegie movement and through it he was to disover the important truth that he 'had no problem turning other people on'.[2] Bartley's biography also reveals that Erhard was periodically visited by astonishing revelations – on a beach at Atlantic City, he 'became the universe', on another occasion he had 'conversations with God'.

We have seen how new therapies tend to arise through the combination of an individual creator and a classic case. In the case of est, the creator and the case are one and the same. It was what happened to Erhard on a freeway in California – 'somewhere between Corte Madera and the Golden Gate Bridge' to be more precise – that was to lead directly to the founding of est and a revolution in the 'ecology of enlightenment'. In the high-ceilinged, lavishly furnished living room of his San Francisco mansion surrounded by primitive pottery, giant plants, his secretary (who turned out to be his first wife) and a watching, anxious and suitably deferential Erhard disciple, we asked Werner Erhard to tell us what happened on the road to the Golden Gate. In the latter part of 1971, he told us, as he was sitting in his car driving towards the city, 'suddenly I got it'. What 'it' was essentially amounted to the realisation that things are in fact exactly the way they are. That is to say, 'what is, is and what is not, is not.' Simultaneously, he realised that he actually knew nothing, 'a startling thing for a person who had dedicated his whole life to learning, to finding out', Erhard assured us, with the curious mixture of naïvete and cunning which is his hallmark.

> I had this enormous pile of knowledge that I had put together . . . . I made it part of my way of life to learn something new every day and to keep adding to the pile. But what I realised was that absolutely everything I knew, I knew towards some end. In other words, I knew absolutely nothing simply because it was so. I knew everything I knew either to become better, or to be more successful, or to become enlightened or to some end and in that instant I realised I knew absolutely nothing.

When that 'devastating experience ' passed – he realised that he knew everything. That is to say, he realised not that he was all-knowing but that 'all things were open to myself. Not necessarily to my system of intellect, but certainly to myself'. Before all this happened, he had thought 'there must be one thing I haven't found out yet which when I find it out will pull it all together and then I'll have it made. And I discovered in that instant that there was no secret, that the secret is what is, is and what isn't, isn't and that's so obvious you cannot call it a secret'. And with that Erhard laughed, a somewhat mirthless, harsh chuckle as if to express conspiratorial agreement with the unspoken suspicion then crossing both our minds, that we might be in the presence of an intellectual gymnast of the very top rank.

He also realised that people are perfect. Even nasty people are perfect, 'They are perfect in their nastiness', that is to say they are exactly as nasty as they are, they are no more nasty than they are, and therefore they are perfect in that degree of nastiness. 'I also recognised,' he added, completing his account of his car-born conversion, 'that one should be whole, that one should be complete, that the point of life is not to make it but to be'.

After this 'transformation', Werner Erhard put his not inconsiderable talents (his mother once said of him 'he could sell you City Hall'[4]) into forming an organisation which would bring the possibility of similar experiences to countless thousands of individuals still mistakenly struggling to make it rather than simply being. In *The Graduate Review*, a sort of house magazine produced by the est organisation, Erhard spelled out the implications of his shattering discovery:

> There are some who think that I have discovered something that other people ought to know. That is not so. What I have discovered is that people know things that they do not know they know, the knowing of which can nurture them and satisfy and allow them to experience an expanded sense of aliveness in their lives. The training is an occasion for them to have an experience – to get in touch with what they actually know but are not really aware of.[1]

The est training is usually carried out over two successive weekends, beginning each Saturday and Sunday at around nine a.m. and ending at around midnight but sometimes later. Early on in its history, est became irreverently known as the 'no piss therapy' since you cannot go to the bathroom, or indeed have a cigarette, eat or sleep, unless the est trainer says so. Included in the training, in addition to the two weekends, are three optional seminars, called the pre-training, the mid-training and the post-training. These are about three hours long and are conducted in the evenings a few days before, between and a few days after the weekend sessions.

The training is held for about two hundred and fifty people at a time, usually in a hotel ballroom or conference centre. The participants are seated on chairs, arranged theatre style around a low platform on which the trainer stands. There are microphones to enable people who want to say something, or ask a question to be heard by the others, and everyone wears a name-tag so the trainer can address people individually. The rigidity of the rules has earned est some criticism, but Erhard dismisses it. It became clear to him, shortly after his transformation, that 'the rules in life do not bend' and he argues that it is important for people 'who are being given the opportunity to discover themselves' to discover too that there are certain facts of life which cannot be persuaded away. The rules of the training are to emphasise the fact that the physical universe 'always goes by the book and that, like gravity, life does not relax the rules just because you want it to or even because you need it to.' A useful message no doubt but it does not alter the fact that the est rules heighten the tension, increase quite subtly the dependence of the trainees on their trainer and provide the latter with another stick (or carrot) with which to manipulate his charges.

And what happens during the training? Three relationships are said to develop. The first is between the trainer and each participant. The training starts with what looks like a lecture but after a while the resemblance fades as the trainer parts with such paradoxical statements as 'If you experience something, it completely disappears' and shouts at them 'I am your trainer and you are the trainees. I am here because my life works and you are here because your lives don't work'.[5] The trainees are told in no uncertain terms that for all their reasonableness, their intelligence, their belief systems, they are 'assholes' – a much-loved word in est vernacular. 'You've just paid one hundred and seventy-two pounds (or three hundred and fifty dollars) to be here' thunders the trainer sarcastically, 'and you'll get nothing from this training.' One person who braved the humiliations and physical privations of Erhard Seminar Training is Valerie Singleton, the well-known television presenter. The trainers' belligerence, she believes, is simply a technique to make people look at themselves honestly.

> They are trying to provoke you and they are not going to do that by coming in and being pleasant and nice and saying 'Hi, how are you all?' I mean they are trying to get a reaction from you. People stand up and say 'I don't have to be spoken to like this. I mean, I don't have to be here'. And they say, 'Well, why are you here?' And people stand up and say, 'My life's working'. And they ask, 'Well, why are you here if your life's working?'

Valerie Singleton believes that the main est message is that you have to accept life the way it is and that when you do it changes. You no longer say I wish life was this or I wish it was that: I wish

I had more money, a better job, a better husband, a new man – whatever. 'By actually accepting your life the way it is and really enjoying it the way it is, it actually gets better, which makes sense, doesn't it?' Well, yes, if it was not too bad in the first place, otherwise, probably not.

Certain other messages are drummed home. Each person must take absolute charge of his or her own life. People are 'assholes' because they live in 'belief systems' that prevent them from experiencing aliveness and making their lives work. Belief in God destroys God – it interferes with 'experiencing' God. Endlessly thinking of what one is going to become tomorrow, of the house one would like to buy, the neighbourhood one would like to live in, the relationship one would like to have, destroys any experience of today, of being in the house you are in, the neighbourhood you are in, the relationship you are in. When a trainee objects that one can have a belief in God *and* experience him and quotes St Thomas Aquinas as someone who wrote seventy-three books about God, the trainer replies dismissively that 'we can be damned sure he didn't have much time to experience him, then'. (It was incidentally an immediate successor of St Thomas Aquinas, William of Occam (d.1347) who wrote 'Id quod est, est, quod non est, non est').

Not surprisingly, a barrage directed against every belief and opinion put forward by the trainees provokes a state of electricity which some find hard to handle. Est has thought of that too and provides vomit bags which assistants hand out rather like air hostesses in a badly pitching plane. But the pace can lag and late in the day the temptation to put one's head down and have a catnap is often irresistible. Those who do nod off promptly get bawled out by the trainer and their lapse can provide the moment for a homily on the fact that one of the reasons why people's lives don't work is that they enter into agreements which they subsequently have not the will to keep.

The process of breaking down belief systems and patterns of 'mind fucking' (the est indelicacy for 'thinking') is arduous, humiliating, even brutal, so that by the end of their training, the inner life of the trainees may be so disturbed that, in Bartley's words, 'their very clothes exude the stench of congested thought'.[2] Not surprisingly, given such emotional intensity, the second relationship that develops is that between the trainees themselves. Here is Erhard's own description of what happens:

Initially people raise their hands. . . .and they talk about something – be it an annoyance, or an insight or their theory of the training etc. Then, as the training goes on, people begin to share more fully what they are actually experiencing until, toward the end of the training, people become able to share in a way we call 'getting off it' – relating things they have held on to perhaps for their entire lives – things they have been stuck with yet were unable to reveal they were holding on to and now find they can let go of.[6]

'The extraordinary thing is,' says Valerie Singleton, 'that you do begin to identify with what all these people are saying and you see problems that you thought were only your problems that other people have. And you do begin to get a tremendous bond with these people and towards the end of the second weekend, there are tremendous friendships'.

The third relationship people experience in the training is with themselves. There are techniques or 'processes' whereby people can switch their attention from concepts about themselves, their lives and the lives of others, to observing directly their own experience. A favoured 'process' is one in which trainees are asked to select a problem from among those they have in life and to see specifically which experiences are associated with that problem – which bodily sensations, emotions, attitudes, gestures, postures, thoughts, judgements, things they have been told to think or things they have read, conclusions, decisions and explanations. People find apparently that there are bodily sensations which they feel when and only when the chosen problem makes its presence felt in their lives. Processes last anything between twenty and ninety minutes and after they have been completed the trainees are invited to communicate whatever insights they experienced during them.

The training, then, is not like a classroom, a seminar, a lecture or any form of orthodox group therapy. In Werner's modest opinion, the training is simply unique and its aim none other than 'a transformed individual', that is to say, someone who can tell the truth, and 'a transformed environment', that is to say one in which the truth can be told.

But first the est trainee must be freed from the restrictions of Mind. In est terminology, Mind is 'uncorrected cybernetic machinery', promoting a strait-jacketing 'life plan', so merely changing your 'Mind' is not what est is about. Only by tran-

scending Mind can a person 'identify with Self', and be transformed. But what is this 'self' of which est trainers, when they
are not engaged in the wheedling and bludgeoning of the training, speak? We put this question to Erhard himself and what
followed illustrates the difficulty in penetrating the obfuscation
and the opacity of much of the est language.

> *Werner Erhard:* Well, let me tell you first what it isn't . . . . If you
> and I examined our lives carefully we would see that we lived
> our lives as if we were things –T-H-I-N-G-S– objects. Now if I
> say, Dr Clare, you live your life like you are an object, you are a
> thing, it's offensive; and yet when we examine our lives, we do
> live our lives as if we were things. Now a thing has a couple of
> qualities essentially. One of the qualities that a thing has is that
> it is located in some place. If it's a thing it's somewhere. It's not
> everywhere, it's not nowhere; things are always somewhere.
> And they always have some particular form . . . . So they are
> located in space and they are located in time and they are
> located in form. If, in fact, that is the self that you are attempt-
> ing to realise then the realisation of that self will lead to a kind
> of narcissism because if I'm this thing, then that thing or any
> other thing is not this thing, and is therefore a threat to this
> thing. And so I've got to watch out for myself.
>
> A.C.: Why should it be a threat to this thing?
>
> W.E.: Er . . . .
>
> A.C.: Why should the existence of other things threaten the exis-
> tence of this thing? (Very long pause).
>
> W.E.: I'm trying to decide at what level of abstraction to answer
> this. I'm left with a very abstract level to answer it on so I'll
> answer it that way. In a given space, if you have a myriad of
> things, you have a kind of disorder, confusion, or whatever
> you like to call it, to which we try to bring some order. The way
> in which we bring some order is to locate one of these things to
> be the orientation point in that space and if you define self as a
> thing you make your thing the orientation point. Therefore any
> attempt to make an orientation point anywhere else becomes a
> threat to your order of things. In addition to which my point of
> view, and I am now calling my thing a point of view, a point
> from which to view, my point of view is strengthened only by
> agreement . . . . Therefore, you have to be in agreement with
> my point of view in order for my point of view to be streng-
> thened. I have to be seeing you as a function of me, I have to be
> seeing you because of me, I have to be seeing you in my terms
> in order not to have my point of view threatened. So that's why
> others are a threat to a thing . . . . In transformation, one shifts

from experiencing oneself as a thing, in a sea of other things to being the space of all things. One experiences oneself as evidenced by many things. So that who I am is not this thing and who you are is not that thing but who I am is the space in which that thing and this thing occur and who you are is the space in which this thing and that thing occur. There's a shift from positionality to space, a shift, a shift from thing to space . . . . Ultimately, the self is space.

Perhaps it is appropriate at this stage to recall the remark of Luke Rhinehart, author of *The Dice* and a much publicised est graduate. 'Est is incomprehensible and valueless nonsense', he said, 'until one has taken the training.'

But in spite of what one might term, in the est manner, the bullshit, this distillate of such raw and dubious essences as scientology, mind dynamics, Zen, Taoism and what Rosen has dubbed 'charm, chutzpah, psychoanalysis and certain oily arts of the American market place'[3] is a response to genuine and widespread needs. Not only in the United States do people become so hooked on the siren voice of the middle-class ethic with its promises of jam tomorrow that they never actually live today. Not only in the United States do people grow up undervaluing themselves and confused by the clash of received directives and personal experience. But perhaps only in the United States would the idea have been conceived that it is possible to do in four days and three evenings what psychoanalysts strive to do over a period of several years and what the more cautious among us might regard as the work of a lifetime.

Est undoubtedly encapsulates certain truths, universal truths, some would call them truisms. But even allowing for the apparent decline in the fashion of literacy might not we expect that the average American could find such insights in say, the *Reader's Digest* or in one of the many know-yourself, how-to manuals produced each year? Would not a library ticket and a spare hour save him three hundred and fifty dollars? Not so, replies Erhard. 'There is a distinction between the truth stated and the truth. That is to say that the truth couched in words, or the truth couched in symbols, or even the truth couched is no longer the truth, it is a representation of the truth.'

And there, perhaps in a Freudian slip, Erhard gives poor, embattled and besieged psychoanalysis (the truth couched?) its final death-thrust. The talking therapy which was itself to revolutionise the world is pushed aside by a therapy, nay a mission, which hurls the couch out of the window and installs in its place the exhilarating, the overwhelming, the transforming activity of – experience.

Trainees express their transformation by shouting 'I've got it, I've got it' which to anyone who has seen *My Fair Lady* sounds like a cue for music. For some this moment is accompanied instead by hysterical laughter, for others equally hysterical tears. Either way there is much hugging, kissing and jumping about as transformation spreads through the group like a particularly virulent form of food poisoning.

Transformation is termed 'a contextual shift' whereby the content of an individual's life moves from attempts to get satisfied, or survive, or to protect or hold on to what has been achieved, to the experience of *being* satisfied right at this moment and of organising life 'as an expression, manifestation and sharing of the experience of being satisfied.'[6] That is getting 'it'. And, in the sense that the 'it' is nothing, est playfully suggests that the training in the end provides 'nothing', thereby demonstrating a little whimsy, and a touch of self-mockery while having a jolly good jab at the competitors in the human potential bazaar who promise the moon itself. But, once you have got 'it', then it is 'natural' to express that in life and share the experience with others. Hence the proselytising quality to est and the fact that once you are absorbed into the organisation as a 'graduate' you may find yourself devoting a great deal of your time to spreading the transformation message.

Much is made of the fact that no one *needs* the training. It is not medicine (if you are ill, see a doctor), it is not psychotherapy (if you are mentally ill, see a psychiatrist). Nor is it religion, exercise or a social activity. No, the training is not about people's problems *per se*. But it is related to those 'rare' moments such as Erhard experienced before he settled down to his disciplines when 'we are fully alive, when we know – without thinking – that life is exactly as it is in this moment.'[6] At such moments we have no unfulfilled wishes, no nagging regrets, no irritating worries. They are perfection in themselves. They are complete.

In short, these moments are the 'peak experiences' described originally by Abraham Maslow, the American psychologist[7] and one of the co-founders, with Carl Rogers, of humanistic psychology, otherwise referred to as the human potential movement. Like Rogers, Maslow, believes that man is propelled by a 'self-actualising' drive and that those who most successfully express it and fulfil it experience many more 'peak experiences' than ordinary people. Such an experience can occur at any time – while you are sitting in a chair, travelling on a bus, cleaning your car. (Only Erhard appears to have had a 'peak experience' lasting as long as three months). Nothing changes in such a moment and yet everything is transformed. The uniqueness of the most mundane stimulus, the sight of the chair, the sound of conversation, leaps at you. The peak experience has been variously described as 'a bubbling over of sheer delight, a moment of pure happiness'[8], as a moment when the mask is swept aside and reality stands revealed[6], as 'a sense of completeness, of absolute value and relevance . . . . a feeling of intrinsic merit, above and beyond the mere conventions of society'.[9]

The peak experience can occur in more auspicious circumstances too. Religious and mystical experiences, sexual climax, drug-induced ecstasy states, sensations experienced as an emotional response to a superb vista or a great work of art – all can be and are categorised as 'peak experiences'. The search for such experiences does not have to be explained by having recourse to any complicated theory of human motivation. They are an end in themselves. 'One simply knows that one has made contact with reality'.

But is est itself merely a peak experience, a brief contact with what seems like reality at the time? Valerie Singleton seems to be not quite sure.

> The last weekend, [she says of her training] I was absolutely exhausted. I think I had about five hours sleep the whole weekend. I remember going into work – I had to do the programme on Monday – and I just felt fantastic. It didn't seem to matter that I had had so little sleep. I was very much more open with people, very much more aware of people, very much more direct with people. . . . and I found that by being more open and warm to people they actually were much more responsive to me.

Later she found, the effects began to slip away, she began to be aware of contradictions in the message, but this was a source of regret.

> I think if you can hang on to it, it does actually make you happier,

more at ease with yourself and more at ease with life. Some people lose it they say and then it comes back suddenly a year afterwards, or two years afterwards. You certainly hear extraordinary stories like that. But when you are with est people, certainly, there is a communication and a directness and an honesty. The only difficulty is that that's lovely when you are with est people; a little bit more difficult with people who haven't done it and don't know what you are on about.

Est has not only made a number of spectacular converts including John Denver the songwriter, John Curry the Olympic gold medal skater, and Yoko Ono, but it has also, and perhaps inevitably spawned a number of imitators. One, called Exegesis, is run by the twenty-nine-year-old son of an Essex meat salesman, Robert D'Aubigny. Like Erhard, the name he bears is not his original one. He was born Robert Fuller and for some years after he left drama school he followed the Erhard trail, investigating and sampling a broad variety of cults and positive-thinking movements in this country and in the United States before launching his own contribution called Infinity Training Seminars. Later, he changed it to Exegesis. The whole business is a straightforward imitation of est with an added emphasis on confrontation shock tactics and protracted verbal abuse. The cost of a three-day session is £175 and the rules controlling the hotel-based encounter are the familiar no smoking, no going to the lavatory, no eating or drinking, no speaking to each other and no talking back to the Exegesis trainer without permission. Exegesis has been the subject of a *Daily Mirror* exposé and a critical television play. D'Aubigny has been accused of using 'mindwarping' techniques, of bully-boy thuggery and of KGB-style psychological intimidation. Playwright Andrew Carr, the author of the play, *Instant Enlightenment Plus VAT*, admitted that having attended an Exegesis seminar with the purpose of exposing its methods he found his brain becoming 'too tired to argue'.[10] 'For two or three days after the seminar I felt I'd do anything for that man'. A documentary on BBC television revealed some of the techniques used and also unexpectedly captured the sinister side of the organisation when Exegesis aides physically prevented a participant from leaving the seminar.

Nor are the rules enforced by moral pressure alone. There is a £10 fine for not carrying your cheap Exegesis 'enlightenment' notebook, a £5 fine for breaking the lead in your pencil, a £1 fine for forgetting to applaud when a leader stands up or speaks. Like est, Exigesis employs 'processes' – one requires trainees to stare at each other through open-ended bags; the idea of such a visual confrontation is to make people understand each other better. At the end, they are supposed to 'see the light'. But not all the sons of est are as aggressive and disturbing as Exegesis. Insight is a New York-based organisation which was launched by an American called John Roger, and has become well-known in Britain through the efforts and writing of Arianna Stassinopoulos. Ms Stassinopoulos is a Cambridge honours graduate, a former President of the Cambridge Union and author of *The Female Revolution* and a biography of Maria Callas. Ms Stassinopoulos brought Insight to Britain in 1979, fifteen months after having herself taken a course of 'experience' in New York. Before it, as she explained in an article in *The Observer*, 'I was living out the tragedy of our culture, seeking to live life, to capture and understand it, through the mind alone.' After: 'I was at last living from my being rather than my head. Everything was the same but two feet off the ground'.[11]

The Insight experience, or 'transformation' to use Erhard's terminology, takes fifty hours spread over three evenings and two full days and at the time of writing costs £150. The numbers involved at any one time are somewhat smaller than in est, about one hundred trainees, but as in est the venue is usually a hotel ballroom. The first London sessions took place at the Café Royal, a suitably portentous beginning. Insight literature suggests that it is laundered est or perhaps est without jackboots. 'The power and regimentation of est is replaced by a sense of compassion and an extraordinary loving inter-action of the group' writes a woman who has taken both trainings, in the Insight brochure. Other trainings, the Insight message goes, subject you to a whole variety of embarrassments. In Insight, nothing unpleasant happens at all. Nobody calls upon you to speak, forces you to do anything you don't want to do and nobody is called an 'asshole'.

But if the atmosphere appears to be one tailor-made for British reserve and psychological caution, the rules are again similar to est's. No smoking, no alcohol, and above all, don't tell. Graduates are advised not to make any big changes in their lives immediately after taking the training. (This may relate to a curious phenomenon we discovered ourselves among people who have been transformed by new therapies. 'I felt so good', we were told on several separate occasions, 'that I went straight out and got a divorce.')

The fifty hours are spent in a variety of ways. There are lectures, guided meditations, exercises, children's party games. At one point, participants choose their own partners for one-to-one conversations, at another they are given something resembling an IQ test. It is, Insight graduates, say, often amusing, often fun. There is also the inevitable 'pain' but, they insist, Insight is one hundred per cent supportive and the support spreads from the trainer to the participants.

Like est, Insight seems easier to define in terms of what it is not rather than what it is. It is not, we are told, a religion despite the fact that Diane Kacic in the Insight brochure testifies to the fact that as a result of taking the training she now feels 'constantly protected, a sensation I have not experienced since I lost my childhood belief in guardian angels'. Diane also reveals that her eyes seem less inclined to go red in spite of London air and contact lenses and her colleagues at work now remark on her 'more positive attitude'. It is not a psychotherapy although the same brochure carries the tale of a lonely self-conscious woman who for years wore wedding and engagement rings to conceal the 'humiliating truth' that she was 'in reality a middle-aged spinster' only to sell them one week after taking an Insight course. The rings were badges of her fears but thanks to Insight 'My hands are both bare now and I enjoy the newness of their unencumbered lightness.' Nor is it a revelation, a cult, a conversion or even further education.

The claims made in the brochure, and echoed by Insight graduates at guest seminars, suggest that it may well be a potent amalgam of all these things. Bernard Levin, for example, spoke movingly and persuasively at a seminar of how it had helped him overcome his difficulties in talking to strangers. Behaviour therapy? George Scott has placed on record his view that Insight led him to an easier suspension of disbelief. 'The training freed me from my compulsion to distrust' he wrote. 'That in itself was a mini-epiphany.' Conversion? Arianna Stassinopoulos, again at the seminar, talked of the guilt and the pain we all carry with us from the past in terms virtually identical with those we heard from Vivian Janov at the Primal Institute in Los Angeles.

Not that it very much matters how such 'enlightenment' courses are described. The validity of the Insight experience, or indeed the est transformation, transitory though the 'shifts' may often be, can hardly be denied when so many reputable personages are prepared to stand up, at the risk one might suppose of considerable embarrassment, and vouch for them. If you *feel* better you *are* better, in some sense at least, even if the symptoms of your particular 'disease' have but temporarily remitted to appear again at some later date.

But of course there is another way of evaluating the impact of the ests and the Insights and the other movements to liberate the self and that is by looking for signs of altered *behaviour* amongst the converted. Does 'transformation' alter the way the transformed behave or is it merely a change in the way they feel? The est training, so the blurb says, is about getting you in touch with you. After it there are no rules to follow or techniques to practise, just the result is left. But having been awoken, surely one wonders what to be doing now that one is awake? A philosopher, Jonathan Lieberson puts the dilemma plainly:

> To wake up, to be stunned by the astonishing variety and richness of world views, to be soaked in wonder: this may be splendid, but what does one do with all this aliveness and enthusiasm? This question is moral: Which direction should I take? Should I try to imitate Jesus or Henry Ford or Lenin? Should I try to master a specific task? Should I try to make money or retreat from the market place? Should I go back to sleep?[4]

Well, Erhard is a sharp and nimble operator and he clearly saw such accusations of self-satisfied narcissism and moral vacuity coming. And so he created The Hunger Project. And what is The Hunger Project? Well, following the est tradition, the project is not about solutions, about fixing up the problem of world hunger. No, the Hunger Project is, in Werner Erhard's own words, about 'creating a context – creating the end of hunger as an idea whose time has come'.

> People don't die of hunger because there is no solution to the problem of hunger. People die of hunger because of the way the world works – that is to say, the forces in the world. Hunger is a function of the forces in the world, not a function of scarcity or a function of an absence of solutions . . . . As a function of The Hunger Project, we will learn what we need to know to make an

idea's time come; then we will learn how to make the world work.

The project was formally launched in 1977 after 'considerable research' and discussions with 'experts on world hunger'. It is separate from est, although naturally many est 'graduates' are associated with it. How does one participate? Quite simple. Choose the fourteenth of any month as a day of fasting; contribute what you can afford to The Hunger Project and have your family and friends participate by joining you in your fast and contribution.

By May 1978, it was clear that The Hunger Project was indeed an idea worthy of its maker. By then, more than 90,000 people in all fifty states of the Union had enrolled and, forty-six countries had taken responsibility for making the end of hunger and starvation an idea whose time has come'. NBC Radio arranged for public service announcements about the project to be aired on the network three times daily, seven days a week 'until the end of starvation'. A 'woman in Washington' changed her $10 pledge to $20,000 after participating in the project and 'experiencing its impact in the world and in her own life'. She has arranged to pay $1000 a year for another nineteen years. A San Francisco participant has made a pledge to donate $250 on each Valentine's Day and Thanksgiving until the end of starvation and has adjusted her will to continue the pledge in the event of her death. The Governor of Massachusetts proclaimed 1978 Hunger Project Year. Musician and est graduate, John Denver, produced and narrated a new film about ending hunger and starvation called 'I Want to Live' while expressions of support came from the Governor of Pennsylvania, the Leiutenant Governor of Hawaii and the Mayor of San Francisco. By Thursday 28 August 1980, no fewer than 1,478,115 people, worldwide had enrolled.

Now that looks a formidable response to those carping critics who portray est as nothing more than a method of generating 'peak experiences' and sadomasochistic trips for the well-heeled and the alienated. After all, to persuade so many people in such a short time to contribute to the relief of starvation suggests an elevated moral consciousness and a transformation that turns people outwards rather than inwards. But take a look at the published accounts of the Hunger Project and you will notice something rather odd. Nowhere is there any mention of money or food actually going to the starving. In fact the whole of the 1,751,000 dollars spent by the organisation in 1979 (out of a total income of 1,810,000 dollars) went on activities other than feeding the hungry.

As a charitable corporation, the Hunger Project is required to classify its expenditure into three areas: management and general administration, fund raising and programme services. The modest 23% spent on the first two categories left 77% or 1,344,000 dollars for programme services, which could be defined as the end-product of the charitable endeavour. But the end-product of the Hunger Project is confusingly similar in character to general administration and fund raising. Enrolment and Committee Activities (649,000 dollars) involve the project in expenses such as data processing, telephone and travel, staff salaries, printing, copying, mailing and other costs to maintain a nationwide volunteer network. Publication of *A Shift in the Wind* (340,000 dollars), a tabloid news sheet distributed four times a year to everyone enrolled in the Project, also involves printing costs, salaries, postage *et al*. Communication, Information and Education Services (355,000 dollars) are described as a wide variety of programmes designed to communicate broadly to the general public about the issue of hunger, as well as the direct funding of projects (such as research) carried out by other organisations, and the money goes on grants, salaries, travel, meeting rooms, advertising, mailing, printing and so on.

However, as issue nine of *A Shift in the Wind* points out: 'Although the Hunger Project does not directly feed people, it does recognise the vital importance of food aid programmes, especially during times of famine.' This astonishing insight led them to pay for ten full page advertisements in major newspapers in the US as an expression of support for those organisations involved in Cambodian relief. The money raised as a result of these advertisements, it should be said, was paid directly to the actual relief organisations and not to the Hunger Project.[12]

What then the Hunger Project amounts to is a gigantic public relations exercise. It can be seen either as a valuable ancillary to the relief organisations who are striving to find the money to buy the food to send to the starving millions or as a further diversion of energy and cash away from that central necessity. One of the people approached early on to participate in the Project was John Maher, the no-nonsense Irish-American who runs the Delancey Street Foundation, a centre for the rehabilitation of young criminals in San Francisco. 'What do we have to do?' said Maher. 'You give up one meal a week', was the reply. Maher asked what should be done with the food, should it be sent somewhere? 'No', said the Project representative, 'you just become conscious of hunger.' Maher could hardly contain himself.

> I said to this bird, [he told us] I've got fifty Puerto Ricans, one hundred black people, all kinds of people who know what hunger is. These people, [he was referring to the people from the Hunger Project] do not understand that thinking about people being hungry does not do anything; sending them some food does something. They think that everything revolves around their internal consciousness. But the people across the Bay are still starving, and the people across the Bay are still going to burn down their houses and ours if they do not get something to eat.

In other words, what is food is food, and what is not food, is not food.

There has been a local Hunger Project committee in London since 1978 and an independent UK branch of the organisation came into being in the autumn of 1979. By 5 September 1980, 12,770 people had been enrolled by a variety of means including street canvassing and 'presentations' to societies, schools and women's organisations.

In 1974, est took its ideas into the community with its 'public service program'. In March of that year it 'donated' three Communication Workshops to Moffett Hospital at the University of California Medical Center in San Francisco. A hundred and thirty-seven members of the Pathology Research Facility participated. Later, two 'trainings' were undertaken for elementary school children, the first in the 97th Street School, Watts, the second in the Sydney School in Castro Valley. Later, that same year, est partially donated trainings to the Black Community in New York City and to the Native Hawaiian Community in Honolulu. In 1975 and 1976, two similar trainings were undertaken in the Black Community in Oakland, the city across the bay from San Francisco whose citizens John Maher believed would find consciousness-raising no substitute for food, work and justice.

Subsequently, est has been involved with the California State Department of Corrections, San Quentin, Leavenworth and Lompoc prisons, McNeil Island Penitentiary near Seattle and the State Paroling Authority of Hawaii. But 'the most comprehensive contribution to the transformation of the quality of life in a community' according to the relevant est brochure is the training donated to the City of Parlier, near Fresno in California, a predominantly Chicano community in the San Joaquin Valley. Parlier, far from being a true city, is more like a village of some three thousand people but it faces the traditional urban problems of unemployment, a lack of basic amenities and an undue dependence on welfare. Est's plan was breathtaking in its simplicity and audacity. If individual people could take responsibility for their lives and their situation through the training then why could not an entire community do the same? Parlier would be helped not by providing the jobs and the shopping centre that studies had shown were needed, but by 'aligning' (an est term) the people of Parlier so that they could 'communicate' and 'work together' towards a 'clarity of purpose'. In the words of *Los Angeles Times* journalist, Barry Siegel[13] 'the self-help potential movement of the 70s, in short, would fulfil the unrealised goals of the Great Society and Cesar Chavez.' The implications, naturally, were enormous. No longer would it be necessary for urban problems to be eliminated. Instead we would have a new way of looking at them.

Early in 1978, est moved in and soon the city's Mayor and City Manager, who had previously never heard of the organisation, became firm enthusiasts. In turn, they convinced the City Council to accept est's offer of a 'training' for the entire community, the Mayor expressing the exuberant opinion that 'Something beautiful is happening . . . . that's all I'm going to say'. By May, they were ready to go with the Mayor, City Council, Police Chief, Superintendent of Schools, and the concerned private citizenry anxious to 'transform themselves into individuals' who 'can tell the truth' and Parlier into a society 'in which the truth can be told'.

Instead of producing alignment, est almost started a miniature civil war. The forceful, even crude, challenge which est routinely mounts against the individual's belief system did not go down too well with the majority of Parlier's traditional, family-oriented Catholics. Erhard could ruminate to his heart's content about giving up a belief system in order to experience belief but 'the citizens of Parlier were simply not going to stand for est leaders kicking Bibles across the floor and calling religion "bullshit".' Of course, there were those who suggested that these accounts were exaggerated but nevertheless one-third of the hundred and eighty who started the training dropped out before it ended. Of the hundred and twenty who remained, only fifty were Parlier residents, the remainder coming from other towns and paying a special $30 fee.

There was trouble too over est's alleged high-pressure tactics which included repeated phone-calls to would-be recruits, trouble over the trainers' 'gutter language' and over what was seen as verbal intimidation. So great indeed was this trouble that Erhard himself had to leave his San Francisco base and appear at a special meeting in the town, signalling incidentally how important the whole initiative was to est's ambitions, public image and reputation. Jauntily attired in pleated khaki slacks and a white shirt with shoulder epaulettes, Erhard displayed his 'homey, impish manner and a non-stop boisterous grin'. While a good number of the town's most outspoken anti-est inhabitants did not show up for the special meeting, many did and Erhard expressed intense enthusiasm for everything that everyone had to say. He quickly defused the situation by insisting that est was neither here nor there and what they should do was sketch out how the community might be transformed. Suggestions poured from the audience. 'An end to drugs, crime and poverty', said the town's senior priest. 'A sense of pride in what Parlier already has' suggested another citizen. 'Everyone participating together in solving problems,' said a third. 'Love,' said the Mayor. Erhard received all these suggestions as if he was in the presence of a galaxy of Nobel Prize winners.

> First we must create a vision. Then we can make up our minds whether we are willing to work to achieve it, to take responsibility, to make a commitment. Are you willing? If you say yes, I am willing to come back and help too.[13]

The crowd broke into spontaneous applause. Future meetings were scheduled and after two and a half hours Erhard withdrew for private consultations with city officials. Since those heady days, est's contact with Parlier has been sporadic. A second meeting with Erhard reportedly drew about thirty people. Parlier stubbornly remains the way it was before the happening. But to feel depressed about the outcome may be to miss the est point. The Mayor's sister, Raquel Benitez, was quoted at the end of the first Erhard meeting saying 'Whether this works or not, I'm just excited that people are excited. Even if it doesn't last.' Erhard replied 'There's nothing wrong with that. That's part of the experience. There's nothing wrong with that.'

Critics of est believe that the organisation has donated trainings free to hospitals, school groups, prison populations and a town like Parlier, not so much out of a desire to help, as a desire to build a documented track record in community work, which would enable it to start selling its training packages to cities and institutions across the country and charging for such a service. Such community projects hold out lucrative possibilities. Instead of collecting $350 per individual, the est organisation could move into group sales grossing over $100,000 for each community programme filled to the three hundred person capacity.

Nor should it surprise anyone that a movement dedicated to personal transformation should be relatively indifferent to socio-economic and political power realities. Est has been accused of helping the rebellious, alienated and protesting adolescents of the 1960s return to mainstream, business-oriented, establishment America by reassuring them that they are perfect the way they are. If they are fed up with roughing it in a hippy commune, subsisting on nut cutlets and wheat germ, and exhausted by their attempts to awaken working class consciousness, then that's OK. Est also suggests that the much-hated 'system' will work if *they* rather than *it* undergo change.

Est, it might be said, is giving capitalism an experiential face. And why not indeed? After all, Erhard's own background is sturdily individualistic and entrepreneurial. He remains a salesman and a very good one too. As Richard Price, the Esalen gestalt therapist, remarked to us, 'You've seen the ads for Macdonalds hamburgers; eighteen billion hamburgers sold, OK, well, it is the same with est, so many thousand people processed . . . . '. For all the reverence shown to the notion of 'small is beautiful'. Schumacher's exhortation derived from Buddha's 'Noble Eightfold Path', there is nothing small about est. Its main office in the heart of San Francisco is large and modish, and exudes the air of a thrusting, dynamic industrial corporation selling plastics. Name-tagged executives scurry around with fixed, have-a-good-day smiles and helpful aides relate the latest graduate figures or Hunger Project gains, for all the world like stockbrokers endorsing an investment in a particular series of shares. But then what else would one expect of an organisation which has as its Board Chairman, the former General Manager of the Coca-Cola Bottling Corporation of California, Don Cox?

Erhard runs a tight organisation too. Great emphasis is laid on the importance of *communication* (there are Communication Workshops for the staff), on relationships (there are Making Relationships Work courses for the staff) and on the truth (Werner appears to take a personal responsibility for ensuring that the truth is always told). An est trainer describes Werner's obsessional attention to detail. If he discovers something wrong he will ring the hapless suspect whatever the time of day or night. The trainer, Randy McNamara, tended to be rung around three in the morning:

> He [Werner] would say, 'Randy, this or that happened. Did you do that?' I would come up with some airy-fairy explanation or justification for what had happened. He would then repeat, 'Randy, I said did you do that?' I would say, 'Werner, I don't recall it very well'. He'd say, 'Good, recall it'. I'd say, 'Werner, it was a long time ago'. He'd say, 'Good, what happened?' I'd say, 'Werner you know there were a lot of things happening then. I don't remember it'. At that point he would just pound the desk. I could hear it. He was using the speaker phone. And then I got off it.[2]

'Getting off it' is the est equivalent of confession. The response would then be a simple 'Thank you, Randy, goodnight' and back to sleep for Randy until Werner felt the need to ensure the truth was told once more. For these and allied reasons, est is regarded by some as a fascist organisation and there are dark hints concerning Erhard's alleged authoritarianism and the docile, submissive sycophancy of those immediately around him.

But, when all has been said about est's organisation, its 'training', its aspirations concerning the transformation of whole communities, its elaborate self-advertising techniques and its relentless expansionism, the movement stands or falls over the package it is selling. 'The proof', says Erhard, 'is in the pudding. The people who have been through the training have reported on the validity of the training and the shift in the quality of their lives. Nothing that I say is as important as that'. Yet, such external evidence as there is suggests that there is nothing objectively 'authentic' or 'truthful' about the transformation experience. One may 'feel' transformed but in the absence of any more tangible evidence it stubbornly remains a feeling and not a fact.

However, it is not so much est's preoccupation with the value of 'transformation' that disturbs (the notion is far, far older than Erhard and is, for example, buried deep in the tradition of Christian mysticism) so much as the shallow, moral relativism which it embraces. For all the emphasis on transformation, est is a recipe for staying whatever way you are while feeling smugly superior about having 'changed'. 'Right action' according to est, is 'contextually determined behaviour' which in turn is defined as behaviour which is appropriate, is fitting. But who decides on whether it is fitting? Establishing objective standards of 'fitting' behaviour is condemned out of hand (it is to become 'stuck in position'). Rather, the judgement on whether this or that behaviour is morally acceptable or not depends purely on the 'context', the 'situation', on 'where you're coming from'. The exercise of reason in weighing evidence and contributing to and drawing on a collective moral system of values yields to the 'demands of the context'. Such a relativist position had led at least one critic to wonder how many of Werner's graduates know how distant such a philosophy is from what was required of him to become the entrepreneurial success they all admire.

> Whatever the training may accomplish, the est theory encourages one to become a Zen harlequin, non-judgemental and non-evaluative, favouring a relativistic stupor over science and argument, cynically distrusting all 'abstractions' and general rules, collapsing with self-conscious laughter at double-talk and Oriental riddles.[4]

Erhard would no doubt reply to this criticism in his not inimitable manner, 'That's great – we find that very valuable'. When cornered he tends to discard the intellectual mode and don something more Rotarian. 'I've had the opportunity,' he says 'and perhaps the privilege and the circumstances and the support to be able to what I call poke in the ribs thousands and thousands of people. But that's really all I've done. That's really all est does. It kind of pokes people in the ribs and says 'Notice this!'

References

1 Erhard, W. 1976 'The Transformation of Est: Getting off it and getting on with it' *The Graduate Review* Erhard Seminars Training. San Francisco, California

2 William Warren Bartley III 1979 *Werner Erhard: The Transformation of Man: The Founding of Est* Clarkson N. Potter

3 Rosen, R. D. 1977 'est: The Self is Fun to the Self' In: *Psychobabble* Atheneum. New York

4 Lieberson, Jonathon 5 April 1979 'Est is Est' *New York Review of Books*

5 Rhinehart, L. 1977 *The Book of est* Sphere Books. London

6 Erhard, W. and Gioscian, V. 1977 'The est Standard Training' *Biosciences Communications* 3: pp.104-122

7 Maslow, A. H. 1968 *Toward a Psychology of Being* 2nd Edition. Princeton, New Jersey

8 Wilson, C. 1972 *New Pathways in Psychology: Maslow and the Post-Freudian Revolution* Gottarcz

9 Brown, R. and Herrnstein, R. J. 1975 *Psychology* Methuen. London

10 *Daily Mirror* 20 March 1980

11 Stassinopoulos, Arianna 20 May 1979. 'In Search of Insight' *Observer*

12 *A Shift in the Wind* The Hunger Project Newspaper Number Nine, August 1980

13 Siegel, B. 16 July 1978 'Est stirs the Dust in a Farm Town' *Los Angeles Times*

8 A Secular Religion?

Although the theories of Freud and Adler come much nearer to getting at the bottom of the neuroses than does any earlier approach to the question from the side of medicine, they still fail, because of their exclusive concern with the drives, to satisfy the deeper, spiritual needs of the patient . . . . In a word, they do not give meaning enough to life. And it is only the meaningful that sets us free.

Carl Gustav Jung[1]

From the very first years of psychoanalysis, there has been an argument over whether psychotherapy more properly belongs to religion than to medicine. Are spiritual well-being and mental health one and the same? In so far as Freud considered the questions of religious practice and belief it was to disparage and dismiss them. In his *Future of an Illusion* he declared religion itself to be a neurosis, indeed *the* universal neurosis of mankind. Refusing to cope rationally with the awesome cosmic realities of life and death, man creates religion as a defence against his unconscious fears. Religious emotions Freud connected to sexual difficulties, conversion he explained as a crisis of puberty and adolescence, and in *Totem and Taboo* he incensed orthodox religious believers by equating Christian and other beliefs with primitive totemism. In 1937, two years before his death, he showed that age had not mellowed his hostility, when he told his friend René Laforgue, who was urging him to leave Vienna on account of the Nazis, that the real enemy of psychoanalysis was not Nazism but the Roman Catholic Church.[2]

In 1927, in his essay on lay analysis (questioning the need to be medically trained to practise psychoanalysis), Freud declared 'I have assumed that psychoanalysis is not a specialised branch of medicine. I cannot see how it is possible to dispute this'.[3] But, as Thomas Szasz, only the latest of a long line of critics of psychoanalysis, was to ask, 'if psychoanalysis is not a specialised branch of medicine, what is it a branch of?.[4] Freud answered thus:

> The words 'secular pastoral worker' might well serve as a general formula for describing the function of the analyst . . . . We do

not seek to bring (the patient) relief by receiving him into the catholic, protestant or socialist community. We seek rather to enrich him from his own internal sources . . . . Such activity as this is pastoral work in the best sense of the word.[3]

If Freud undermined religion by dubbing it neurosis and substituted his secular therapy in place of the priestly and the rabbinical mission (provoking the great Viennese hammer of psychoanalysis, Karl Kraus, to observe with characteristic sarcasm 'Psychoanalysis is the disease of emancipated Jews; the religious ones are satisfied with diabetes'), Carl Jung struggled to incorporate religion into the body of his particular psychoanalytic theorising. Jung used the terms 'soul' and 'psyche' interchangeably. Sin and psychopathology, grace and mental health likewise became synonymous. Religion becomes, in such a model, a form of psychotherapy, a means whereby man can be made not merely *holy* but *whole*. Conversely, psychotherapy, the cure of the sick mind, becomes an alternative to religion.

Publicly, psychoanalysis to this day maintains a Freudian stance. It distances itself from religious notions and emphasises its medical, nay its scientific roots. But its basic model owes more to religion than to medicine, more to Jung than Freud. In medicine, there is presumed a *health* from which the diseased organ, system or individual deviates. Cure is the return of the diseased object to the presumed state of health. It is a discontinuous model securely founded on a notion of health which, while never explicitly defined, is always assumed to exist in the absence of clear-cut disease. Psychoanalysis, in contrast, uses a model of disease from the outset. Man is flawed, imperfect, incomplete. From the moment of birth, indeed from conception, he is engaged in a constant struggle for perfection, for completeness. No man is free from the contamination of 'sickness'. In the last interview he gave before he died, Erich Fromm, the last survivor of the influential post-Freudian school (the others being Adler, Rank, Horney and Sullivan), was asked if the people we generally term normal are actually sick. Fromm replied:

Oh yes. The most normal are the sickest. And the sick are healthy. I know that sounds witty and exaggerated. But I am very serious about it. The sick person shows that he has not yet suppressed certain human things that can no longer clash with cul-

> tural patterns, but that they do clash and this causes symptoms of illness. Like pain, such a symptom is only a sign that something is wrong. Lucky are those who have symptoms . . . . But many people – I mean the normal ones – are so adapted, have rid themselves of everything that is their very own, they are so alienated and so much a robot-like instrument that they no longer feel a conflict.[5]

This is not the language of the physician but of the pastor. Man is a fallen animal who knows not that he is sick. He is to be redeemed through the healing power of love, variously defined as we have seen, as the empathy, caring and genuineness of the encounter, the transference of the psychoanalytic interchange or the 'transformations' of the experiential movement. As the language of psychotherapy borrows more and more freely from the language of religion, so the therapist abrogates more and more of the functions of the priesthood. Three functions in particular form the basis of the take-over. The first is religion's role in explaining the unknown. The origin of the universe, predictable natural events, irrational behaviour, anti-social acts, all have been variously explained as acts of God, devilish possession or the fruits of Original Sin. The expansion of psychotherapeutic psychiatry, with its explanation of irrationality in terms of infantile complexes and unconscious conflicts, eroded and overthrew the religious interpretations. Where once adultery was explained by the priest as unbridled lust and the wages of sin, it is now explained by the psychiatrist as due to low self-esteem and difficulty in getting close to others. Commenting on such a trend, two American psychiatrists remark that 'in the past twenty-five years more and more socially unaccepted behaviour is explained in these terms to the apparent satisfaction of more and more people'.[6]

The second religious function taken over by psychotherapy is its ritual and social function. In American culture, the Church was, and in many smaller communities still is, the centre of social activity. The post-Freudian era has seen the Church giving ground steadily to the analyst's office, the encounter group, the Community Mental Health clinic, the hundreds of growth centres mushrooming across the American continent and beyond. For many otherwise lonely, lost and hitherto empty people, these are the places which now function as the major social focus of their lives.

The third religious function that has been 'psychiatrised' is the definition of values. Until the Freudian revolution, man tended to turn most frequently to the priest, the rabbi, the minister and the vicar for advice and guidance on how to live. Yet, as has been pointed out[6], the marked alterations in public attitudes towards abortion, gambling, alcoholism, crime and the problems of marriage and family life owe much more to the influence of psychiatrists and psychologists than to the men of God. As moral questions have steadily been moved from the ambit of the preacher to the psychotherapist, so the Churches, intimidated by the successful assault on their power and influence, have turned to the secular priests to learn the secrets of their ministry. Wherever we went in America, be it to Esalen with its nudity and encounter groups, to Erhard's est or to the rolfers with their massage beds, we were told, by the proud practitioners that numbered amongst their clients was a Father John of the Redemptionists or a Sister Mary Lou from the Little Sisters of Mercy. Pastoral counselling booms and the orthodox clergy seek through consciousness-raising, meditation exercises and Rogerian self-actualising to discover how to make the message of God more relevant than the message of Freud that has displaced it.

There is, however, one 'religious' function that has neither been eliminated nor absorbed by Freud's 'secular pastoral worker'. The question of the ultimate purpose of life, the existential problem of meaning, has been a question which while it has been the central study of theology and philosophy alike has been shunned by medicine. The religious answer, namely that life's purpose is to be lived for the greater glory of the Creator, served for many until the steady inroads of scientific materialism began to throw it in serious doubt. Now the religious answer fails to satisfy all but a minority of believers, but the question itself does not disappear. Indeed, it seems to take on an even more desperate, and more insistent urgency. As might have been predicted, psychiatrists have recently bestowed a 'diagnosis' on the resultant state of uncertainty and purpose-lessness. It is 'existential neurosis' and, like many another diagnosis, its 'discovery' was but a prelude to an outbreak of suffering due to it of epidemic proportions. According to the analyst Viktor Frankl, 'more and more patients are crowding our clinics and consulting rooms complaining of an inner emptiness, a sense of total and ultimate meaninglessness of their lives.'[7] The wheel, it would appear, has turned full circle. It began to move when Freud observed that although he had confined himself to 'the ground-floor and the basement of the edifice called man' he had already found 'a place for religion by putting it under the category of the neuroses of mankind'. It gathered speed as thousands of people, their faith devalued and denigrated by scientific reductionism and secular psychotherapy, took themselves in increasing numbers to the very experts whose professional activities had helped create the vacuum in the first place. The circle is complete as these thousands of religiously dispossessed, pose across the psychotherapy room the question formerly fit for the pastor and the priest: 'What is the meaning of my life?' 'If a man finds a satisfying answer to the question what is the meaning of his life', declared Einstein, 'that man I would call religious.' And what would Einstein call the man who provided the answer? A secular pastoral worker perhaps?

But in so far as the psychoanalyst, Freudian or Jungian, tried to provide an answer he more often than not failed. Too elaborate, opaque and time-consuming, the theory was ill-suited to feed a hunger that was at once more stark and immediate. Even more damaging, was the fact that psychoanalysis, for all its metapsychological speculations and artistic pretensions, came out of the scientific stable. And was it not science that had so imperilled man's confidence as to reduce him to a speck of inconsequential matter in a universe so awesome that the human mind 'faints in its attempt to grasp its immensity'?[8] So once more whole chunks of psychoanalytical theory are discarded like burnt-out, redundant stages of a space-rocket and the slimmed-down capsule that remains turns on to a new course to meet this new navigational demand.

The public searches for meaning as it searches for growth, for self-actualisation, for transformation. They can have it through the frank mysticism, the Eastern philosophies, the meditation and the mantras that are part and parcel of the burgeoning therapy and growth centres in America, Europe and the East itself. In one sense, the human potential movement has the ground to itself. Orthodox psychiatry, psychoanalytical or otherwise, today keeps at an arm's distance from anything that smacks of the mystical or the occult. The medical materialists explain mysticism to their own satisfaction as an epiphenome-

non superimposed upon underlying physico-chemical alterations. From such a vantage point, St Paul's transformation on
the road to Damascus is the manifestation of a discharging
epileptic focus in his occipital cortex. St Teresa is dismissed as
an hysteric. St Francis of Assisi is tagged as a man with a personality disorder. The psychoanalytically inclined, while characteristically assuming a position of detachment and understanding, actually manifest more sympathy. A report by the Group
for the Advancement of Psychiatry on *Mysticism: Spiritual Quest
or Psychic Disorder?*, appeared to hedge its bets concerning the
answer to the question it had set itself. Here and there, however, the true feelings of the members showed:

> The psychiatrist will find mystical phenomena of interest because
> they can demonstrate forms of behaviour intermediate between
> normality and frank psychosis, a form of ego regression in the
> service of defense against internal or external stress; and a para-
> dox of the return of repressed regression in unconventional
> expressions of love.[9]

In the face of such scientific reductionism and psychoanalytical
indifference, however the religious need does not diminish.
This need, it should be said, is wider than just the desire to
answer the riddle of existence. It is a religious need in the sense
that William James employed the term 'religion' in his Gifford
Lectures on Natural Religion in 1901 and 1902. William, the
brother of the novelist Henry James, was a distinguished
psychologist who was particularly interested in personal rather
than institutional forms of religious thought and practice. His
particular definition of religion reflects such a preference:

> the feelings, acts and experiences of individual men in their sol-
> itude so far as they apprehend themselves to stand in relation to
> whatever they may consider the divine.[10]

Such a wide-ranging definition has not met universal favour
amongst orthodox religious believers. One priest-psychologist
has observed that such a definition 'brings religion into the
domain of the empirical, the observable and, ultimately, the
measurable' and has argued instead that religion 'is a public set
of beliefs, associated with a set of public behaviour patterns,
whose function is to express a transcendental relationship,
man's dependent relation on his Creator'.[11] James, however,

did not interpret 'religion' or 'the divine' narrowly because he was struck by the fact that there are systems of thought which the world usually calls religious (such as Buddhism) which do not positively assume a God. When we speak of the individual's relation to 'what he considers the divine' we must interpret the term 'divine', says James, 'as denoting any object that is godlike whether it be a concrete deity or not'. A key element in such a notion of religion is the element of transcendence. 'I accept the universe' was a favourite phrase of the New England transcendentalist, Margaret Fuller (provoking a 'Gad! She'd better' from a sardonic Thomas Carlyle). The whole concern of religion is with the manner of our acceptance of the universe. Do we accept it in part and grudgingly or heartily and altogether? It makes a sizeable emotional and practical difference to us whether we accept it with a drab, resigned stoicism or with the passionate happiness of say the Christian mystic.

And it is transcendence that brings us back to mysticism, defined by Goethe as 'the scholastic of the heart, the dialectic of the feelings'. A somewhat more prosaic definition portrays it as the assertion of an intuition which transcends temporal categories of understanding which rely on speculative reason. Rationalism cannot conduct us to the essence of things. Therefore, we need intuitive vision. The Indian philosopher, Radhakrishnan, terms mysticism 'integrated thought' in the sense that it integrates things into a new pattern instead of, as in analytical thought, breaking them down into parts. It thus relates them into a meaningful whole – a notion we have come across already in the new psychotherapies.

Mystical states are classically described as having five main characteristics.[8,10] It is interesting to dwell on these for a moment for it will instantly be seen that we have also already encountered these, albeit in different guises, in encounter groups, gestalt therapy and, most notably, in est. The first quality of mysticism is its so-called *ineffability*, that is to say it defies expression in terms which are fully intelligible to one who has not undergone some analogous experience. It is thus a state of feeling rather than a state of intellect. Secondly, mystical states have a *noetic* quality, that is to say they result in insight into depths of truth and knowledge inaccessible to mere reason. Even though the mystic may not be able to say what he *knows* in the language of the intellect he is convinced with absolute certainty that he does *know*. The third quality of mystical states is their *transiency*. They rarely last for any length of time but the pursuit of a particular way of life is believed to increase their frequency. In the words of the great Christian mystic, St John of the Cross, 'the soul has it in its power to abandon itself, whenever it wills, to this sweet sleep of love'. Fourthly, there is the quality of *passivity*. The mystic feels, in Happold's words, 'as if his own will were in abeyance, as if he were grasped and held by a power not his own.'[8] Finally, there is the quality, characteristic of many mystical states, which convinces the mystic of a *consciousness of the Oneness of everything*. In theistic mysticism, God is felt to be in everything and everything to exist in God. In the Chinese philosophy of Taoism, the nature of the universe is conceptualised as coming out of Tao, the primal meaning and undivided unity behind everything. This sense of the Oneness of everything, while expressed differently, is at the heart of the most highly developed mystical movements. It is to be found in Hindu and Sufic mysticism as in the mysticism of Christian contemplatives.

It is a common error to confuse mysticism with such sensate experiences as visions or revelations by spirits, physical feelings such as warmth or fire. However, mystical literature repeatedly stresses that such experiences are not the goal of mysticism; rather it is only when these are transcended that one attains a direct, intuitive knowledge of fundamental reality. Such a distinction is to be found in Yoga texts:

> When all lesser things and ideas are transcended and forgotten, and there remains only a perfect state of imagelessness where Tathagata and Tathata are merged into perfect Oneness . . . .[12]

The goal, particularly of the Eastern mysticism, is not visions of angels or Buddhas but 'enlightenment', the awakening of an inherent capacity to perceive the true nature of the self and the world. Visionary experiences, when they occur, are generally regarded as illusions for the poorly prepared or the misguided.

While in California, we had the opportunity of talking with an American psychoanalyst who has been preoccupied with the relationship between mysticism and psychotherapy for many years. Arthur Deikman is in private practice in Mill Valley, just outside San Francisco. Author of *Personal Freedom*[13], an account of personal transformation interwoven with Buddhist stories,

Zen paradoxes, Sufic insights and psychotherapeutic terminology, Deikman accepts the notion of an 'existential neurosis' with alacrity, and identifies strongly with the disillusion of his clients concerning Western scientific materialism. One of the initial questions we posed to him, after we had eaten a delightful supper in his spare hillside home, was why so many of the searchers for meaning looked to Eastern mysticism, of which they could know little, when Western mysticism had for thousands of years addressed very similar problems? To Deikman, the appeal of Eastern philosophies to the clientele of the growth of centres and the therapy groups was quite simple – such philosophies are essentially optimistic. In contrast to the Western mystical tradition, which Deikman regarded as riddled with the noble ethos of existential courage enabling the individual to face the loneliness, meaninglessness and isolation of life with mature acceptance and determination, Eastern traditions offer an alternative way of knowing.

But of what did this alternative way of knowing consist? Deikman gave us each a copy of his book and a short lecture. We learned a little of Sufism, the Muslim mysticism which so strongly emphasises the doctrine of Oneness. The Beloved is the nearest to a deity in the Sufic tradition and the Beloved is also the Truth which admits of no duality either in fact or idea. There is the story of the lover who knocks at the door of the Beloved. 'Who is there?' asks the Beloved. 'It is I' announces the lover. 'This house will not hold Me and thee' comes the reply. The lover goes away and weeps and prays in solitude. After a long time he returns and knocks again. The Voice asks 'Who is there?' 'It is Thou' answers the lover. Immediately the door opens, lover and Beloved are face to face at last. The Sufic message – the self must die absolutely, must blend totally in the experience of God as the Divine Lover.

Deikman tells of Tassajara, a Zen monastery, some twenty miles from the Big Sur coast in California.[13] 'Everyone in it is American and rather young.' The gateway, however, is very Japanese and time is regulated by the notes of bells and wood clappers. The meals are vegetarian, very ceremonial, full of wrapping and unwrapping of bowls, placing spoons and chopsticks in ritual order, and chanting verses in Japanese. Sometimes, there is a lecture about Zen, very philosophical, full of paradoxes, 'usually a translation of everyday events into

Buddhism'.

> There are perhaps three kinds of creation. The first is to be aware
> of ourselves after we finish zazen (meditation). When we sit we
> are nothing, we do not even realise what we are; we just sit. But
> when we stand up, we are there! That is the first step in creation.
> When you are there, everything else is there; everything is cre-
> ated all at once. When we emerge from nothing, when every-
> thing emerges from nothing, we see it all as a fresh new creation.
> This is non-attachment.[13]

Zazen involves sitting cross-legged for forty minutes. The students are told 'Be the pain, watch it, don't move, don't complain, accept it.' (Shades of rolfing). The student should not
strive for enlightenment, he is told, because if he is truly 'just
sitting' he is enlightenment personified. Deikman analyses the
emphasis on sensation, the focus of the breathing, chanting,
saying mantras and 'just sitting', the monastic simplicity, the
training to be 'spiritual'. He is not, however, sure that what we
need at this time is 'something from a foreign country which
existed in an alien time' but he accepts that studying such a
monastic system may cast light on the nature of the spiritual life
which many contemporary Americans yearn for and avidly seek
out. Of course, their search may just be another example of a
greediness fanned by a fiercely materialist consumer society.
'You can cross your legs in the full lotus position and be greedy
for enlightenment,' observed Deikman, 'and you are worse off
than someone who is greedy for money because a person who is
greedy for money knows he is being greedy whereas you think
you are being spiritual.
Deikman was clearly sincere, yet it did seem to me from what
was happening around him in Mill Valley and neighbouring
Marin County and down the coast at Esalen, that many did
believe that not only could transformation occur over two
weekends but one could become an Eastern mystic in a matter of
days. The Esalen catalogue for July-October 1978 offered a
five-day course on 'Living Your Own Tao' and a seven-day
workshop on meditation while for the slower enthusiast, the
American Institute of Buddhist Studies, with Esalen's co-
operation and the hospitality of the University of California at
Santa Cruz, was offering a four-week intensive programme
devoted to Zen and Tantra, the evolution of an 'American

Buddhism', the Lotus Garland Universe and 'Buddhist Ecology and Sociology'.

It was difficult to suppress the suspicion that the flight to Eastern mysticism might have more to do with the fact that it is novel, fashionable and mystifying than that it is truly enlightening and a genuine panacea for the 'existential neurosis'. As was said to us many times by critics and supporters of the trend alike, people in California have always been on the move, searching for new experiences, new explanations, new meanings. They stop at the Pacific Ocean but the wander-lust and the search for the novel cannot be assuaged. Inevitably, they turn their gaze earnestly across the ocean to the mysterious East, still looking like latter-day Gatsbys for their particular green light at the end of Daisy's dock.

Some of them cross the ocean and savour the Eastern philosophies on their home territory. At Esalen, we first heard of the Indian holy man, Bhagwan Shree Rajneesh and his Ashram at Poona. Richard Price, who had been to Poona, left us in no doubt that while the writings of Rajneesh were 'fine' and the acts of meditation prescribed by him were 'cathartic' and 'invigorating' all was not well. He referred darkly to the 'dangerous' quality of some of the groups there, some led by group leaders from the defunct Quaesitor organisation. In Price's group at Poona, a participant had her arm broken, so fierce and uncontrolled were the 'encounters'. In another group, another woman had her leg broken. Price found the authoritarian structure of the Poona Ashram very disturbing and referred disparagingly to the Rajneesh's 'top sergeants' setting up situations ostensibly reflecting the will of the holy man but actually working out 'their own unprocessed violence'.

From Price's account it was difficult not to dismiss the Bhagwan as one of the examples of what Erich Fromm, in that last interview before his death, called 'pure fake'.[5] 'It is the commercialisation of Buddhism and Zen, Buddhism and Tao' Fromm declared of the newfound enthusiasm for the mystic East. 'What's happening today is not serious, it is salesmanship with modern business methods, complete with advertising, trying to sell something that will satisfy religious feelings and longings.'

A very different account, however, of the Poona Ashram has come from a most unexpected source. In Britain, *The Times'* columnist, Bernard Levin, a man not noted for his 'experiential' enthusiasms (unless idolatry for Wagnerian music qualifies) wrote glowingly of a visit he paid to Poona and his encounters with the Bhagwan Shree Rajneesh. He described the 'Buddha Hall' itself – 'a huge makeshift auditorium, roughly oval in shape, a marquee with a flat stone floor', the colourful garments of the fifteen hundred faithful followers, as they waited expectantly for the holy man's arrival, and then the arrival itself of 'a figure dressed in a white robe, beneath which his feet are clad in simple sandals' in a 'large gleaming yellow Mercedes'. The message of the Rajneesh is discussed with similar attention to detail but not before Levin has loitered over the 'showmanship' in which the whole performance is wrapped. Two of 'Rajneesh's Praetorian Guards' stand at either side of the entrance and 'as the long queue shuffles forward they sniff each discourse-goer as he or she passes between them'. The reason given – the Rajneesh is allergic to perfumes of any kind – Levin finds difficult to believe for the Rajneesh is never closer than eighteen feet to any of his followers. No, it is one of the 'trimmings' which include the legends propagated about his extraordinary powers. (he is said to read fifty to seventy-five books a week), the tape recordings of his every discourse, the mandatory donning by each disciple of an orange garment, the wearing of the *mala* (a string of 108 beads from which Rajneesh's portrait is suspended from a locket), 'not to mention his triumphantly stage-managed entrance'. The trimmings, needless to say, must be digested before 'the kernel of his mystery' can be approached.

And the kernel? At the end of the path that leads to the discourse hall, there is a sign reading 'Shoes and minds to be left here'. Levin, as befits a tough-minded journalist, blanched a little at the second provision but quickly pulled his new Eastern self together:

. . . . it does not require years of meditation to recognise that all the most important, and all the most forceful achievements and influences that affect human beings bypass the mind altogether to have their effect – art, faith, sleep, joy, death, hate, laughter – none of them can be understood in terms of the mind nor the workings of any of them understood by the mind.[14]

None of them? No, none and certainly not love which is also the business of Rajneesh as it was of Christ, Buddha and all the enlightened masters. Drop the mind, exhorts Rajneesh, drop the ego, be ordinary and you will become extraordinary, be true to your inner being and all religions are fulfilled.

It is all very reminiscent of est and in Levin's account an actual discourse strongly resembles one of Erhard's post-'graduate' seminars. Rajneesh's voice is 'low, smooth and exceptionally beautiful', his gestures are 'hypnotically graceful and eloquent', his eyes 'penetrating and clear', he uses his hands in 'an endless variety of expressive forms'. He uses quotations (freely though not necessarily accurately) has a penchant for paradoxes (if you choose to go to Hell willingly you will be happy there – if you are forced into Paradise you will hate it) and has a mesmeric effect on his listeners. Long after he has left the hall, devotees wander round as if in a trance, some prostrating themselves on the marble platform on which he has earlier stood.

Levin is excited at the liberating effects. A young married couple he met spoke within ten minutes of a marital problem not usually discussed between strangers ('or indeed at all' emphasises the clearly incredulous Levin). They come from far and near though the examples given by him look like a typical cross-section of any American Express tour through the great shrines of the Orient. Levin himself was prevailed upon in one of the encounter groups to get up and engage in a liberating sequence of dance steps 'and even this limited experience of the disembarrassing process made me see its necessity and efficacy' he adds somewhat disingenuously.

Indeed, Levin's endorsement of the Bhagwan was so enthusiastic it provoked a counterblast from an Indian critic, Dominik Wujastyk, who took him gently to task for, among other things, referring to the 'trifling admission charge' of ten rupees; 'astronomical', Wujastyk calls it, pointing out that it would buy three meals at an Indian restaurant or more at home. The sniffing on entrance? This is no more nor less than 'an intimidation technique'. As for the content of the Rajneesh's discourses – 'I am not unsympathetic to eastern spirituality', declared Wujastyk, setting himself up for the kill, 'but the talk was of an extremely low standard, often factually wrong and wearingly repetitive. Most of the audience,' he added 'was in some sort of hyper-suggestible state'.

Never having met or heard the Bhagwan I cannot pass comment. I have read some of his writings though and I am inclined more towards Wujastyk's judgement than to Levin's. They appear to be an ill-digested mish-mash of Zen insights and pseudo-psychology.

Epigrams such as 'We eat, excrete, sleep and get up, this is our world. All we have to do after that is to die' jostle with primal therapy-type speculations about the traumas of passing through the birth canal and the 'unbearable' pain of our arrival into this world. There is little that one would not find in any of the original Christian or Buddhist mystical texts which the Bhagwan plunders and nothing new of comparable luminosity.

Yet Westerners still flock to the Ashrams and the therapy centres of India in search of transcendence and the sensations of a tradition which for most of them is entirely alien. But cannot similar insights and experiences be derived from the equivalent traditions feeding their own culture? Whose instructions are these?

> In order to arrive at having pleasure in everything,
> Desire to have pleasure in nothing.
> In order to arrive at possessing everything,
> Desire to possess nothing.
> In order to arrive at being everything,
> Desire to be nothing.

The Sufi mystic Muhammed Iqbal? The Bhagavad Gita? No, they are part of the immense spiritual outpouring of St John of the Cross. Few of the earnest, charismatic Westerners who marvel at the luminous simplicity of Eastern philosophical truths are aware of the fact that their own Western Christian civilisation itself rests on a storehouse of similar insights.

Levin in Poona contrasted the faces there, 'alive, expressive, contemplative, serene, interested, eager, in a word, innocent', with the lost, resigned, exhausted faces of people in say, London's busy Oxford Street but Assisi still boasts similarly uplifted faces – in its Piazza della Commune young, charismatic Christians exult in the liberation of Christianity with an exuberance no less striking.

This is not to suggest an unseemly competition between the virtues and values of Western and Eastern mysticism. Rather it is to underline a paradox whereby some people seek in the Indian Ashrams what others appear to find closer to home.

Deikman is quite wrong to attribute the movement eastwards to an optimism in the mystical teachings to be found there, for optimism is the essence of all mysticism, Christian as much as Buddhist, Sufic as much as Hindu. An alternative explanation might be that the religious nature of the search for meaning needs to be concealed in these secular days and is less apparent to Westerners at least if expressed through Sufic insights and Zen paradoxes than by having recourse to the mystical outpourings of Teresa of Avila or Thomas a Kempis. Arianna Stassinopoulos expresses her religious longings in terms of a classical post-Freudian emptiness, and finds the answer in a transatlantic pot-pourri of psychotherapy, commonsense and mystical teachings. Young, serious-minded Americans join a Zen monastery not a hundred miles from Los Angeles, the very epicentre of the commercial, capitalist, technological world from which the intuitive, ineffable, transcendent path leads away. It is, as Rollo May remarked to us at the end of our trip to the United States, a search for a way to live, a search which in this century led first to the early, tentative steps of psychoanalysis and now, seventy years later, leads *back* to the religious sensibilities and mysticism psychoanalysis was intended to supplant.

The end result is that many people no longer seem to know whether they are in need of spiritual assistance or psychological treatment. Some ask whether any line can actually be drawn dividing the spiritual path from therapeutic progress. Can the absorption of methods and concepts from religious teachings, particularly Eastern ones, result in an increase in our understanding of the meaning of existence and our role in the divine mystery of life? Or will it result only in a reduction of the profoundly religious to the conventionally therapeutic? Is the search for the self, part of a secular pursuit of mental health and psychological stability, or is it directed towards re-establishing the link between man and the universe?

'Spiritual guides and psychotherapists, what do your names mean?' asks the American philosopher, Jacob Needleman, in an essay which points out that the idea of 'self-knowledge' with which both groups work, actually amounts to very much more than the mere acquiring of psychological strength, personal independence and 'meaningful relationships' so solemnly held out by spiritual guides and psychotherapists alike as the fruits of therapeutic and spiritual exploration.[15]

But as the orthodox religions have back-peddled with regard to such potentially mystical concepts as self-revelation as transcendence, so the new psychotherapies have exuberantly run to adopt them. While the priest seeks to restore the receding value of his spiritual message by discarding troublesome notions of supernatural intervention and the Godhead, the psychotherapist vigorously endorses the liberating effects of mystical experience and personal transformation.

Such development in psychotherapy poses difficultues when it comes to any attempt to evaluate the new talking therapies as treatment. When asked how long he would give his already lengthy psychoanalysis, Woody Allen replied one more year and then he would try Lourdes, a characteristically ironic comment on the need for some kind of miracle to bring about any improvement in his gargantuan neurosis. However, his comment may contain an even more profound truth. Lourdes, after all, in the words of a recent and sympathetic commentator, 'is a phenomenon perpetuated by its own momentum'.[16]

Asking whether what happens there can or can not be scientifically evaluated may be as meaningful or meaningless as making a similar enquiry concerning some of the projects reviewed in this book. To go to Lourdes is to share in the stimulation and refreshment of 'a common act of faith and fellowship'. In the final analysis, religious experiences, such as Lourdes, are personal, intuitive, subjective and are knowable by anyone other than the individual actually undergoing them. It is these personal qualities, possessed by or claimed for the new psychotherapies which moved them from the therapeutic to the religious arena. The extent to which what they offer is genuine and lasting or merely novel and transient may indeed be tested but it is more likely to be by time than by any scientific trial that the test will occur.

References

1 Jung, C. J. 1932 'Psychotherapists or the Clergy' in his *Modern Man in Search of a Soul* Harcourt, Brace. New York
2 Quoted in Freud: 1980 *The Man and the Cause* R. Clark. Jonathan Cape and Weidenfeld and Nicolson
3 Freud, S. 1927 'Postscript to the Question of Lay Analysis' *Standard Edition of the Complete Psychological Works of Sigmund Freud* Translated by J. Strachey Vol.20 p.252 The Hogarth Press 1953-1974. London
4 Szasz, T. 1978 *The Myth of Psychotherapy* Anchor Press/ Doubleday. New York
5 Wykert, J. 1980 'Fromm's Last Interview' *Psychiatric News* 16 May p.4
6 Nelson, S. H. and Torrey E. F. 1973 'The Religious Functions of Psychiatry' *American Journal of Orthopsychiatry* 43, (3), pp.362-367
7 Frankl, V. E. 1969 'Reductionism and Nihilism' In: *Beyond Reductionism* Editors, A. Koestler and J. R. Smythies Hutchinson. London
8 Happold, F. C. 1963 *Mysticism. A Study and an Anthology* Penguin Books. London
9 Group for the Advancement of Psychiatry *Mysticism: Spiritual Quest or Psychic Disorder* New York. 1976
10 James, W. 1902 *The Varieties of Religious Experience* Fourt Paperbacks. Collins. 1960
11 O'Doherty, E. 1974 'Religious Therapy' In: *Psychotherapy Today* Editor, V. Varma. Constable. London
12 Goddard, D. 1938 *A Buddhist Bible* Dwight Goddard, Thetford, Vermont
13 Deikman, A. 1977 *Personal Freedom* Bantam Books. New York
14 Levin, B. 1980 'An Extraordinary Journey to the Interior' *The Times* 9 April
15 Needleman, J. 1976 *Psychiatry and the Sacred. On the Way to Self Knowledge.* Edited by J. Needleman and D. Lewis Knopf. New York
16 Marnham, P. 1980 *Lourdes: A Modern Pilgrimage* Heinemann. London

9 Innovations in Orthodox Psychotherapy

In Britain, despite the contributions of several prominent British psychoanalysts, both native and foreign born, the influence of psychotherapeutics on psychiatry has been much less than in the United States. The principal reasons for this difference include the long-standing links of British psychiatry with the main body of general medicine . . . . and, most important of all the existence of a health service that determines not only the structure but to some extent the function of the practice of medicine. From the inception of the NHS professional psychotherapy has come traditionally within the private sector, and its place in a national health service raises several stinging administrative, ethical and scientific questions.

Professor Michael Shepherd[1]

Given the fact that the great majority of the 'new' psychotherapies originated and flourished in the United States, our account so far has tended to have a predominantly transatlantic flavour. The apparent barrenness of British psychotherapy might be taken by some as evidence in support of Janov's view of the British as psychologically immature or of the view propounded by a British psychologist, Dougal Mackay to the effect that they are 'emotionally constipated'.[2] Freud himself, certainly in his early years, was somewhat disdainful towards British psychiatry. In a letter to Jung in 1909 he referred to the psychiatrist and neurologist Frederick Walker Mott as 'a psychiatrist but of the English breed: knows how to catch pike and salmon, sails and rows very well but has only a few barbaric notions of the psyche'.[3] There are those who would even now share Freud's view, stopping only to cast doubt on the fishing abilities! A more dispassionate account of British psychiatry over the past fifty years would acknowledge its pioneering work in social and community psychiatry, its impact on general medicine, its contribution to improved methods of classifying psychiatric disorders, its role in the evaluation of physical treatments such as drugs, and its vigorous interest in behavioural theories and techniques.

This is not to suggest, however, that everything within the British psychiatric garden is rosy. Far from it. A submission made by the Royal College of Psychiatrists in 1974 to the Central Manpower Committee of the Department of Health and Social Security declared that 'the average standard of psychiatric practice in Britain is abysmally low', adding that while psychiatrists were understandably reluctant to publicise this fact 'the evidence is overwhelming'[4]. Since 1974 the situation has marginally improved but repeated hospital scandals including St Augustine's, Normansfield and Rampton together with continuous criticism of the excessive prescribing of psychotropic drugs by Britain's 25,000 general practitioners hardly provide the basis for complacency. An excessive emphasis on drugs and electrical treatment and a remarkable lack of time are among the more persistent criticisms made by psychiatric patients, their relatives and observers of the contemporary British psychiatric scene. 'It's drugs, drugs, drugs all the time . . . . cannot medical students be taught that part of their job is to listen?' complains the mother of a young schizophrenic patient, while in a report on the need for more 'talking' treatments with the NHS, the National Association for Mental Health (MIND) expressed the view that many patients complain of being treated as objects, given drugs instead of the opportunity to talk about their feelings and their problems. 'Even when pills are the right answer' declared the Report, 'there is a need for discussion and, perhaps most important of all, for a willing ear to listen to their problems, anxieties and fantasies.'[5]

Such a dismal situation might appear to provide a very fertile breeding ground for the emergence of 'fringe' therapies of the kind we have encountered in the United States. Yet, by and large, British psychiatry has not sported a 'fringe' to anything like the extent of its American counterpart.

Why has it not done so? The simple answer is that Britain, unlike the United States, did not adopt Freudian psychoanalysis as its major orientation. British psychiatry, both before and after the Second World War, retained its strong links with medicine, and the development of a national health service with an emphasis on the provision of psychiatric services across the nation, made the prospects for psychoanalysis, a time-consuming and expensive approach even less likely. In the US, on the other hand, the leaders of American psychiatry in the post-war years were overwhelmingly analytically oriented. Psychoanalysis flourished in a free-market medical system and, until relatively recently most of the bright young American psychiatrists on completion of their training turned away from the massive American State Hospitals with their huge populations of chronic psychotic patients and towards the rich pastures of office-based psychoanalytical practice. In 1971, the average private mental hospital in America employed 502 full-time professional staff per thousand in-patients while the comparative figure for the public mental hospitals was 106.[6] Because of the cost, such private hospital staff and facilities were effectively denied to the poor and the disadvantaged. An American psychiatrist, Fuller Torrey, points to the experience of Washington DC where there are thirty-five psychiatrists per 100,000 population 'more than in any place in the world'.[7] These psychiatrists, in the words of a British psychiatrist, Robin Murray, 'huddle together in the affluent districts profiting from the generous health-insurance benefits of federal employers'[8] while the public psychiatric services are probably the worst in the nation and standards at the once renowned St Elizabeth's Hospital have deteriorated so badly that the Joint Commission on American hospitals removed its accreditation.

While the average British psychiatrist may be responsible for the treatment of over seven hundred individual patients a year[9], an American psychoanalyst, Dr John Gedo, reveals that in the first two decades of his career he treated a grand total of thirty-six people, twenty-eight of whom 'terminated analysis on the basis of a consensus about the satisfactory outcome of the enterprise'.[10] Not surprisingly, Dr Gedo's revelations did not go without a comment on the cost-effectiveness of such an approach. Despite the fact that the two major national psychoanalytic organisations, the American Psychoanalytic Association and the American Academy of Psychoanalysis, have been making vigorous efforts to have psychoanalytic therapy included in any national health insurance programme, even a committed advocate of psychoanalysis like Professor Judd Marmor of the University of California at Los Angeles is forced to concede that 'the sheer logic of cost analysis makes it highly unlikely that a technique involving four to five expensive visits per week for an indeterminate (and sometimes 'interminable') number of years can be included in such a programme'.[11] Marmor believes that at best any viable insurance programme will have to set some fiscally tolerable limit on the number of psychotherapeutic visits per year that it can subsidise and that limit will certainly be below a four to five times per week, fifty weeks per year frequency.

There are, of course, British psychoanalysts. A 1968 survey revealed that there were 235 classically trained analysts in this country, of whom 164 were medically trained. At that time there were a further thirty-nine analysts in training. However, given that psychoanalytical training takes up to six years, it seems unlikely that the number of medically-trained psychoanalysts in the country exceeds two hundred. The bulk of these are in whole-time or part-time private practice in the major metropolitan areas.

The lack of psychoanalysts and the relative shortage of psychotherapists within the NHS have certainly contributed to the lack of 'fringe' psychotherapies in Britain. However, this is not to suggest that within Britain's NHS psychotherapeutic approaches are absent. Treatments based on talking or containing a significant element of psychological intervention and manipulation are to be found within the mainstream of British psychiatry and they have been fertilised by other treatment approaches, biological, social and behavioural, which also flourish within this system. However, given the manpower and training realities mentioned at the outset of this chapter, such treatments are not distributed equably throughout the country and in parts of Britain they can be extremely difficult to obtain. We are speaking here of psychotherapies directed at moderately specific interpersonal problems and we include orthodox group therapy, family therapy, marital and sex therapy, and behaviour therapy. Such approaches are also to be found embedded within orthodox American psychiatry though once again they are not widely available. One of the first post-war developments in talking treatments in Britain was group-based psychotherapy. During the war itself, a number of British psychiatrists in the armed forces became interested in the therapeutic potential of group processes. This interest was initially aroused by the realisation that many soldiers became psychiatric casualties when put into the wrong jobs. To ensure a more adequate placement of service personnel, new methods of choosing suitable candidates for training as officers were evolved. These new procedures made use of a number of situational tests and, in particular, of the 'leaderless group' test that had been suggested by a leading psychoanalyst of the time, Dr W. R. Bion. Bion, working with a colleague, John Rickman, had developed ideas concerning the usefulness of group processes while working at Northfield Military Hospital. These ideas mainly concerned how to develop a group and a communal spirit among men dissatisfied with military discipline and anxious to return to civilian life. Bion stayed at Northfield for only six weeks during which time 'he temporarily changed a troublesome community into an organisation that functioned adequately'.[12] His ideas were subsequently developed in the second 'Northfield Experiment' when his administrative innovations were applied to a whole hospital. Another of the group therapy pioneers, Dr Tom Main, described Bion's attempt as 'an experiment designed to use a hospital not as an organisation run by doctors in the interests of their own greater technical efficiency, but as a community with the immediate aim of resocialisation of the neurotic individual for life in an ordinary society'.[13] The attempt involved turning the hospital into a 'therapeutic community' (Main's article in the *Bulletin of the Menninger Clinic* in 1946 was the first to use this term) and using psychoanalytically-derived group psychotherapy to promote 'emotional growth and social learning' in a positive way.[14] Bion took the unprecedented step of relinquishing the authoritarian role with which the military and the hospital traditions had both endowed him. The soldiers, and subsequently the patients and staff, had to choose between suffering the discomforts of a chaotic and unstructured communal life or of shouldering the responsibility for organising their communal and social life themselves. They could no longer blame the army or the hospital when things went wrong and had now to deal with their own anti-social and disruptive tendencies. It is interesting to note that some of the practical group 'processes' used at Northfield were derived from the psychodrama theories of Jakob Moreno.

Therapeutic community approaches have proliferated on both sides of the Atlantic since those early post-war days, as indeed, have the methods of group psychotherapy upon which they rest. Foulkes has distinguished three different forms of group therapy.[15] First, there are group activities of all sorts which arise spontaneously in life or are found in organised forms. Such groups would include the Oxford Movement and the Women's Institute, physical culture and yoga movements, various kinds of discussion groups and so on. Secondly, there are groups in which there is deliberate therapeutic intent. Virtually anything can be the focus of such activity including music, dancing, films, dramatic performances, games, reading classes, painting, basket weaving and the like. In most instances, it is the *activity* which is seen to be essential to the process of treatment and recovery and, as a consequence, such groups are more accurately termed occupational therapy groups. If, on the other hand, the occupation is incidental and it is the *group situation* which is essential then what is involved is indeed group therapy. The distinction, needless to say, is not always clear. Thirdly, there is group therapy itself. Most therapists would demand that three conditions be fulfilled before they would bestow the description 'group therapy' on some form of activity coming under their scrutiny. These conditions are:

1 That verbal communication and formulation are the principal occupation of the group.
2 That such treatment must do full justice to the individual members and their interaction.
3 That a therapist who has a group before him will want to avail himself of the forces and dynamics which present in the group situation.

The majority of group therapists in Britain are permissive and non-directive rather than suggestive and educative. Their groups, whether of in-patients or out-patients, generally range in size from six to ten patients and the majority of them meet weekly for approximately one and a half hours. Foulkes described the groups he ran and supervised at the Maudsley Hospital just after the war as 'face-to-face' groups in which 'no programme or plan of any kind as to matters discussed' was established and in which the group's occupation was 'to tell about anything its members wish'. The members were encouraged to voice their thoughts freely and every contribution was admitted at the time whether or not it appeared to have any bearing on the current discussion.[15]

Underlying most therapeutic groups is the assumption that group therapy provides individuals who have difficulty in initiating and sustaining interpersonal relationships with an opportunity to identify, understand and eliminate such difficulty. People form relationships within the group as it proceeds. They begin to behave in the group vis-à-vis each other and the therapist as they behave outside the group with their families, neighbours, work colleagues and friends. Within the group each member can compare his or her view of each group member with the views of the others. This can be done too in a relatively unthreatening situation because the relationships, such as they are, exist for a therapeutic purpose and are accordingly less emotionally loaded than orthodox personal relationships. In short, orthodox, psychoanalytically-derived psychotherapeutic groups bear a striking resemblance to the encounter groups of the human potential movement and the Rogerian school.

It is axiomatic in group therapy that everything that happens in a group involves the group as a whole as well as each individual member. Foulkes makes this point:

> In what precise way it involves any of them or even which aspects of each (individual) are actually mobilised, is a matter of paramount interest. An unending variety of configurations, including the conductor (leader) in his particular position, can be observed. To this category of concepts belongs for instance the idea of a disturbance in a therapeutic group.[15]

We will hear again of this notion of a disturbance in a group (in contrast to disturbed individuals) when we go on to discuss family therapy. The kinds of groups discussed by Foulkes and others are now used extensively within and outside of hospital. Many of the more modern ones make liberal use of techniques borrowed from Gestalt, psychodrama and transactional analysis, though the debt is not always acknowledged. Others rely on orthodox psychoanalytical ideas. While not everyone favours the use of psychoanalytical methods in groups, concepts such as 'transference', the unconscious and mental mechanisms such as projection, repression and regression, derived from classical psychoanalysis are still widely employed. The selection of patients also reflects preferences associated with the psychoanalytical method. Verbally skilled, reasonably intelligent and socially functioning individuals obtain preference over less socially competent individuals, although recently there have been a number of attempts to utilise group therapy methods in the teaching of social skills to individuals who have considerable difficulty in such basic social functions as sustaining ordinary conversation and meeting strangers.

Some therapeutic groups are 'closed', that is to say they begin and they end with the same membership (less of course those who drop out).

Other groups are 'open' and as people leave, because of improvement or dissatisfaction, others replace them. The life of 'open' groups can continue indefinitely whereas 'closed' groups generally last for up to two years. According to Professor Henry Walton of Edinburgh University's Department of Psychiatry, 'the effects of treatment will begin to be evident after six months and definite improvement can be expected after one year'.[16] Contrary to the often expressed lay opinion, professional experience suggests that it is better to ensure a mixture of problems within any group than to have it entirely composed of, say, depressed housewives or indecent exposers. Specialised groups do, of course, exist and particularly for such groups as alcohol abusers, their relatives, drug addicts, compulsive gamblers and people troubled by sexual or aggressive impulses.

Robin Skynner, one of Britain's most enthusiastic group therapists, and a founder member of the Institute of Family Therapy in London, admits quite openly that it was the need for the National Health Service in Britain to meet the demand for psychotherapeutic help rather than to allow 'this expensive skill to be restricted to those who can afford it' which provoked the development and application of group methods.[17] Similar developments in technique occurred in the United States during the 1960s as a consequence of increasing government interest there in community mental health and the mobilisation of public funds. However, in addition to group therapy being more economical in terms of time and money, it is, its exponents insist, more effective. One protagonist of this view is Irvin Yalom of Stanford University in California. On the basis of interviews with patients who claimed to have found group therapy beneficial, Yalom drew up a list of factors which appeared to be of particular therapeutic significance. The factors which appeared to affect recovery and help bring it about included:

Discovering and accepting previously unknown or unacceptable parts of oneself.

Being able to say what bothers one instead of holding it in.

Other members expressing their opinion of one.

Learning how to express feelings.

Learning what sort of impression one makes on others.

Expressing negative and/or positive feelings towards another.

Learning of the need to take ultimate responsibility for the living of one's life, no matter how much advice and support others give.

Seeing others reveal embarrassing things and take other risks and benefit from this.

Feeling more trustful of groups and of others.[18]

Inevitably, the vogue for group therapy led to a growing interest in the family, the main social group in society, as a more suitable subject for therapy in certain circumstances than any individual member of it. *Family therapy*, as it has become known, derives much of its theoretical foundation from psychoanalysis and psychoanalytically-derived therapeutic formulations, as well as from behavioural and sociological notions. The protagonists of the family approach tend to be scornful of psychiatry's classic preoccupation with the individual. Salvador Minuchin, one of America's best known family therapists, has compared the individually-oriented therapist to 'a technician using a magnifying glass'. He sees a highly detailed and defined field but it is severely circumscribed. The family therapist, on the other hand, is a technician working with a zoom lens – 'he can zoom in for a close-up whenever he wishes to study the intra-psychic field but he can also observe with a broader focus'.[19]

Robin Skynner, in his book, *One Flesh: Separate Persons*, emphasises the extent to which the family as a system contains within it a variety of sub-systems formed by generation, sex, interests and functions.[20] Within any family there is a parental sub-system, a system involving father and sons, mother and daughters and so on. Whereas Skynner is interested in how the power is shared out in families and how, for example, decisions are reached, Minuchin and the so-called 'structuralists' emphasise the need for the healthy family to designate and maintain boundaries or rules defining how each individual member is meant to participate within a particular sub-system. Indeed, Minuchin argues that one measure of a family's health is the clarity with which it designates boundaries. Minuchin provides the example of a parental sub-system being defined by a mother who tells her older child, 'You aren't your brother's parent. If he is riding his bike in the street, tell me and I will stop him'.[19] A parental sub-system which includes a child is defined by the mother telling the children, 'Until I get back from the store, Annie is in charge.' Such a parental child can develop responsibility, competence and autonomy beyond his years but there may be difficulties if the delegation of authority is not explicit or if the parents abdicate their position leaving the child as the main source of guidance, control and decisions.

The preconditions of family therapy are such as to limit its usefulness. This needs to be said because family theorists, as a general rule, are optimistic, particularly in their writings, and give the impression that moving the object of one's therapeutic endeavours from the individual to the family is tantamount to being halfway to cure already. In fact, before therapy can even begin you need an intact family unit, an acceptance by the family of a family treatment approach and the need to construct a particular formulation of the family problem particular to that family. What sorts of problems are particularly appropriate? This simple enough question poses difficulties for it reeks of the much-derided 'individual' approach with its 'enuretic' schoolchild, its truanting adolescent, its alcoholic father or housebound mother. Family theory does not specify individual so much as family pathology. A recently published British psychiatric text suggests that the following 'family situations' respond particularly well to 'a whole family treatment approach':

1 Pathological scapegoating – a situation in which one individual persistently carries the blame for all the family woes. Complaints about a child's behaviour frequently serve to camouflage marital difficulties.

2 Inappropriate or excessive dependency demands by one individual upon another.

3 Ambiguous communication patterns – the use of modes of expression which can mean contradictory things and which often serve to protect the individual using them from taking responsibility for his/her actions and intentions.

4 Vicarious gratification in the deviant behaviour of a family member.

5 Deviant behaviour arising in several members following bereavement.

6 Successful individual treatment in one family member followed by the appearance of symptoms in another.[21]

Contra-indications include families within which relationships are characterised by 'sadistic gratification' or 'chronic, widespread dishonesty and deceit'.

Family therapy uses a variety of therapeutic methods which range from the taking of a detailed family history (it helps draw attention to painful and repressed events in the family chronology) to methods borrowed from psychodrama such as the construction of an individual's social atom, the use of role playing and the 'empty chair' technique. How many sessions of family therapy are recommended? Wolberg notes that in America most lower-class families will not be able to afford more than a half-dozen sessions, which he feels is scarcely enough to do more than tide them over the emergency which led them to treatment in the first place.[22] More affluent families may have up to thirty sessions although in Britain the average number is usually less.

As Virginia Satir, a leading exponent of family therapy, has pointed out[23], family therapy is in one sense a form of marital therapy even though the family therapist also deals with the marital partners in their parental roles. In taking a family history, the therapist usually starts with the marriage and what led to it. Not surprisingly, therefore, *Marital Therapy* has grown up alongside family therapy.

Desirable goals of family therapy, which include resolution of conflicts, improved understanding and communication between family members, enhanced solidarity and a greater tolerance for and appreciation of individuality, depend on the existence of a sturdy and healthy marital relationship between the parents.

The problem with marriage today, as Pietropinto and Simenauer have ironically observed, is not the question of its continued existence as a social institution (over ninety-five per cent of the population marries at some point in their lives) but the quality of its existence.[24] Marriage has been compared to a besieged city with all those within wanting to get out and all those outside wanting to get in. In the United States, the national divorce rates have increased fifteen-fold during the last century and doubled during the past decade. The association with family difficulties is highlighted by the fact that more than half of the divorced couples in the US have children under eighteen and at least forty per cent of the schoolchildren there will spend part of their lives in a single-parent household. In Britain, in 1977, there were 129,000 divorces while between 1971 and

1976 the number of one-parent families rose from 570,000 to 750,000, an increase of one-third due largely to a dramatic increase in the number of divorced lone mothers. Much divorce occurs in the early years of marriage and it has been calculated that if remarriage rates in Britain remain at current levels, one in five men and women born around 1950 will have entered a second marriage by the age of fifty.[25]

Given the shattering sound of breaking marriages and the ever-present preoccupation with perfection and growth, it was inevitable that the word 'therapy' would sooner or later become linked to marriage. So linked have these two notions become that experts can speak of the divorce of fifteen million Americans as 'a national health emergency'. Emergency it may very well be, but a social classification rather than a medical one might seem more appropriate. The great problem of referring to marital problems as if they were 'illnesses' is that there is an assumption that there is something called 'a healthy marriage'. How elusive that notion can be is illustrated by a paper which appeared in the prestigious *New England Journal* entitled 'Frequency of Sexual Dysfunction in "Normal" Couples'.[26] The placing of inverted commas around the word 'normal' seemed justified by the contents of the paper for the authors found that in analysing the responses of 'a hundred predominantly white, well-educated and happily married couples to a self-report questionnaire' forty per cent of the men and sixty-three per cent of the women reported some degree of sexual difficulties and/or dissatisfactions. After much discussion of the possible methodogical shortcomings of the study, the authors concluded that sexual dysfunctions 'were more likely to reflect a combination of education deficits, inhibitions, physiologic conflicts and interpersonal conflicts'! And these were a hundred 'happy' married couples! The authors did, however, draw some tentative comfort from the fact that 'these couples were apparently able to tolerate a relatively high frequency of specific sexual dysfunctions and difficulties and still feel very positive about their sexual relations and their marriages'. But, given the heightening of marital and sexual expectations by, amongst others the therapists themselves, how long can our one hundred 'happily married' couples refrain from adding their clamour for 'therapy' to the swelling murmur?

Given the difficulties of establishing marital or sexual norms, there is confusion about what precisely the objectives of marital therapy are. Wolberg is quite clear that the task of marital therapy is to help keep 'a shaky marriage' together when there is even a small chance of its success while strengthening the couple's psychological resources in the process or, if the marriage cannot be saved, to help the partners separate with a minimum of conflict and ill-will, particularly where children are involved.[22] However, marital therapy is also used to describe such diverse activities as providing each of the individuals concerned with a greater degree of self-understanding, treating sexual difficulties and identifying and managing specific psychiatric disturbances in one or both partners. The British marital therapist, Dr Sidney Crown, admits that 'marital therapy' is a bad name though not for any semantic reasons but because contemporary mores and customs suggest that 'couple therapy' is better. 'This is because', explains Crown, borrowing from the American idiom, 'significant ongoing relationships have never taken more varied forms than they do at present'.[27] He points out that a marital therapist these days may be called upon to 'treat' a boyfriend and girlfriend, an engaged couple, two couples living together, spouse-swapping, and homosexual couples as well as 'more exotic combinations'.

Given the transfer of marriage from the arena of moral problems to that of psychiatric disturbance, the layman may wonder whether the possible impact of the therapist's own marital mores and attitudes is a factor to be reckoned with. Not according to Dr Crown. It is his practice to make plain that he is not 'trying to force any couple into a pattern' but to help them discover 'a way to their own self-realisation' which may be marriage, separation or divorce or, indeed, one of the many other combinations, exotic or otherwise, detailed in his and others' accounts of such therapy.

In general, when a couple come for therapy, they are assessed by the therapist together as well as individually; less often, they may be seen in groups with other married couples. Key areas of the relationship are explored with particular emphasis on the type of problem, the way in which the various roles within marriage are allocated and fulfilled, and how decisions are arrived at and adopted. Areas of disagreement and conflict are identified and noted and the aims of therapy are then stated, bearing in mind the age of the partners and the type and severity of the problem. Two main therapeutic approaches are currently favoured in Britain, namely the psychodynamic and the behavioural.

As we discuss in more detail in the section on sex therapy below, behavioural approaches are concerned with the identification and removal of marital 'symptoms', that is to say, highly specific problems or difficulties which lend themselves to direct behavioural modification. Psychodynamic approaches, on the other hand, aim to eradicate such 'symptoms' through the traditional psychodynamic methods of uncovering, recognising and 'working through' their basic cause (the latter almost invariably buried deep in the 'unconscious'). Despite the obvious incompatibility between these two approaches, many psychodynamic therapists and behaviour therapists assure each other and their clients that such therapies can be combined. This says something about the actual importance of the underlying theoretical formulations of the behavioural and psychoanalytical schools respectively!

Psychodynamic marital therapy stresses the differences between it and marital counselling. Counselling avoids working with 'unconscious' mental processes and uses instead a Rogerian-type, client-centred, non-directive approach. Such an approach has been the mainstream of marriage guidance in Britain for years, and over the past decade such counsellors have been attached to the growing numbers of group practice and health centre based general practitioners in the British primary health care system.

Psychodynamic therapy stresses its legacy from classical analysis but in practice seems less involved with unconscious motivation and more involved with the here-and-now situation. The therapist attempts to establish whether the marriage is husband or wife-dominated, whether one or the other spouse is more or less affectionate, how decisions are reached with regard to such areas as money, holidays, social arrangements, leisure, child-rearing and religious practice. The therapist also explores the sexual relationship and the extent to which the marriage is characterised by excessive 'acting-out' or by excessive containment and inhibition. In so far as there is a psychoanalytic emphasis, it comes with the assessment of a marriage in terms of the pathological use of such mental mechanisms as repression, projection, denial and rationalisation, the characteristic ego defences and superego functioning, and the level of psychosexual development. The classical analyst will exhibit intense interest in whether or not his clients have reached 'a three person (oedipal) level (with relationship problems)' or whether their psychosexual development is 'at a more infantile and individual (need-fulfilling, holding-back, torturing) level'.[23] Satir emphasises an analysis of the marriage in terms of how the partners attempt to accomplish, in their relations with one another, what was lacking in the families of their origin and her description resembles to a quite remarkable extent the ideas of Eric Berne and the transactional analysis school. (See Chapter 6).

The efficacy of the various methods of marital therapy is discussed briefly elsewhere. Here it only remains for us to comment on the remarkable movement of psychiatrists and psychologists into the marital arena. Once again, the vacuum created by the decline of religion and religious values has sucked in the psychotherapies and the proliferation of journals, conferences, workshops and seminars on family and marital approaches, testifies to the extent to which these therapies have seized the opportunity. On the credit side, is the cultivation of the notion that marriages can develop, can grow, are organic and living relationships, not static and fixed. Whether or not the average Briton suffers from 'emotional constipation', there is more than a suspicion that, until relatively recently, many people on this side of the Atlantic endured marital and sexual inadequacies not so much out of stoic resignation as dumb help lessness. Marriages might be private heavens or private hells but they were to be negotiated with equal public aplomb. The growth of group therapy with its emphasis on speaking in public the hitherto unspeakable, has provided the impetus for change, the walls of reticence have begun to crack and the private and the public faces of British marriage have begun to approximate more closely to each other. Against these very real benefits has to be placed the fact that the growth of therapy does not, as yet, appear to have been accompanied by a growth in what one might term marital maturity. Marriage is, in one sense, a testing-ground for the theories of self-growth and self-realisation. Rollo May tells of how he periodically meets some of his old friends in a San Francisco club and invariably the conversation turns somewhat melancholic as each of them wonders why after a lifetime of searching they have not found someone to love. Most of them have had a series of relationships which lasted some time and then broke up. 'It seems to me' says May, 'that they never really loved anyone long enough to get below the superficial problems that come today and are gone tomorrow. How to love is a situation one ought to be struggling with one's whole life long'. There is something poignantly old-world about May's sentiments. They cohabit uneasily with assertions of the primary need to find oneself, and assert oneself. They conjure up ideas of self-sacrifice, of the denial of the self for the other, of the greater demands of a relationship over the self. The modern couple, affected by the axioms of the 'Me Decade' and the vigorous self-asserting philosophy of the new therapies, struggles to live for the present and values the dictates of 'gut feelings' over logic and judgement. The public message often appears to be that marriage is for couples whereas of course, in reality, it is about families. Although the vast majority of couples have them at some time, children are shunted off-camera as husbands and wives attempt to preserve the image of carefree passion and self-discovery that the modern media messages emphasise. (In Ingmar Berman's much-acclaimed *Scenes from a Married Life*, the serious, self-obsessed mutual and self-analyses engaged in by the two protagonists were never interrupted by requests for the marmalade or arguments over who was driving little Bjorn to school.)

In defence of the marital therapists, it should be said that most of them realise this, and that much marital therapy merges into family therapy involving the older and occasionally all the members of the family (even, in some brave instances extending to the in-laws and the extended family members!) Most orthodox marital therapy is a form of brief psychotherapy, rarely lasting longer than six months and rarely more frequent than one treatment session a week. The therapy may be conducted by one therapist or two opposite-sexed therapists. It is concentrated on clarifying the nature of the difficulties between the couple, linking aspects of past with present experience of one or both of the spouses, confronting one or both when little progress seems to be being made or when behaviour inside or outside the therapy sessions is becoming destructive, interpreting motivation of which the participants may be unaware and generally encouraging them to spend some time taking a cool or at least cooler look at what is going on between them.

Many of the marital problems that are brought to therapists are related directly or indirectly to sex. As we have seen from the *New England Journal of Medicine* report quoted earlier, estimating the prevalence of sexual problems is a somewhat difficult task. Nor should it be thought that this American report is atypical. In his survey of sexual behaviour in young people, the British social researcher, Michael Schofield, reported that fifty-seven per cent of the British subjects interviewed reported sexual problems of some sort, lending support to the view that having sexual problems is, statistically speaking, the 'norm'.[28]

What kind of sexual problems do therapists treat? The answer is any and every sexual behaviour, impulse or experience that is causing the individual or his/her partner distress and/or dissatisfaction. Such problems include impotence, premature ejaculation, vaginismus, consummation difficulties, fear of sexual intercourse, failure to reach orgasm and dislike or refusal or sex. Until the mid-1960s, the main therapeutic approach relied heavily on classical psychoanalytic theories and techniques. Change came with the publication of Masters and Johnson's account of their pioneering work in the United States. Sexual problems were traditionally treated as problems of individuals (and indeed there are, it is important to remember, a number of physical and psychiatric causes of sexual difficulties). One of the major contributions of Masters and Johnson, according to the British marital and sex therapist, Dr Michael Crowe, has been their recognition that a sexual problem exists in a relationship between two people and their insistence on treating the couple as a unit.[29]

The Masters and Johnson therapy programme is a two-week residential treatment package.[30] The couple stay in a hotel and attend seven days a week in therapy. After a comprehensive medical and sexual history has been taken there is a series of meetings between a male and female co-therapist and the couple at which problems are clarified and important instructions given. From then on, in the privacy of their hotel room, the couple carry out what is termed 'sensate focus' therapy. This consists of a ban on intercourse and involves instead a session of alternate body massage, using skin lotion and covering every part of the body *except* the breasts and genitals. The aim is the rediscovery of the sensations of touch, smell and bodily contact and 'of learning to get pleasure by giving pleasure'. After this stage, the couple move on to 'genital sensate focus' in which genital contact is permitted on the same 'give-to-get' principles. 'Both these stages', points out Crowe, 'and the ban on intercourse, are necessary to get over the performance anxiety that many dysfunctional partners have'. In fact, it is a form of the behavioural technique known as 'desensitisation' whereby the individual is exposed in small, graduated doses to the stimulus or activity which causes him anxiety or panic, the whole process being conducted in a highly relaxing and reassuring atmosphere. From the genital sensate focus, the couple then progress to more specific techniques related to their particular problems, be they impotence, frigidity or whatever.

The methods of Masters and Johnson have been used within the National Health Service by, among others, the psychologist, Paul Brown in London and the psychiatrist Dr John Bancroft in Oxford. Others, such as Dr Patricia Gillan, have combined the approach with relaxation and other behavioural techniques and with the use of sexually explicit literature and films. However, most applications in Britain represent modifications of the American method. It is not clear, for example, how necessary it is to have the couple treated away from home in a residential setting. A related approach to sexual problems, and one which strongly resembles in its theoretical approach the transactional analysis theories of Eric Berne (Chapter 6), involves so-called 'contract therapy'. The therapist asks the couple what they would like of each other, such desires being expressed in specific, positive and repeatable terms. The man may ask that his spouse 'nags less', the woman that her spouse 'shows more affection'. Specific examples of the affection to be shown would be agreed (e.g. 'kissing me before going out in the morning') while the desire for less nagging would be turned into a positive desire such as 'listening to what I say for a few minutes before criticising'. Quoting Crowe once more, 'What is expected is that, as a result of the exchange of positive behaviour, the couple become more attractive to each other, and that the whole relationship is improved, to the point that the exchange of rewarding behaviour becomes automatic'.[29] In short, 'contract therapy' is teaching people to give each other positive instead of negative 'strokes'.

Therapists such as Crowe and Brown use a variety of these

techniques and Crowe himself has gone on to compare the Masters and Johnson method with that of a basically 'interpretative' approach and a control procedure involving non-directive intervention. (Chapter 10). Sexual and marital problems are now the stock-in-trade of increasing numbers of psychiatrists and psychologists, and clinics within and outside the NHS are rapidly developing, as a specialist back-up to the non-directive marital counselling offered by lay marriage guidance counsellors and marriage guidance clinics attached to general practices and health centres. In their detailed book, *Sex Therapy Today*[31] Drs Patricia and Richard Gillan provide the addresses of over sixty NHS and Family Planning Association sex therapy clinics, scattered the length and breadth of Britain, as well as those of a number of private centres and clinics devoted to this work.

Does this trend represent 'a humanisation' of a national health service hitherto excessively and narrowly concerned with medical and technological notions of 'sickness' or is it further evidence of a progressive 'medicalisation' of problems formerly identified as social and moral? There is certainly much evidence of a technology in sex therapy; the literature is replete with vibrators, the length of pre-ejaculation erection time, the counting of orgasms and the measurement of penile and vaginal blood flows. The criticism of transactional analysis too, as just the sort of theory of interpersonal relations a capitalist, economically-exploiting materialist society would apply to sexual and marital relations is not as extreme as it sounds – the 'trade-offs' of this approach amount to little more than sophisticated and eroticised versions of 'you scratch my back and I'll scratch yours' in many instances.

There is, of course, a titillating curiosity concerning the activities of sex therapists and much speculation concerning the use of sexual surrogates, partner-swapping, group 'gropes' and sex between therapists and clients. This is indeed a long way from Freud who once was so disturbed to hear that one of his analyst friends, Sandor Ferenczi, let his patients kiss him that he wrote to Ferenczi in 1931 'that with us a kiss signifies a certain erotic intimacy' and that hitherto in psychoanalytic technique analysts had stuck to the conclusion 'that patients are to be refused erotic gratifications'.[32] Freud anticipated that such goings-on between therapist and patient would not necessarily stop at a kiss. Eventually we would have 'the whole repertoire of *demiviergerie* and petting parties' which would result, remarked Freud sarcastically, 'in an enormous increase of interest in psychoanalysis among both analysts and patients.' According to Marmor[33] Freud's misgivings concerning Ferenczi's technical innovations proved to be 'prophetic'. In 1966, a Reichian psychoanalyst, J. McCartney, reported that thirty per cent of his female patients in analysis expressed 'some form of overt transference as sitting on the analyst's lap, holding his hand, hugging or kissing him' and that about ten per cent 'found it necessary to act out extremely, such as mutual undressing, genital manipulation, or coitus'.[34] McCartney explained that in working through the 'overt transference' (i.e. the eroticised emotional relationship between client and therapist) the analyst should allow himself to be reacted to as though he were a parent. As the analysed client proceeds through the various stages of psychosexual development, she expresses her infantile and adolescent needs but eventually she must work through her adult sexual feelings with the help of the therapist's participation.

Marmor recoils from such a revelation (there have since been others from American psychiatrists and sex therapists) but to rest his revulsion on appropriately non-moral grounds, he too has recourse to the same metapsychological explanations that McCartney employs. He observes somewhat primly that while it is not his purpose to expound on the variety of 'inner needs' that may be involved in such behaviour, 'unconscious hostility towards women, reaction-formations against feelings of masculine inadequacy or against unconscious fears of homosexuality' may be involved. Simpler and more psychologically immature souls may merely suspect lust, but that would be to rob the whole business of its non-moralistic jargon its aura of detached expertise and its scientific flavour. Yet clearly the ethical values and constraints of therapists in sensitive areas such as marriage and sexuality are of as much relevance as their technological, behavioural and psychological skills.

One observer of the psychotherapeutic scene in Britain, and a person who can speak as a consumer as well, Professor Stuart Sutherland, makes the point that whatever psychotherapists may say, their values, attitudes and moral beliefs do intrude.[35] He points out that many patients become quite dependent on their therapists and are greatly influenced by their personal views even though these views may not be overtly stated in therapy. Behaviour therapy, on the other hand, relies less on ideas and talk and more on techniques. Such techniques can be adapted to help the patient pursue those goals that he thinks are worthwhile.

As Professor Hans Eysenck, Professor of Psychology at the Institute of Psychiatry in London and one of the protagonists of behavioural approaches in Britain points out, behaviour therapy does involve talking. The therapist talks to the client to find out what is wrong, what he is complaining of, what needs to be done. But the essential feature is not the talking. What happens in behaviour therapy, and we have seen excellent examples of this in the techniques of Masters and Johnson, is that the patient is required to *do* something. If he is afraid of open spaces you let him go out, first a little bit and then a bit further, with somebody accompanying him, then later alone. If he is afraid of flying in an aircraft, then you get him to go to the airport and look at planes first, then go nearer, then perhaps sit in one without flying. 'The essence', points out Eysenck, 'is activity, behaviour and the essence of success is behaviour'. That is to say, if he couldn't fly before can he fly now and not have we done something to his ego or to his personality or has he grown, or is he self-actualising?

The basic principle of behavioural approaches is that a neurotic reaction is acquired through the simple process of conditioning. What is being conditioned is an emotional feeling of fear or anxiety. Such reactions easily give rise to more complex neuroses. A person with a conditioned fear of dirt may end up severely crippled by his or her compulsive need to wash off any dirt and rid himself of his fear of contamination. The behaviourist's answer to this problem is not to seek within his patient's unconscious for the underlying trauma-related cause but to treat it as a problem in its own right. For the behaviourist a symptom is not a symptom of anything. There is nothing behind or underneath it (other that is to say than the original conditioning experience in childhood or in earlier life linking the stimulus, in this case dirt, with the fear). The answer is to submit the individual to a process of deconditioning or counter-conditioning. One such method of deconditioning is *extinction*. In the case of the famous Pavlov dogs experiment, extinction was implemented by ringing the bell on a large number of occasions without presenting any food. Gradually, the dogs ceased salivating at the sound of the bell (which had originally been brought about by pairing the sound of the bell with the appearance of food). Simple 'extinction' may be one of the processes which operates in so-called 'spontaneous remission' whereby some neurotic illnesses spontaneously remit without treatment.

However, not all neurotic symptoms remit and this may be due to the fact that, unlike the Pavlovian dogs, human beings can avoid things that frighten them and this avoidance, by relieving anxiety, serves to further link the avoided object with the fear. A man afraid of flying avoids flying and obtains relief from his fear. But the feared stimulus, flying, is now enhanced in his mind as a source of anxiety. In such a case, behaviour therapy may be required to help the individual face his fear.

In *systematic desensitisation*, mentioned briefly in the description of the techniques of Masters and Johnson, an attempt is made to condition an alternative response to the fear-producing stimulus so that the occurrence of one inhibits the occurrence of the other. For example, anxiety involves the tensing of muscles. By systematically persuading the patient to relax his muscles while asking him to imagine the feared object (be it a spider, open space, flying in an aircraft) in its least feared state, the therapist relieves the associated anxiety. In the example given, the patient may admit that he fears aircraft least when he just looks at them and so the process of desensitisation would begin with him relaxing while imagining looking at aircraft and would proceed from there. Relaxation rather than anxiety is conditioned as a response to the stimulus of flying and gradually the therapist works through a 'hierarchy' of ever more threatening situations so that eventually the patient is able to tolerate sitting in an aircraft and taking off. Desensitisation can be carried out by means of actually exposing the individual to each state of his hierarchy of fears or by getting him to 'imagine' them. In both instances, treatment only progresses to the next stage when he is able to contemplate experiencing the stage under discussion without becoming anxious.

Another technique, known as *flooding*, has been used with some success in the treatment of certain crippling neurotic states, particularly the severe obsessive-compulsive disorders. This involves making the patient experience his fear fully until it reaches a peak and then diminishes. It involves prolonged contact with the feared object or situation and the patient is encouraged to live through the intense anxiety so aroused. For example, a patient with an intense fear of spiders might be required to remain in close contact with spiders for an hour or more. Flooding is thought to be particularly useful in the treatment of so-called *agoraphobia*, the fear some people have of open spaces, crowds and travelling.

A behavioural treatment which has earned for the whole behavioural approach much criticism and contumely (it figured prominently in the Stanley Kubrick film, *A Clockwork Orange*), is *aversion therapy*. It has been used in the treatment of sexual deviations, such as exhibitionism and paedophilia, in alcoholism and in drug dependence. The therapy involves pairing the unwanted behaviour with a noxious stimulus such as a painful shock or a nausea-producing or paralysing drug. Following such a course of 'treatment' the patient is negatively conditioned to the stimulus in question.

Other behavioural approaches draw on the theory of *operant conditioning*, developed by the American psychologist, Burrhus Skinner. Stated simply, the theory strongly resembles Berne's theory of transactions. The idea is that if a particular action is consistently followed by a reward (Berne's 'stroke') then that particular action is likely to be repeated. If however it is followed by punishment or by nothing at all then the action is likely to cease. It is crucially important that the reward or the punishment follows quickly on the behaviour in question. Too long a gap results in a failure by the individual to connect the two and hence the conditioning quality of the reward or punishment is low. Whereas Pavlovian conditioning involved salivating dogs, Skinner's approach involved pigeons. Skinner waited for his pigeons to behave in a certain way and when they did he stepped in and provided a reward. Gradually the behaviour in question became more frequent. A similar technique, called *token economy*, is increasingly used in the management of certain mentally ill and handicapped individuals. Many such patients are socially withdrawn and do not participate in group activities. But whenever they do therapists and nurses reinforce such positive behaviour by rewarding them with tokens which can be exchanged for desired rewards such as cigarettes, sweets, visits to the cinema etc. The patient's social life can be gradually reshaped and lead to him living a relatively normal life outside hospital.

Such an approach is used in marital contract therapy. It is also part and parcel of life itself – child-rearing practices, industrial relations, education. There are some striking adaptations too. One group of marital therapists employ a complex feed-back system of 'traffic lights', green for approval, red for disapproval, which are used by either member of the couple or by the therapist during discussions with the pair.[29] A significant increase in so-called 'positive' talk and a corresponding decrease in negative contributions have been claimed. Other therapists administer fines for unwanted behaviour while others get action replays on video of desired and unwanted behaviours engaged in during therapy.

Much is made by theorists such as Skinner and Eysenck of the fact that behavioural approaches ignore such factors as the couple's personal and family background, their developmental histories, their emotional interactions and the social system in which they operate. Many marital therapists are not indifferent to the behavioural aspects of their patients' problems and one can detect in the work of such dynamic psychotherapists as Salvador Minuchin and Robin Skynner examples of behavioural techniques such as operant reinforcement being used. Likewise, more behaviourally oriented therapists, such as Crowe in Britain and Liberman in the US, recognise and exploit the possible contribution to cause and treatment of non-behavioural factors.

Yet the dispute between the psychoanalytically-derived psychotherapies and the behavioural therapies persists and is at its most virulent in any discussion of efficacy. (Chapter 10). In behaviour therapy's defence it can be said that originally at any rate it devoted its efforts and resources to the most seriously afflicted. Crippling phobias and obsessions were its main targets. In the past few years, however, behaviour therapists have begun to move further afield and to concern themselves with the less specific and more complex problems of marriage, sex and family relationships. In this broader area, the issue of what is 'normal' becomes even more of an irritant. Both groups of therapists, psychotherapists and behaviourists, insist that it is the clients and not they who decide what requires treatment but there is more than a touch of special pleading here. Is a woman who only achieves an orgasm on average once in every ten occasions of sexual intercourse someone in need of treatment? Does she suffer from the condition of 'anorgasmia'? How often does a man have to fail to achieve an erection to qualify for treatment? The answer that it is a problem if the person concerned says it is, may help to preserve the therapists' spurious notions of professional detachment but it is no answer. In these instances the public is heavily dependent on what the experts define as 'problems', and what resources they, the therapists argue are necessary for 'treatment' to be provided for the 'need' they have themselves identified. There are, of course, many people who have very real problems in their marriages, their sexual lives and their families which deserve help. However, when experts sally forth and declare that one half or two-thirds or three-quarters of the population have sexual problems or unsatisfactory marriages or psychologically unstable families, it is necessary to take a sceptical and critical look at their definitions of sexual health, marital stability and family adjustment before automatically assuming that a case has been made for turning yet more of life's experiences into opportunities for therapy.

'I'm afraid this rage for happiness is rather vulgar' declares a character in Shaw's cynical play, *Getting Married*. The vogue for therapy, one is tempted to speculate, is merely a sublimated version of this same rage. If this be true, then the therapies and their protagonists had better beware. Whatever their abilities to provide self-growth, maturity, ego strength, peak experience, and transformation, happiness seems certain to prove too much for them.

References

1 Shepherd, M. 1979 'Psychoanalysis, Psychotherapy and Health Services' *British Medical Journal* 2: pp.1557-1559
2 Mackay, D. Quoted in 'Blocked emotions cripple marriages' by Denise Winn *The Observer* 21 September 1980
3 *The Freud-Jung Letters* Editor, William McGuire 1974 Letter 140J. p.220 Hogarth/Routledge & Kegan Paul
4 Royal College of Psychiatrists 1974 *Memorandum on Psychiatric Manpower as it Affects the Psychiatric Service* London
5 National Association for Mental Health (MIND)

Psychotherapy: Do We Need More Talking Treatment? Mind
Report No. 12 London

6 National Institute of Mental Health 1972 'Staffing Patterns in
Mental Health Facilities' *NIMH* Series B. Washington

7 Torrey, E. F. *Washington Post* 4 September 1977

8 Murray, R. M. 1979 'A Reappraisal of American Psychiatry'
The Lancet i: pp.255-258

9 Russell, G. F. M. 1973 'Will there be enough psychiatrists to
run the Psychiatric Service based on district general hospitals?' In: *Policy for Action* Editors, R. Lawley and G.
McLachlan Oxford: Nuffield Provincial Hospitals Trust
and OUP

10 Gedo, J. E. 1979 'A Psychoanalyst Reports of Mid-Career'
American Journal of Psychiatry 136: 5, pp.646-649

11 Marmor, J. 1973 'Changing Trends in Psychotherapy' In:
Psychiatry in Transition Selected papers of Judd Marmor
1974 Brunner/Maazel. New York

12 Bion, W. E. and Rickman, J. 1943 'Intra-group Tensions in
Therapy: Their study as the task of the group' *The Lancet* 2:
pp.678-681

13 Main, T. 1946 'The Hospital as a Therapeutic Institution' *Bulletin of the Menninger Clinic* 10: pp.66-70

14 Mandelbrote, B. 1979 'The Therapeutic Community' *British
Journal of Psychiatry* 135: pp.369-371

15 Foulkes, S. H. 1950 'A short survey and orientation with
particular reference to group analysis' Paper read at Quarterly Meeting of the Royal Medico-Psychological Association. London February 1950

16 Walton, H. J. 1978 'Group Psychotherapy' In: *Companion to
Psychiatric Studies* Editors, A. D. Forrest, J. W. Affleck and
A. K. Zealley. Churchill Livingstone. Edinburgh

17 Skynner, R. 1974 'Group Therapy' In: *Psychotherapy Today*
Editor, Ved Varma. Constable. London

18 Yalom, I. 1975 *The Theory and Practice of Group Psychotherapy*
Basic Books. New York

19 Minuchin, S. 1974 *Families and Family Therapy* Tavistock Publications. London

20 Skynner, R. 1976 *One Flesh: Separate Persons* Constable. London

21 Hill, P. 1979 'Constant Family Therapy' In: *Essentials of Post-
graduate Psychiatry* Editors, P. Hill, R. Murray and

A. Thorley. Academic Press. London and New York.
22 Wolberg, L. R. 1977 *The Technique of Psychotherapy* Grune and Stratton. New York
23 Satir, V. 1967 *Conjoint Family Therapy* Science and Behaviour Books Inc. Palo Alto, California
24 Pietropinto, A and Simenauer, J. 1979 *Husbands and Wives: A Nationwide Survey of Marriage* Times Books. New York
25 Dominian, J. 1980 *Marriage in Britain 1945-1980* Study Commission on the Family. London
26 Frank, E., Anderson, C. and Rubinstein, D. 1978 'Frequency of Sexual Dysfunction in "Normal" couples' *New England Journal of Medicine*
27 Crown, S. 1976 'Marital Breakdown: Epidemiology and Psychotherapy' In: *Recent Advances in Clinical Psychiatry* Editor, K. Granville-Grossman. Churchill Livingstone. Edinburgh
28 Schofield, M. 1976 *Promiscuity* Gollancz. London
29 Crowe, M. 1976 'Behavioural Treatments in Psychiatry' In: *Recent Advances in Clinical Psychiatry* Editor, K. Granville-Grossman. Churchill Livingstone. Edinburgh and London
30 Masters, W. H. and Johnson, V.E. 1970 *Human Sexual Inadequacy* Churchill Livingstone. Edinburgh and London
31 Gillan, P. and Gillan, R. 1976 *Sex Therapy Today* Open Books. London
32 Freud, S. Quoted in *Life and Work of Sigmund Freud* Vol.3 pp.163-164 Basic Books Inc. New York
33 Marmor, J. 1972 'Sexual Acting-Out in Psychotherapy' In: *Psychiatry in Transition* Ibid
34 McCartney, J. 1966 'Overt Transference' *Journal of Sex Research* 2: pp.227-237
35 Sutherland, S. 1976 *Breakdown: A Personal Crisis and a Medical Dilemma* Weidenfeld and Nicolson. London

10 Talking — Does it Work?

Psychotherapy has become a major lucrative American industry catering to the needs of millions of consumers. It is crowded with entrepreneurs, each of whom proclaims the unique virtues of his product while largely ignoring those of his rivals, and backs his claims with speculative pronouncements supported by a few case reports. Solidly based objective information as to the nature and efficacy of the product is, by contrast, sadly lacking.

Professor Jerome D. Frank[1]
1974

The remarkable proliferation of talking treatments, might be easier to understand had psychotherapy, orthodox or unorthodox, been shown to be significantly more effective than other, less demanding approaches. Yet despite a vast literature on the subject, the evidence, such as it is, offers little comfort to those who assume that Freud opened the gates to psychiatric salvation. Up to relatively recently, many analysts remained indifferent to demands that they subject what they were doing to some form of objective assessment. Some adopted the view that their approach, like penicillin, self-evidently worked so what was the point of testing it? Others pointed to the very real technical difficulties of attempting a rigorous assessment. However, two recent developments, the first chronicled in this book, have dramatically altered the position.

The rise of psychotherapies much less complicated than psychoanalysis, much cheaper and more immediate in their alleged impact, has sharpened the question of whether psychoanalysis and psychoanalytically-derived psychotherapy 'work'. The second stimulus is the growing involvement of the State in the financing of psychiatric treatment. The first is discussed in more detail in this chapter but the second point, while not central to our concerns, does deserve some comment, for the question of who pays the psychotherapist has as it turns out, a crucial bearing on the issue of establishing efficacy.

If Woody Allen is prepared to pay for psychoanalysis for twenty-two years it does not very much matter if it has been shown to be no more effective in the treatment of introverted, narcissistic, highly intelligent and neurotic individuals than, say, a trip to Lourdes, the comparison Allen himself has made. Once the responsibility for payment is taken over by some agency other than the individual, the situation changes rapidly. In the United States, within the Federal Government's Health Care Finance Administration, within the private health insurance groups and particularly within the Senate Finance Committee, there is considerable anxiety over the cost of providing health cover for individuals undergoing psychotherapy. Suddenly it is the health policy administrators, the civil servants and the politicians who are asking for evidence that psychotherapy is in fact superior to drug, behavioural and social treatments in the management of psychiatric disorder.[2]

Nor are we just talking about the cost of covering payments made by patients to such therapists. The cost of training an analyst is itself substantial. Recently, Dr Judd Marmor of the Department of Psychiatry at the University of Southern California, reported that a review of the length of the average training analysis of all the applicants to the American Psychoanalytical Association indicated that only three of the 191 applicants over a four year period underwent a training analysis lasting less than four hundred hours. Eighty-seven had analyses lasting more than a thousand hours, thirty-three of more than fifteen hundred hours and six of more than two thousand hours. The overall average for the entire 191 applicants was approximately 1025 hours.[3] Not surprisingly, a recent study of some 890 psychoanalytic candidates and their spouses reported that the psychoanalytic training was creating a strain in their relationships with their children and spouses, leaving out the impact of the financial burden of paying the training fees, a burden that eighty per cent of the respondents found either 'substantial' or 'horrendous'.[4] Should we be surprised that professionals, having negotiated a training experience only surpassed in length and intensity by the Jesuit novitiate, should prove somewhat reluctant to embark on research exercises aimed at discovering whether the whole business actually amounts to anything significant?

Despite the lack of convincing evidence, there is no lack of faith in the efficacy of psychotherapy. A report on the subject published by Britain's National Association for Mental Health (MIND) tended to justify that organisation's advocacy of more psychotherapy and psychotherapists on the grounds that patients seemed to want them. However, it is interesting to note the nature of such patient demand, at least as described by MIND.[5] Patients saw psychotherapy as a corrective to the tendency in medicine and psychiatry to treat people as 'cases' and to prescribe pills. The MIND Report also pointed out that many patients don't just want to *feel* better, they want to *be* different. In the early part of the 1970s, Britain's psychiatrists appeared to agree for they sanctioned manpower expansion plans which would multiply by a factor of five the number of full-time consultant psychotherapists working within the National Health Service. However, these new psychotherapists would not necessarily see patients, for their main task would be 'to provide all members of the caring professions with basic psychological understanding, personal skills in human relationships, and that degree of psychotherapeutic skill appropriate to their professions'.[6] Such an expansive brief, of course, only adds extra impetus to the demand that we attempt to establish what precisely psychotherapy is and what skills it embodies. An experienced British general practitioner made this very point when commenting on the conventional wisdom concerning the 'need' for psychotherapy in the setting of primary health care:

> If psychotherapy implies no more than steady support, a sympathetic and understanding attitude, a sophisticated understanding of the complexities of human behaviour and at best a certain wisdom about life then clearly this is needed in all patient care. But has it a place in future general or hospital practice in the sense that it is defined by the psychoanalytical school with its special lights? Psychotherapy aims to restore the normal milieu, yet its classical technique does not favour immediate gain and may favour adjustment to chronicity.[7]

Dr Tom Madden, the author of these views, rubbed salt in the wound by observing pointedly that if psychotherapy is as vital as so many of its protagonists suggest, then how has it come about that it is almost unobtainable at the specialised level, and then only after intensive screening of the potential case as 'suitable for treatment'? This is a particularly stinging barb for the issue of selectivity is a burning one in the whole talking treatment arena, ever since Schofield pointed out that psychoanalysts tend only to treat the mildly neurotic YAVIS patients, that is to say Young, Attractive, Verbal, Intelligent and Successful.[8]

So what can be said of the state of the evidence some forty years after Freud's death? As we have already indicated, there have been many studies reported but the majority are seriously flawed and repeating them here would serve little purpose. But there has been a handful of serious attempts undertaken in recent years and it is upon these that we have chosen to concentrate. One of the earliest intensive and longitudinal studies was undertaken at the Menninger Clinic in Topeka, Kansas.[9] The purpose of the study was to explore changes in patients brought about by 'psychoanalytically-oriented psychotherapies and psychoanalysis'. Psychoanalysis was defined in this study as

> a technique employed by a neutral analyst resulting in the development of a regressive transference neurosis. The ultimate resolution of this neurosis is achieved by techniques of interpretation alone.

Psychotherapy, in contrast, includes approaches derived from the theory of psychoanalysis but which do not aim to induce a full transference neurosis. ('Transference neurosis' refers to the process which is said to occur during analysis by which the patient displaces on to his analyst the feelings, ideas and beliefs which derive from previous figures and experiences in his life). In psychoanalysis, interpretation, confrontation and clarification are used as the main therapeutic interventions whereas in psychotherapy other interventions are used such as suggestion, advice, reassurance, prohibitions and persuasion based on rational factors.

On the basis of the results obtained with the forty-two patients studied (there was no non-treatment group for comparison), the authors of the report concluded that for patients with 'high Ego Strength, high Motivation, high Anxiety Tolerance and high Quality of Interpersonal Relationships, psychoanalysis is the treatment of choice.' 'Ego Strength' was defined in this study as a combination of the degree of integration, stability and flexibility of the personality, the degree to which relationships with others are 'adaptive, deep and gratifying of normal instinctual needs' and the degree to which the individual's disturbance is manifested by symptoms. Stripped of the jargon, the study is saying that psychoanalysis is useful for reasonably healthy, well-motivated, socially functioning and reasonably personable individuals. Plainly it is not for the sick.

More recently, the findings of the Penn Psychotherapy Project have been published and suggest a similar situation.[10] This project aimed to discover what sort of patients and what sort of therapists predicted a good therapeutic response. A total of seventy-three patients were treated in 'psychoanalytically oriented psychotherapy', the average number of treatment sessions devoted to each patient being forty-four. Two-thirds of the therapists were senior trainees in psychiatry while the remainder were more experienced. Most patients improved (again there was no control, non-treatment group) but in so far as anything predicted who would improve and who would not, it seemed to be the pre-treatment characteristics of the patients. A glance at the demographic characteristics of the patients in the study reveals that the mean age is twenty-six, two-thirds are female, ninety per cent are white, eighty-five per cent have had a College education and sixty per cent are single.

In 1979, a study was published claiming to clarify the extent to which such therapeutic effects as do occur are due to specific techniques, (such as interpretations and suggestion) as opposed to so-called non-specific factors inherent in any benign human relationship.[11] 'Highly experienced' psychotherapists treated fifteen male college students selected because of their high score on the depression, anxiety and social introversion scales of the Minnesota Multiphasic Personality Inventory. A comparable sample was treated by a group comprised of 'professors of English, history, mathematics and philosophy' while another comparable group, matched for symptoms, underwent no therapy but were merely tested at intervals for comparison with those in treatment. On average, the young men treated by the professors showed as much improvement as those treated by the professional therapists, despite the fact that the five professional therapists had on average twenty-three years of experience and had been selected 'on the basis of their reputation in the professional and academic community for their clinical expertise'. More sobering still is the fact that the group of young men who received no treatment at all did almost as well.

As one might expect, the analytically-trained psychotherapists and the college professors behaved differently with their respective patients. The analytically-oriented therapists fostered a 'professional' relationship characterised by respectful listening, questioning, making psychoanalytic interpretations (on the basis of such notions as transference, oedipal conflicts etc.) and maintaining a notable interpersonal distance. The college professors, whose behaviour resembled experientially-oriented psychotherapists, tended to be more relaxed, more willing to engage in a free-and-easy exchange with their patients, more ready to provide direct advice and guidance, and more likely to discuss issues other than feelings, conflicts and difficulties. In the words of the authors of this study,

> the professional therapist's unique contribution to treatment outcomes . . . . did not appear *to be linked with* specific skills in dealing with resistances or in interpreting neurotic patterns but rather with his ability to potentiate therapeutic gains in individuals who appeared to be highly motivated for therapy and whose resistance to change is low.[11]

The fact that a matched group of patients would do virtually as well with minimal treatment as a group given more active psychotherapy, emerged once again in a celebrated comparison of behavioural methods of therapy and psychodynamic psychotherapy conducted at Temple University in Philadelphia.[12] In this study, ninety-four patients presenting at a psychiatric outpatients department and diagnosed as suffering from moderately severe neurotic disturbances or personality disorders were randomly assigned to one of three groups. One group was treated by experienced psychoanalytically trained psychotherapists. Another group was treated by experienced behaviour therapists while the third group had no formal treatment other than the initial 'in-depth' assessment interview common to all three groups, and a monthly telephone call assuring them that they had not been forgotten and would be assigned to active treatment as soon as possible. The three groups were assessed at four months, twelve months and two years. At four months, all three groups had improved significantly in so-called 'target' symptoms, that is to say those particular symptoms which the patient himself spontaneously identified as being a specific problem at the outset of the study. Both treatment groups improved significantly more than those on the waiting list, but there was no significant difference in the amount of symptomatic improvement, social adjustment and work ability between the psychotherapy and the behaviour therapy groups. The one and two year follow-up assessments supported the view that those who had shown most improvement at four months continued to do well.

The results of this study, as Professor Marmor pointed out in a foreword, 'offer little comfort to those adherents of either group (psychoanalytically derived psychotherapy and behaviour therapy) who are involved in passionately proclaiming the inherent superiority of this particular brand of therapy over all others'. Indeed, the study strongly suggested that despite their mutual antagonism, there was a remarkable overlap in the approaches of the psychotherapists and the behaviour therapists, suggesting that any differences may be more matters of degree than substance. Behaviour therapists tended to be more directive, more concerned with symptoms, less concerned with childhood memories and, despite their reputation for coldness and lack of clinical involvement, warmer and more active therapists. Tape-recorded interview analysis showed that they made as many interpretative statements as did the psychotherapists. Given the similarities between the two approaches in practice, it is not clear from this study whether the behaviourists and the psychotherapists did actually use fundamentally different approaches to reach the same therapeutic end or whether the effectiveness of their treatments was due to factors common to both schools of thought. But the patients themselves seemed less in doubt. Those who improved attributed their response less to the theoretical framework within which they had been treated and more to the personality, enthusiasm and involvement of the therapists.

A similar picture emerged from an extensive study of the outcome literature undertaken by a group of American researchers and entitled provocatively 'Comparative Studies of Psychotherapies: Is it True that "Everyone has Won and All Must Have Prizes"?'[13] These authors compared various psychotherapeutic approaches: individual psychotherapy versus group psychotherapy, time-limited versus time-unlimited, client-centred versus traditional, and so on. Only those studies which met fairly basic research standards were chosen and the total number of research reports analysed exceeded one hundred. The major conclusion of the review was that the different forms of psychotherapy do not make significant differences in the proportion of patients improving by the end of therapy. The other conclusion of note was that most patients who go through *any* form of psychotherapy gain from it. Of thirty-three studies comparing psychotherapy with no therapy at all, twenty showed therapy to produce significant improvement, thirteen indicated no difference. The authors, faced with the lack of difference between the major therapies, were forced to conclude that certain common elements, most notably the personality of the therapist, must account for the therapeutic impact.

A very similar result has been published by Glass[14] who in a most remarkable review of psychotherapy research, surveyed the results of more than a thousand studies. Glass made no attempt to screen out poorly designed studies and used a fairly broad definition of psychotherapy, although he did exclude encounter groups from consideration. Daniel Hogan, whose review of the nature, types, efficacy and professional standards of psychotherapy is perhaps the most exhaustive available, has recently concluded that 'psychotherapy is an effective process and does bring about an improvement in the mental health of many of those who participate in it'.[15] But it is clear from Hogan's impressively marshalled evidence that there is scant support for the view that psychoanalysis or psychoanalytically-based psychotherapy are superior to more simple and straightforward methods of psychotherapeutic intervention.

None of these studies greatly resemble the randomised, controlled clinical trial, such as is used to evaluate drug and other physical treatments in psychiatry and which is now generally accepted as the most rigorous test of safety and efficacy. Yet elements of the approach are present. Critics of applying scientific tests to the efficacy of psychotherapy, object that psychotherapy is not a specific technology like drugs. They accept the importance of the individual therapist's personal characteristics and ask how can one ensure that the type of psychotherapy provided by psychotherapist X is equivalent to that given by psychotherapist Y? If one ingests a hundred milligrams of a well-known anti-depressant one can be reasonably certain that it has the same chemical composition as an equivalent does of the same substance in San Francisco, London or Moscow. But can the same be said of Freudian psychoanalysts, behaviour therapists or encounter leaders?

These are, it has to be admitted, formidable objections but

they are hardly insuperable. Yet difficulties in mounting respectable and respected trials of psychotherapy are well-known. A celebrated study that failed in the early 1970s involved psychotherapists in the NHS (the Maudsley Hospital) and the private sector (the Tavistock Clinic).[16] This was a most carefully designed trial in which it was agreed from the outset that the aim should be to include only those patients 'who appeared to be highly suitable for the particular form of psychotherapy to be used'. Selection of patients took place in three stages. First, psychiatrists working within a reasonable distance of the two centres referred patients who appeared to them to fulfil particular criteria for psychotherapy. These criteria included

1 No evidence of serious physical or psychotic illness.
2 No serious drug addiction, sexual deviation or sociopathic disorder.
3 Discernible and lasting problems in interpersonal relationships.
4 No evidence suggesting the need for hospital admission.
5 Average intelligence at least.
6 No previous formal psychotherapy.
7 Active motivation for treatment.
8 Willingness to participate in a research programme.
9 Age between 18 and 45.
10 Willing for a relative to be seen.

A hundred and thirteen patients were referred. Of these, twenty-three failed to return the screening questionnaire (which asked for details of the individual's difficulties, family circumstances and history, sexual experience and occupation). Ninety patients were left. However, on the basis of the Tavistock psychotherapists' assessments of the questionnaire responses, only twenty-seven of the ninety were accepted to pass on to the third stage of selection. Each of the twenty-seven was given an interview with one of the four Tavistock participants, an interview which lasted at least one and a half hours and which was tape-recorded. The Tavistock participants then met and discussed each case and agreed to accept – eight. These eight represent approximately nine per cent of those individuals who had completed screening questionnaires and seven per cent of the patients identified as candidates for psychotherapy by participating psychiatrists! A more dramatic example of the selectivity of contemporary psychotherapists would be hard to come by. The authors of the study estimated that it would take thirteen years to accumulate sufficient patients to allow the study of efficacy to proceed!

Some observers concluded on the basis of this experience that psychotherapists just do not want their work evaluated. Others, most notably Professor Michael Gelder of Oxford University, believe that the answer is to select sub-groups of patients with specific problems, such as phobias or depression, and assess the efficacy of psychotherapy applied to them. An additional problem is the high rate of what is termed 'spontaneous improvement', that is to say, improvement occurring in the absence of therapy. A considered estimate currently states that about forty-five per cent of people who suffer from neurotic symptoms spontaneously improve while the overall outcome for all forms of psychotherapy is estimated at around sixty-five per cent.[17]

Lest it be thought that we are extrapolating unfairly from what psychotherapists do in a research programme to what they do in everyday clinical life, consider the conclusions concerning the assessment of patients for psychotherapy reached at the end of an extensive review of the literature by Dr Sidney Bloch, a colleague of Professor Michael Gelder.[18] Replying to his own question concerning the features in a patient which are favourable for 'long-term, insight-orientated psychotherapy', Bloch identifies seven. They are a familiar seven, the magnificent seven as it were of classical psychotherapy's selectivity:

1 a reasonable level of personality integration and general functioning (i.e. patients 'who have the strength to face their disturbing feelings and to carry on their lives independently of therapy');
2 motivation for change;
3 realistic expectations of the therapeutic process involved, reflecting 'psychological-mindedness';
4 at least average intelligence;
5 non-psychotic conditions, namely the neuroses and the milder personality disorders;
6 the presence of strong emotion like anxiety and depression at the time of assessment;
7 life circumstances free of any unresolvable crises.[18]

These are remarkably similar to the selection criteria of the

Maudsley-Tavistock study – which yielded seven per cent of those originally referred for treatment! The first criterion raises the question of the morality of providing an expensive and time-consuming therapy for people who can function independently without it. There is no objective and agreed measure of motivation (the second criterion) while what constitutes 'realistic expectations' is difficult to establish in the absence of evidence that psychotherapy works. The fifth and seventh criteria merely echo the constant message that psychotherapy is not for people who are in serious mental difficulties. The fourth criterion has the virtue of testability while the sixth serves to remind us that it is therapy that we are considering and not the provision of a course in self-exploration or a professional friend.

Perhaps it is not surprising that Anthony Storr, in his recently published book *The Art of Psychotherapy*[19], should so boldy state that the analytical schools as discrete entities will soon disappear. The labels of 'Jungian', 'Freudian', 'Kleinian' will become less and less important in his view 'as research discloses the common factors which lead to a successful outcome in psychotherapy which, to my mind is largely independent of the school to which the psychotherapist belongs'. However, Storr clings to the notion that personal analysis is an important part of the training of a psychotherapist, although it is difficult to see why, since such research as has been done seems to indicate that the theoretical experience and knowledge possessed by the individual psychotherapist are largely irrelevant to the outcome.

Twenty-five years of psychotherapy at Johns Hopkins Hospital in Baltimore led Professor Jerome Frank to concede that the therapeutic qualities of caring, empathy and genuineness, identified by Carl Rogers as the significant element in all psychotherapy, do appear to exert an important therapeutic effect.[1] Yet attempts to assess the efficacy of Rogerian encounter groups are not easy to come by in the literature. The most quoted study is that by Morton Lieberman and his colleagues at Stanford University which looked in some detail at the array of therapies flourishing in California during the early 1970s.[22] In all, seventeen groups, each composed of ten group members, were studied. These were made up of two 'T' groups (non-directive groups in which the goal is the enhancement of the individual's sensitivity to the feelings of others), two Gestalt groups, two psychodrama groups, one psychoanalytic group, two groups devoted to applying transactional analytic methods, two 'Marathon' groups (a marathon group meets for 24-48 hours without pause, apart from short breaks – the intensity of prolonged interaction, perhaps facilitated by sheer physical exhaustion, is said to produce more personal change than months or even years of more 'dilute' therapy), two 'Personal Growth' groups (Rogerian encounter groups), a Synanon confrontation group, a body awareness group and two Tape Programme groups which had no appointed leaders but which were supposed to be guided by a set of encounter tapes.

The intention of Lieberman and his colleagues was to discover who benefits from the new psychotherapies, who is harmed and what aspects of the group experience explain these effects. The question is clearly not an academic one. Today's American, the authors point out, is fairly likely to come face to face with the question of membership of an encounter group. He may personally consider enrolment in a 'growth center' or joining a 'living-room group' or he may find himself confronted by an encounter group connected with his work or his church. Or 'he may be puzzling over a request from his offspring to sign a permission slip for participation in a school group'.

The sample in this study was derived from volunteers responding to articles placed in student publications and posters placed around the Stanford campus. The main measures of outcome, in addition to the client's own self-report, included the reported experience of a 'peak experience' and the assessment of people who knew the participants as to whether they had changed as a result of the 'therapy'. With regard to the possibility that the sample was 'atypical' of the Stanford student population, it is worth nothing that at the time of the project perhaps as many as fifty per cent of the campus's eight thousand students had had experience of encounter groups!

Lieberman and his colleagues found that the differences between groups of supposedly the same type were as great as differences between different theoretical approaches. What actually happened in each particular case appeared to be more a function of the kind of person the leader was, the sort of leadership actually practised, the persons convened and the atmosphere they created than of the theories that the leaders actually professed and implemented. Thus far Rogers' views appear confirmed. But the authors' general conclusion merits quotation:

> Based both on the number of individuals who experienced
> benefit from the groups and on the comparison of the different
> areas in participants and their controls, it was concluded that
> overall encounter groups show a modest positive impact, an
> impact much less than has been portrayed by their supporters,
> and an impact significantly lower than the participants' view of
> their own change would lead one to assume.[22]

In this study, there was little evidence of what has been termed
the 'late blooming' effect; that is to say, only ten per cent of
those who showed no benefit at termination of therapy showed
signs of benefit six months later. In contrast, another ten to
twenty per cent were less enthusiastic about benefits experienced after such a time interval than they were at termination of
the groups, an example of 'late wilting'. It is interesting to note
that approximately sixty per cent of the participants claimed to
have had emotionally intense, conversion-like 'peak experiences' within the six months after their group experience, a
finding which may go some way to explaining the continued
popularity of these approaches in the absence of any clear-cut
evidence that they have any lasting therapeutic impact.

However, there have been criticisms levelled at the Stanford
study which suggest that its conclusions have to be regarded
with caution. There is evidence that the group leaders may have
been somewhat atypical – one of the leaders was the only person ever banned from conducting groups at Esalen while
another was excluded for a period of several months. These two
leaders accounted for five of the sixteen casualties. Problems
also plagued the design of the project and there is a serious
question-mark opposite the extent to which one can safely
generalise from the overall finding about the value of encounter
groups. However, in the intervening years, there have been
numerous studies of the value of encounter groups, most of
them collected and assessed most efficiently by Gibb.[21] Of 127
studies comparing encounter groups with a no-treatment control group, the encounter-group participants changed significantly more in 102 of these studies. In twenty-one studies no
difference was found and in eight the control group obtained
superior results. Gibb found that approximately one-third of the
studies utilised follow-up measures, mostly one week and six
months after the group experience and this follow-up revealed

that the changes brought on by the encounter group persisted over this time.

What is far from clear, however, in these thoughtful assessments is what it is that has changed as a result of the encounter. According to Bebout and Gordon[22] self-esteem increases, the self-concept changes in a variety of positive directions, 'self-actualising tendencies are greater, alienation is reduced and individual problems are lessened.' In addition, interpersonal relations become more empathic, interpersonal values change and 'people become close with each other and feel less lonely'. Whatever one thinks about these claims, there is much less certainty expressed concerning the efficacy of encounter groups to improve the *social* functioning of clients, whether this be occupational functioning (for which purpose, the T-group form of encounter was actually founded), marital functioning or functioning within the family.

But of course it has to be questioned whether asking about the efficacy of some of the new therapies and their ability to bring about measurable changes is appropriate. It is one thing to try to assess a treatment which is said to relieve agoraphobia or depression or anxiety, quite another to establish whether a self-actualising approach actually self-actualises. The difficulties have been illustrated by a somewhat ill-fated attempt to apply the ideas of the so-called humanistic psychology movement to politics. The trouble started with a book by experiential therapist, Everett Shostrom, entitled *Freedom to Be*.[23] In his introduction to the book, which is a relatively straightforward presentation of some of the basic theoretical assumptions of the human potential movement, Shostrom expresses his intellectual debt to a number of 'magnificent' men who served as his models of actualisation, among them Abraham Maslow, Carl Rogers, Rollo May, Frederick Perls and Alan Watts. So far ritualistic stuff but then Shostrom mentions Richard M. Nixon as someone who 'has exemplified many of the growth processes expressed in this book through his rise to the presidency'. Shostrom offered Nixon as a supreme example of self-actualisation. When Abraham Maslow spoke in his book *Toward a Psychology of Being* of the significance of such human needs as safety, security, belongingness and love, he might well have been speaking of Nixon himself who, according to Shostrom, began his career 'with the satisfaction of many of these needs uppermost in his existence'. At another point in the book, published in 1972 before Watergate, Shostrom declares simply that 'President Nixon . . . . is a public example of "where it's at'''. Indeed.

So incensed was another encounter therapist, Walt Anderson, at this betrayal of humanistic psychology, that he wrote a snappy attack on Shostrom's book in *The Journal of Humanistic Psychology*.[24] In it, Anderson recounts the shift in cultural values which is said to occur in the process of engaging in 'growth'. Such a shift is supposed to move

From	*Toward*
Self-control	Self-actualisation
Independence	Interdependence
Endurance of Stress	Capacity for Joy
Full Employment	Full Lives
Mechanistic Forms	Organic Forms
Competitive Relations	Collaborative Relations

Shostrom likes to think that 'man's inner journey is being guided by the set of values in the right-hand column' and Anderson likes to think so too. Where they disagree is over where to place Nixon, Anderson's perception being that 'he is one of the world's foremost embodiments of the left-hand column, a superb example of what it is we must all outgrow'. Poor Anderson chivvies Shostrom for picking on a figure of power to emphasise the value of growth and expresses shock and dismay that the 'persecutor' of Alger Hiss and the Vietnamese people should be held up for admiration as the supremely actualised Universal Man. But it is not just a case of Shostrom getting it wrong. Rather it is a case of a theory which can mean all things to all men. As Rollo May said, growth is a poor word on which to rest a system for it takes many and varied forms. And what would Mr Nixon make, one wonders, of that Perls poster which covers many a wall in many a growth centre and which is a veritable paean of exultation for the flamboyant assertion of the self:

> I do my thing, you do your thing. I am not in this world to live up to your expectations and you are not in this world to live up to mine! You are you, and I am I, and if by chance we meet, it's beautiful, if not, it can't be helped.

A slogan of autistic, blind egoism or authentic, confident realism? Who is going to say? Deciding would be like trying to assess the efficacy of est. But then there have been attempts to prove that est 'works' and the est foundation, in spite of its own assertions that est is not about anything, has not been slow to include various scientific-looking reports testifying to the usefulness of the package in the propaganda material it circulates concerning training weekends and graduate courses. The best known study is the evaluation by Babbie and Stone of the est experience of a number of 'graduates'.[25] The original study was designed and conducted by an 'independent' team of researchers. A probability sample of two thousand graduates was selected from among the twelve thousand who in November 1973 had been out of the est training for at least three months. A lengthy self-administered questionnaire was mailed to the sample and 1,024 individuals replied, a sixty-four per cent return rate based on the 1,895 persons who were reached by mail and sixty per cent of those originally sampled. The authors seem sure that those who failed to reply were indistinguishable from those who did. However, it is hard to see how they can be certain that the two groups did not differ on one rather important variable, namely the extent to which each felt like getting involved with est again. Most of those who did reply were positive about the effects of their est training. Majorities said that their relationships with others, their health and their work had improved after the training but no third-party reports were sought and no independent evidence of such benefits was available. Despite the fact that est explicitly states that it is not offering 'therapy', a sizeable number of the respondents in this study had expected that the training would have a positive effect on various aspects of their lives, including their sexual relationships and their mental functioning. Much is made of the fact that this is an independent study yet it is surely worth noting that one of its two co-authors, Earl Babbie, is Chairman of the Advisory Council of est's Hunger Project (rubbing shoulders with such luminaries as Milton Friedman, Buckminster Fuller, Ramsey Clark and Dick Gregory). The only 'independent' study which has been published shows that the effect of adding est to the therapeutic programme of alcoholic patients has no discernible effect on outcome.[26]

What is the evidence that other types of psychotherapy 'work'? Although the number of controlled evaluations of transactional analysis is rather small, its beneficial effects compare reasonably well with more orthodox psychodynamic therapies. TA and Rogerian client-centred therapy appeared roughly similar in their effects and much superior to Gestalt therapies. The last group of talking treatments, however, are relatively untested and such studies as have been performed suggest little positive impact. Smith and Glass' extensive review of over four hundred controlled evaluations of psychotherapy consistently reports that of the psychotherapies, the behavioural approaches appear to be the most effective overall, followed by TA, Adlerian-based psychotherapy and Rogerian counselling, with Gestalt therapy further behind.[27] There have been no worthwhile systematic evaluations of Primal therapy, psychodrama or Rolfing.

The extraordinary growth in popularity of marital, family and sex therapies has tended to outstrip efforts made by researchers to assess them. The growth, it has to be remembered, is a relatively recent phenomenon. Most of the journals devoted to such innovative psychotherapies, such as *Family Therapy, Journal of Family Counselling, Journal of Sex and Marital Therapy, Journal of Divorce, Alternative Life-Styles* and *Family Therapy*, have started in the past fifteen years.

An exact assessment of current practice is hindered by the difficulty of defining precisely what marital-family therapy actually is. In the words of two American reviewers, 'There are few licensing boards and no standard educational requirements or recognised national organisations'.[28] Yet there is a vast literature and several reviews of it have concurred in their cautious optimism concerning the general efficacy of marital and family approaches compared with individually-based therapy. One study, that of Dr Michael Crowe at the Maudsley Hospital,[29] is unusual in that it has attempted to establish the comparative efficacy of not one but several therapeutic approaches employed in contemporary marital therapy and for this reason it is briefly considered here.

In the Maudsley study, forty-two couples with marital difficulties were randomly allocated to one of the three types of conjoint treatment (by conjoint is meant that the partners were treated as a couple). The first treatment approach employed a 'directive' style and used a simple model of marital disturbance. The couple was seen as not producing enough rewarding interpersonal behaviour (what in TA language we might term 'posi-

tive strokes') and an attempt was made by the therapist to persuade the partners to increase such behaviour. The therapist
therefore provided advice on so-called 'give-to-get' principles.
The partners were asked to request a change in each other's
daily specific behaviour so as to make it more rewarding to the
partner making the request. Dynamic interpretations were
expressly excluded from the 'directive' approach. The second
therapeutic approach did use an 'interpretative' style with the
therapist actively analysing and interpreting the feelings and
behaviour of the couple and exploring the manipulations of the
relationship, any avoidance of responsibility and any underlying emotional states such as anxiety or anger. A third approach,
described as 'supportive-control', was designed to avoid both
advice and interpretation, the main object being for the therapist
to remain passive and impartial, to encourage the couple to talk
to each other, and to intervene 'only to make peace during prolonged quarrels or to prevent long silences'. A variety of outcome measures were employed including a self-rating questionnaire relating to marital, sexual and general life adjustment,
a six-question questionnaire devoted to major symptoms and a
rating scale of overall well-being.

With regard to marital adjustment, the interpretative
approach produced the first significant improvement after three
sessions, but from then until a follow-up three months after
treatment had been completed (treatment consisted of approximately ten sessions per couple), all three approaches showed
significant improvements with no differences between treatments. At nine and eighteen months follow-up, the supportive
group failed to maintain its initial improved scores whereas both
the other groups remained improved. The directive group,
however, was the only group to show significant improvement
with regard to sexual adjustment and general adjustment.

What makes this study stand out from the vast mass of
studies in the literature is the fact that it was carefully designed
and controlled, distinguished between treatment and control
procedures, had clearly stated its outcome criteria, used an
independent assessor of the effects of treatment, and employed
a reasonably lengthy follow-up period.

Its general findings do suggest that interpretive marital
therapy may exert a long-term effect upon general adjustment,
but overall it compared less favourably with the Masters and

Johnson-style directive approach. Far from being purely of symptomatic value, the directive approach appeared to exert the 'deepest' effects, to judge by Crowe's results, at nine and eighteen months follow-up.

The behaviourally-oriented work of Crowe, and his colleagues working in the marital and sex therapy clinics of the NHS represents an approach which does attempt to identify 'target' symptoms and then concentrate on affecting these. But, as we have seen, many people coming to psychotherapists, orthodox and unorthodox, do not complain necessarily of specific symptoms so much as a general malaise, a non-specific feeling of anomie and dissatisfaction. The problems of assessing the efficacy of what they are offered are truly horrendous. In so far as there are reports in the literature of such interventions as meditation and yoga, they are almost entirely eulogistic. Reports abound testifying to the effects of meditation practices on depression, anxiety and irritability and on internal self-control, self-actualisation and even happiness. However, as West points out in a recent review[30] the majority of these studies employ inadequate or no controls to assess the effects of placebo or spontaneous improvement, do not take into account biases operating in the selection of patients and do not allow for patients' expectations. For example, a widely reported finding concerning transcendental meditation related to its power to enable people to stop or dramatically to reduce their usage of non-prescribed drugs. However, what was overlooked was the fact that all practitioners of TM are required to abstain from using non-prescribed drugs for fifteen days prior to learning the meditation technique and only those who are less severely addicted in the first place are likely to achieve this.

It is exceedingly difficult to contemplate assessing the therapeutic effects of a mystical experience. Inner happiness and moments of sheer, overwhelming transcendence do not always go hand in hand with an exterior comportment of sanctity, sensibility and 'growth'. What immediately feels 'good' is not always most 'true'. The difference between Philip drunk and Philip sober is the classic instance in corroboration. If merely 'feeling good' could decide, 'drunkenness would be the supremely valid human experience'.[32] But such revelations as occur in the drunken state, however acutely satisfying at the moment, are inserted into an environment which often refuses to bear them out for any length of time. This dilemma is cogently summed up by William James:

> There are moments of sentimental and mystical experience . . . . that carry an enormous sense of inner authority and illumination with them when they come. But they come seldom and they do not come to everyone; and the rest of life makes no connection with them, or tends to contradict them more than it confirms then. Some persons follow the voice of the moment in these cases, some prefer to be guided by the average results. Hence the sad discordancy of the spiritual judgements of human beings.[31]

Despite these reservations however, there have been a number of attempts to assess the effects of such essentially religious activities as meditation on psychological ill-health and maladjustment. One of the more detailed of these has suggested that yoga and meditation can significantly reduce anxiety levels and do so to a greater extent than can be achieved by more orthodox forms of psychotherapy.[32] There is, in addition, a steadily growing literature (mostly composed, it is true, of poorly controlled studies) testifying to the usefulness of meditation in the treatment of such stress disorders as insomnia, high blood pressure and headache. The contemporary growth in evangelical sects has highlighted the overlap between notions of therapeutic improvement, borrowed from medicine, and conversion, a term with frankly religious overtones. We have seen how the advocates of organisations such as est and Insight, as well as many of the participants in counselling sessions, psychodrama and primal therapy, testify to the 'transformation' which they have experienced. Their testimony echoes that of William James' convert who declared of his experience –

> Realisation of conversion was very vivid, like a ton's weight being lifted from my heart, a strange light which seemed to light up the whole room . . . . a conscious supreme bliss which caused me to repeat 'Glory to God for a long time'.[31]

Can the lifting of 'a ton's weight' lead to changes which, in a more frankly psychiatric setting, would be called therapeutic? Two American psychiatrists, Drs Marc Galanter and Peter Buckley, attempted to answer just such a question when they assessed the psychological effects of membership of a religious sect, the Divine Light Mission.[33] Responses given by 119 members to a questionnaire indicated a significant decline in the incidence of neurotic symptoms and of alcohol and drug use from the period prior to joining the sect to that immediately after joining. This lower incidence persisted over the course of membership (an average of twenty-one months) and symptomatic improvement was related significantly to group activities, most notably ritual meditation. Transcendental experiences occurred commonly during the kind of meditation practised by this sect and the authors of the study noted that each of these transcendental experiences helped facilitate a decline in one or more of the symptoms. Their findings lend support to the claim that patients' religiosity is significantly correlated with success in psychotherapy.

But what about the 'harm' that psychotherapy, orthodox or unorthodox, can do? It is as difficult to answer this question as it is to answer the question 'Does psychotherapy work?' and for the same reasons. Two examples illustrate what we mean. One definition of a psychotherapeutic casualty includes an individual who expresses negative feelings about his or her experiences in a sensitivity or behavioural therapy setting.[34] Given the fact that such groups, by definition, encourage an open and honest expression of feelings and emotions, this definition by casualty might appear somewhat wide. In contrast, others have argued that psychotic experiences may actually constitute examples of significant personal growth for some individuals,[35] a definition so elastic that it effectively denies the term 'casualty' any meaning. Restricting the term to include only those participants in therapy who appear worse when therapy is terminated, than when therapy started, might seem reasonable but it does depend on accurate assessments of participants being made on both these occasions. The study of various kinds of psychotherapies undertaken by Lieberman and his colleagues discussed above, employed the term 'psychological harm', which they defined as 'reports of greater discomfort of the subject during or following the group experience and/or the utilisation of more maladaptive defences by the subject'.[20] In that particular study, casualties were identified by a number of cross-checks including patient testimony, evaluations made by friends and acquaintances of the patients and the need of patients to seek psychiatric treatment following participation in the therapies. The psychological casualty rate so described approached ten per cent, a sizeable proportion when one considers that the benefit rate was only thirty per cent. If one adds the number of casualties to the number of participants who reported disimprovement following participation, the overall negative outcome rate rises to nearly twenty per cent.

The psychological casualty also occurs in dynamic, orthodox one-to-one psychotherapy. An analysis of some thirty controlled studies led Bergin[36] to estimate that about ten per cent of patients treated in this way deteriorated, a figure which while lower than that reported in the Stanford encounter group study is still not inconsiderable. There is little dispute in the literature concerning the possibility that serious psychological damage can be inflicted upon participants in any of the newer (and the old) psychotherapies by irresponsible, ignorant and charismatic group leaders and individual therapists. Many of the newer approaches implicitly acknowledge this fact by stating that they do not accept participants who have had a previous history of serious psychiatric ill-health. However, it cannot be said that the methods of screening out such individuals are necessarily effective. For example, est makes much of their emphasis on such pre-training screening yet the Babbie and Stone survey shows that of the 1904 graduates surveyed, twenty-eight (2.3%) reported having had a 'nervous breakdown' during the year prior to taking the est training, six of these having been hospitalised.[25] Ten respondents reported having a nervous breakdown after undergoing the est training.

There is general agreement that seriously mentally ill individuals, that is to say patients suffering from schizophrenia, paranoid illnesses, manic-depressive disorders, brain damage and serious disturbances of personality development, are unsuitable for psychotherapy and respond badly to it.[37] Although this is reflected in the selection criteria drawn up by psychotherapists, it is usually not known by the seriously ill, many of whom languish under the illusion, which they share with many members of the general public, that psychotherapy is the treatment which everyone should have but cannot for economic and manpower reasons. But non-psychotically ill individuals can suffer in psychotherapy too. The emphasis which many of the newer approaches place on 'ventilation' and 'letting it all hang out' can produce unwanted effects, particularly if after a participant has done just that the group promptly disbands! A fifty-two-year-old divorcee, who described herself as an isolated woman with a 'tendency to hide' summarised her experience of a women's consciousness-raising group:

> I was able to reveal that I had an abortion many years ago. This was significant because I was unmarried and at that time that situation was a disgrace – and I made up my mind at that time I'd never tell anybody about it. I have since regretted telling the group since shortly thereafter the group disintegrated.[38]

There is a widespread assumption that appropriately trained psychotherapists produce less 'damage' than relatively untrained ones, an idea which lies at the root of calls to establish a register of 'approved' practitioners. The problem once again is that such an assertion lacks any significant evidence to support it. Sir John Foster, considering this question in his *Enquiry into the Practice and Effects of Scientology*,[39] concluded that such a register was necessary if vulnerable people were to be protected against the possibilities of abuse by 'the unscrupulous'.

> The trained and selfless practitioner is concerned only to convert the deep emotional dependence on him which his patient develops during the treatment into an ability on the patient's part to wean himself from the therapist . . . . But it is totally easy for the unscrupulous therapist, who knows enough to create the dependence in the first place, to exploit it for years on end to his own advantage in the form of a steady income, to say nothing of the opportunities for sexual gratification.[39]

Foster's faith, for faith it unquestionably was, in such a distinction between the safe and the dangerous therapist, led him to argue that psychotherapy (in the general sense of the treatment, for fee or reward, of illnesses, complaints or problems by psychological means) should be organised as a restricted profession open only to those who undergo an appropriate training and are willing to adhere to a proper code of ethics. In 1975, the Department of Health and Social Security formed a working party to consider the question of statutory registration. There were seven organisations represented on the working party – the Association of Child Psychotherapists, the British Association for Behavioural Psychotherapy, the British Association of Psychotherapists, the British Psychoanalytical Society, the Institute of Group Analysis, the Royal College of Psychiatrists and the Society of Analytical Psychology. Three years later, the working party produced a report which endorsed Foster's view that a statute enacted by Parliament is required to regulate a 'profession' of psychotherapists.

However, one of the participating bodies, the British Association for Behavioural Psychotherapy, dissented. This organisation differs from the others in that it does not equate psychological treatments with psychotherapeutic interventions derived from the ideas of Freud and his analytic successors. (Neither does the Royal College of Psychiatrists but its representative on this particular working party was an orthodox classically trained psychoanalyst). The dissenting argument merits quotation:

> There is no general agreement as yet on what constitutes a valid psychotherapeutic training, nor is there good evidence that patients benefit from treatment by most qualified psychotherapists, with a few exceptions. That some professional groups approve training courses is of little help to the public until it has been shown that the psychotherapy which is the subject of the courses in fact benefits the patients . . . . However, registration outlined in the main report is suggested on the basis of training which is largely of unproven value at the present time. This is likely to do more harm than good to the public by unnecessary restriction of access to those treatments which are useful and by retarding innovation in a field which is changing rapidly. The future may well bring ways of sorting out which forms of psychotherapy training produce skills which are and which are not useful for clients, and at that time registration on the basis of such training might be feasible.[40]

Hogan's meticulous review[15] concluded that 'one may say with reasonable certainty that encounter groups do cause harm' but he added that 'one cannot help but be struck by the number of studies that have found encounter groups to pose only minimal dangers'. However, Hogan and others admit that much of the outcome research in this area does not concern itself with those groups generally conceded to be the most dangerous, namely 'those conducted on a fly-by-night basis by somebody with little or no training and advertised in underground newspapers'. Indeed, the very fact that one of the so-called 'new' psychotherapies is being researched may significantly decrease the amount of risk involved.

Given that the vast majority of people who practise psychotherapy in Britain do belong to one or other of the so-called 'caring' professions (medicine, psychology, social work, nursing) which are governed by various ethical and professional restraints, it might be wondered quite what the fuss is about. In fact, the fuss is about many of the therapies and the therapists discussed in this book. It is the spectre of rolfing, primal therapy, Reichian massage, marathon nude groups and the rest of what one critic rather unkindly referred to as the 'transatlantic psychotherapy zoo' which looms large over the psychotherapeutic orthodoxy in Britain. The fact that the DHSS Working Party came to a virtually unanimous recommendation, despite the fact that the various members normally fight acrimoniously among themselves about the relative merits of Freud, Jung, Adler and Klein, eloquently testifies to the degree of anxiety felt by the psychoanalytic establishment concerning the possibility that the new psychotherapies will erode their power and influence in Britain as they are currently doing in the US.

It might be said that people are free to spend their money however they like and if individuals are silly enough to place their faith in ill-trained and unscrupulous practitioners then that is their own fault. However, as Foster pointed out, it is impossible to avoid noticing that those who feel they need psychotherapy

> tend to be the very people who are most easily exploited; the weak, the insecure, the nervous, the lonely, the inadequate, and the depressed, whose desperation is often such that they are willing to do and pay anything for some improvement of their condition.[39]

'A great many of us', declared Bishop Latimer in 1552, 'when we be in trouble, or sickness, or lose anything, we run hither and thither to witches, or sorcerers, whom we call wise men . . . . seeking aid and comfort at their hands.' In four hundred years, little has changed. The mentally distressed, like the poor, are always with us and the wizards, the witches, the sorcerers, wise men and sages are with us too, purveying the same potent or impotent brew of medicine, magic and myth. Attempts to distinguish the potent from the impotent, the charlatan from the genuine, continue but these are dogged by many problems, not the least being the fact that in psychotherapy more than in any other form of treatment the charismatic personality of the therapist may be one of the most important elements in the overall efficacy. In this respect, it is worth noting that in the Stanford study of encounter groups, those therapists who seemed to possess particularly powerful, even invasive personalities, appeared to wield the most therapeutic influence – in both positive and negative directions.

It is fashionable to attribute the growth of psychotherapy in California to the affluence and easy living. A more relevant factor may be the extent to which traditional personal, family, social and communal supports have been eroded in cities like Los Angeles. It is interesting to note that Foster's scientology report distinguished between psychotherapy practised for fee or reward and the 'kind of psychotherapy we all practise on each other in our personal relationships' and that provided by many voluntary organisations involved in 'counselling'. The first is needed when the second is less available. May's observations that psychotherapy flourishes when a civilisation disintegrates is also relevant for it suggests that psychotherapy too is 'symptomatic' treatment and, indeed, it can blind us to the need to examine and perhaps even overhaul radically those aspects of the way we live which foster the need to undergo psychotherapy in the first place. In that sense, the burgeoning 'self-help' movement reflects a growing irritation and dissatisfaction with the tendency to assume that all manner of problems of life and living require appropriate experts, be they trained partly trained or untrained, to provide solutions. Some self-help movements are long-standing – Alcoholics Anonymous being the most obvious. Others such as Gamblers Anonymous and TOPS (Taking Off Pounds Sensibly) are of more recent origin. There are now hundreds including the intriguing, but as yet unconfirmed, Analysands Anonymous which is 'open to anyone who has been in psychoanalysis for twelve years or longer and needs the help of a power greater than his own – or that of his analyst – to terminate the analysis'![41] The characteristics of self-help groups include the mutual help and support members provide, the notion that it may be the helper who benefits most from the therapeutic exchange, the valuable notion of normality which such groups foster, the promotion of greater factual understanding, the action-orientated philosophy (the notion that members learn by doing and are changed by doing – rather than by developing intrapsychic understanding) and the collective will-power and belief which enables each person to look to others in the group for validation of his feelings and attitudes. As described by the British sociologist, David Robinson, the self-help movement may represent a significant alternative response to what hitherto has been an assumption at the heart of the psychotherapies, both old and new, that life's problems require a system, a technique, a body of skill, be it Freudian, Rogerian, transactional, primal or psychodrama theory.[41]

Nothing in this book should be interpreted as suggesting that the authors disparage the search which leads many people to the talking therapies. Many of the people flocking to the growth centres and the ashrams, the encounter groups and the rolfing sessions seem to us to be unhappy, bewildered and disoriented people searching for some philosophical principle, some system of values by which to live. The questions they ask are often the ultimate questions concerning existence, purpose, the meaning of life, happiness, pain and death. Nor is there any doubt that psychotherapists are willing to be cast in the role of 'secular pastoral workers' providing values and meanings of their own. Yet we do feel that the announced agenda of psychotherapy, with its heavily medical, secular and pseudoscientific flavour, insufficiently reflects its frankly religious undertones. In the newer therapies, in particular, this dichotomy is becoming less easy to maintain. The search for peak experiences, 'the fireworks of life' as Maslow called them, is a search which cannot without consummate difficulty be termed a search for 'therapy' but rather a search for something hitherto provided (and, in some cases still provided) by orthodox and unorthodox religious movements. Questions of efficacy, in this situation, are irrelevant. 'How few things there are which can be proved' declared Pascal, adding that proofs only convince the mind.

> Who has ever been able to prove that tomorrow will come and that we shall die? And what could be more generally believed? . . . . In short, we must rely on faith when the mind has once perceived where truth lies, in order to quench our thirst and colour our minds, with a faith that eludes us at every moment of the day.[42]

But more urgent perhaps than the desire for meaning is the need of every human being for love. For those who have failed to find it in the parental home, in friendship, or in an enduring sexual relationship, for the thousands of drifting, desperate souls whose lives are empty, whose relationships are fragmented, whose self regard is precarious, psychotherapy offers the intimacy, interest and support that they lack, cash on the nail. 'Unconditional positive regard', Rogers called it, whereas British social workers talk, in the way social workers will, of 'personal skills informed by professional values in the context of interpersonal relationships as an integral part of the helping process'. Many people certainly find in sessions with their psychotherapists opportunities to express feelings they are unable or unwilling to communicate elsewhere, but it is unlikely that those other elements of love, the spontaneity, the unqualified concern of one person for another, and the denial of the self can be provided through transitory, though intense encounters, where commitment is defined by the clock, and where the ostensible purpose is not only to discover the self but to outgrow dependence on the relationship which expedites that discovery.

This book opened with a quotation from an article in *Time* magazine concerning the state and the future of contemporary psychiatry. The article ended prophesying that psychiatry would split into so-called 'biological' psychiatry, with its emphasis on the physical organism, the central nervous system, drugs and other physical treatments, and the human potential movement with its emphasis on meaning, growth, earthly salvation and earthly perfection. Allowing for its characteristic exaggeration, *Time* may be close to the truth. In the fifty years since his creation by Freud, the 'secular pastoral worker' has worn the clothes of the man of medicine while actually engaged in the work of a man of God in a godless society. As the century moves to its close, it is becoming harder to conceal the true nature of the psychotherapies. We cannot believe it is in the interests of anyone to continue to try.

References

1 Frank, J. K. 1974 'Therapeutic Components of Psychotherapy. A 25-year progress report of Research' *Journal of Nervous and Mental Disease* 159: pp.325-342
2 Klerman, G. L. 1980 'The Inter-relationship of Psychotherapy and Psychopharmacology' Reported in *Psychiatric News* XV, 15 August 1980

3 Marmor, J. 1979 'Psychoanalytic Training' *Archives of General Psychiatry* 36: pp.486-489

4 Levy, N. B. 1977 'The effect of psychoanalytic education on the candidate's family as viewed by the spouse' Read at mid-winter meeting of the American Psychoanalytic Association. New York

5 Mind Report No 12 1974 *Psychotherapy: Do we need more "Talking Treatment?"* National Association for Mental Health. London

6 Royal College of Psychiatrists 1975 *Norms for Medical Staffing of a Psychiatric Service – Psychotherapy* Report to Central Manpower Committee. London

7 Madden, T. A. 1979 'The doctors, their patients and their care: Balint Reassessed' *Editorial. Psychological Medicine* 9: pp.5-8

8 Schofield, W. 1964 *Psychotherapy: The Purchase of Friendship* Prentice-Hall. Englewood Cliffs, NJ.

9 Bulletin of the Menninger Clinic 1972 'Psychotherapy and Psychoanalysis': Final Report of the Menninger Foundation's Psychotherapy Research Project Vol.36, Nos.1-2

10 Luborsky, L. Mintz, J. Averback, A. Christopher, P. Bachrach, H., Todd, T., Johnson, M., Cohen, M. and O'Brien, C. P. 1980 'Predicting the Outcome of Psychotherapy' *hives of General Psychiatry* 37: pp.471-481

11 Strupp, H. and Hadley, S. W. 1979 'Specific vs non specific factors in Psychotherapy' *Archives of General Psychiatry* 36: pp.1125-1136

12 Sloane, R. B., Staples, F. R., Cristol, A. H., Yorkston, N. J. and Whipple, K. 1975 *Psychotherapy Versus Behaviour Therapy* Harvard University Press. Boston

13 Luborsky, L., Singer, B. and Luborsky, L. 1975 'Comparative Studies of Psychotherapies: Is it True that "Everyone Has Won and All Must Have Prizes"?' *Archives of General Psychiatry* 32: pp.995-1008

14 Glass, G. V. 1976 'Primary, Secondary and Meta-Analysis of Research' Paper presented as presidential address to the 1976 Annual Meeting of the American Educational Research Association, San Francisco 21 April 1976

15 Hogan, D. B. 1979 *The Regulation of Psychotherapists* Volume 1. *A Study In The Philosophy and Practice of Professional Regulation* Ballinger Publishing Company. Cambridge, Mass.

16 Candy, J., Balbour, F. H. G., Cawley, R. H., Hildebrand, H. P., Malan, D. H., Marks, I. M. and Wilson, J. 1972 'A feasibility study for a controlled trial of formal psychotherapy' *Psychological Medicine* 2: pp.345-362

17 Bergin, A. E. and Lambert, M. J. 1978 'The evaluation of therapeutic outcomes' Editors, S. L. Garfield and A. E. Bergin *Handbook of Psychotherapy and Behaviour Change: An Empirical Analysis* 2nd edition pp.139-190 Wiley

18 Bloch, S. 1979 'Assessment of Patients for Psychotherapy' *British Journal of Psychiatry* 135: pp.193-208

19 Storr, A. 1979 *The Art of Psychotherapy* Secker and Warburg Heinemann. London

20 Lieberman, M. A., Yalom, I. D. and Miles, M. B. 1973 *Encounter Groups: First Facts* Basic Books. New York

21 Gibb, J. R. 1974 'The Message from Research' In: *The 1974 Handbook for Group Facilitators* Editors, J. W. Pfeiffer and J. E. Jones. University Associates, La Jolla. California

22 Bebout, J. and Gordon, B. 1972 'The Value of Encounter' In: *New Perspectives on Encounter Groups* Editors, L. N. Solomon and B. Berzon. Jossey-Bass. San Francisco

23 Shostrom, E. 1972 *Freedom to Be: Experiencing and Repressing your total being* Prentice-Hall, Englewood Cliffs, NJ

24 Anderson, W. 1975 'The Self-Actualisation of Richard M. Nixon' *Journal of Humanistic Psychology* 15, 1, pp.27-34

25 Babbie, E. and Stone, D. 1977 'An Evaluation of the est Experience by a National Sample of Graduates' *Biosciences Communications* 3, 2, pp.123-140

26 Simon, J. 1977 'An Evaluation of est as an Adjunct to Group Psychotherapy in the Treatment of Severe Alcoholism' *Biosciences Communications* 3, 2, pp.141-148

27 Smith, M. L. and Glass, G. V. 1977 'Meta-analysis of Psychotherapy Outcome Studies' *American Psychologist*

28 Gurman, A. S. and Kriskern, D. P. 1978 'Research on Marital and Family Therapy: Progress, Perspective and Prospect' In: *Handbook of Psychotherapy and Behaviour Change* Editors, S. L. Garfield and A. E. Bergin pp.817-901 Wiley. London

29 Crowe, M. J. 1978 'Conjoint Marital Therapy: a controlled outcome study' *Psychological Medicine* 8: pp.623-636

30 West, M. 1979 'Meditation' *British Journal of Psychiatry* 135: pp.457-467

31 Vahia, N., Doongaji, D., Jeste, D., Kapoor, S., Ardhapurkar,

I. and Ravindra Nath, S. 1973 'Further experience with the therapy based upon concepts of Patanjali in the treatment of psychiatric disorders' *Indian Journal of Psychiatry* 15: pp.32-37

32 James, W. 1902 *The Varieties of Religious Experience* Modern Library. New York 1929

33 Gallanter, M. and Buckley, P. 1978 'Evangelical Relgion and Meditation: Psychotherapeutic Effects' *Journal of Nervous and Mental Disease* 166: pp.685-691

34 Batchelder, R. L. and Hardy, J. M. 1968 *Using Sensitivity Training and the Laboratory Method: An Organizational Case Study in the Development of Human Resources* Association Press. New York

35 Laing, R. D. 1967 *The Politics of Experience* Ballantine. New York

36 Bergin, A. E. 1971 'The evaluation of therapeutic outcomes' In: *Handbook of Psychotherapy and Behaviour Change: An empirical analysis* Editors, S. L. Garfield and A. E. Bergin 1st edition Wiley. New York

37 Wolberg, L. R. 1977 *The Technique of Psychotherapy* 3rd edition Grave and Stratton. New York

38 Lieberman, M. A., Selow, N., Bond, G. R. and Reibstein, J. 1979 'The Psychotherapeutic Impact of Women's Consciousness-Raising Groups' *Archives of General Psychiatry* 36: pp.161-168

39 Foster, J. G. 1971 *Enquiry into the Practice and Effects of Scientology* HMSO. London

40 Profession's Joint Working Party on Statutory Registration of Psychotherapists, 1978 *Statutory Registration of Psychotherapists: A Report* Tavistock Centre. London

41 Robinson, D. 1978 Self-help Groups *British Journal of Hospital Medicine* September pp.306-311

42 Pascal, B. *Pensées*

Index

141; assessment 142;
efficacy of 227, 228
Transactional Analysis for
Customer Treatment
(TACT) 134
*Transactional Analysis in
Psychotherapy* (Berne) 123
transference neurosis 215
Trauma of Birth, The (Rank) 117
Treacher, A. 39, 50
Tseng, Wen-Shing 24

Unfinished Animal (Roszak) 26
Union Theological College, New
York 18
Union Theological Seminary,
New York 34
universities 48, 51
University of California 68
University of Chicago 35
University of Göttingen 56

Van Acker, Erika 135
verbalisations 43
Vidal, Gore 117
Vietnam 48, 88, 89
vocational training 39

Walton, Professor Henry 192
Watergate 48, 51
Watts, Alan 63, 145
Weiss, Eduardo 125
Welfare State 23
Wertheiner, Max 55
Westerbake Ranch 66
*What Do You Say After You Say
Hello?* (Berne) 135
Who Shall Survive? (Moreno) 103
*Wholistic Dimensions in
Healing* 64
Wilson, Danny 112
Wilson, Woodrow 32, 36
'Wino' (transactional
analysis) 139
Wolberg, Lewis 12, 195, 197

Wolfe, Tom 13, 65
Worth, Gail Stewart 66
WR – Mysteries of the Organism
(film) 79
Wujastyk, Dominik 180

Yablonsky, Lewis 102
Yalom, Irvin 192
'yin and yang' 65
yoga 230, 231

zen 145, 176-8, 182
Zazen 177